SHAKESPEARE AND RENAISSANCE LITERATURE
BEFORE HETEROSEXUALITY

Previously Published:

Colonial Transformations: The Cultural Production of the New Atlantic World 1580–1640, Palgrave, 2000.

SHAKESPEARE AND RENAISSANCE LITERATURE BEFORE HETEROSEXUALITY

Rebecca Ann Bach

SHAKESPEARE AND RENAISSANCE LITERATURE BEFORE HETEROSEXUALITY
© Rebecca Ann Bach, 2007.

First published in 2007 by
PALGRAVE MACMILLAN™
175 Fifth Avenue, New York, N.Y. 10010 and
Houndmills, Basingstoke, Hampshire, England RG21 6XS
Companies and representatives throughout the world.

PALGRAVE MACMILLAN is the global academic imprint of the Palgrave Macmillan division of St. Martin's Press, LLC and of Palgrave Macmillan Ltd. Macmillan® is a registered trademark in the United States, United Kingdom and other countries. Palgrave is a registered trademark in the European Union and other countries.

ISBN-13: 978-1-4039-7654-3
ISBN-10: 1-4039-7654-6

Library of Congress Cataloging-in-Publication Data

Bach, Rebecca Ann.
    Shakespeare and Renaissance literature before heterosexuality / by Rebecca Ann Bach.
        p. cm.
    Includes bibliographical references and index.
    Contents: Before heterosexuality—The homosocial King Lear : sex, men, and women before the valorization of lust and greed—Restoration Shakespeare 1: adultery and the birth of heterosexuality—Restoration Shakespeare 2: friends and libertines—"Domestic tragedy" and emerging heterosexuality—Othello in the seventeenth and eighteenth centuries and the colonial origins of heterosexuality.
        ISBN 1-4039-7654-6 (alk. paper)
        1. English drama—Early modern and Elizabethan, 1500-1600—History and criticism. 2. Heterosexuality in literature. 3. English drama—17th century—History and criticism. 4. Heterosexuality—England—History. 5. Shakespeare, William, 1564—1616—Criticism and interpretation. 6. Sex in literature. 7. Adultery in literature. 8. Lust in literature. I. Title.

PR658.H44B33 2007
822'.309353—dc22   2006051371

A catalogue record for this book is available from the British Library.

Design by Newgen Imaging Systems (P) Ltd., Chennai, India.

First edition: April 2007

10 9 8 7 6 5 4 3 2 1

Printed in the United States of America.

Transferred to digital printing in 2008.

For Julia

CONTENTS

ACKNOWLEDGMENTS

I am fortunate to have a long list of institutions, colleagues, friends, and family to thank for their contributions (witting and unwitting) to this book. Without the boon of a year-long National Endowment for the Humanities Fellowship at the Newberry Library, I would never have had either the resources or the time to write it. My year at the Newberry (2000–2001) was a delight from start to finish. The staff provided materials, guidance, and general collegiality in all situations, including an initiatory emergency room visit. Despite my disturbing the peace that way, the staff embraced me from the beginning of my year to the end. Thanks so much to Jim Grossman, Sara Austin, and Hjordis Halvorson, among others. No one at the Newberry was ever anything but a huge help. I could not have accepted that grant from the NEH without the kind cooperation and the sabbatical leave provided by the University of Alabama at Birmingham. In addition, my Dean at UAB provided a grant for travel to the Furness Shakespeare library at the University of Pennsylvania as well as the subvention that enabled me to index the book. I very much appreciate that support. I did the preliminary research for the book and additional research and writing at Furness. Furness and the Walter and Leonore Annenberg Rare Book Library at Penn are glorious places to work, thanks to the depth and breadth of their collections and to their superb staff. I owe thanks in particular to John Pollack, Dan Traister, and Lynne Farrington, who have so amply supported my work over the years.

Work at these libraries was made wonderful as well by the people working alongside me. The group of scholars at the Newberry with me fertilized my scholarship and provided care and support as well as extracurricular enrichment. For lunches, dinners, conversations, baseball games, shoe shopping, and general fun, I want to thank April Alliston, Catherine Brown, Alan Frantzen, David Gants, Deborah Kanter, Victoria Kirkham, Ellen McClure, Peggy McCracken, and Carolyn Podruchny. At Furness, I often worked across two desks from Beth McGowan. Sharing work space, living space, and childcare in summers with her has vastly improved my life and work and even saved my sanity when times were very rough. I owe my ability to keep working to her.

Conferences and workshops also enriched this project immeasurably. The University of Chicago Renaissance Workshop invited me to present an earlier version of chapter 5, and our energetic discussion, especially with Richard Strier, helped me to think through objections to the project. Over the years, I have presented a number of other pieces from the book and related work at conferences of the Group for Early Modern Cultural Studies, the Shakespeare Association, and at the Waterloo Elizabethan Theatre conference. I thank the audiences at those conferences, whose questions have helped me to develop my ideas. Thanks are due also to the participants in my seminar "Early Modern Texts and the History of Sexuality" at SAA in 2001. I want to thank especially the group of Renaissance women who have traveled, roomed, and eaten with me through these last ten years or so: Mary Bly, Alison Chapman, Julie Crawford, Kim Hall, Liz Hanson, Natasha Korda, Beth, Mary Janell Metzger, and Cristine Varholy. A larger community of Shakespeareans and scholars has embraced my work, shared ideas, and kept me from too many bloopers—all that remain are certainly my own. I thank Mario DiGangi, Fran Dolan, George Haggerty, Jean Howard, Lynne Magnusson, Jeffrey Masten, Susan O'Malley, Nick Radel, Rick Rambuss, Peter Stallybrass, Goran Stanivukovic, Valerie Traub, and Ginger Vaughan. Scholarly debts to them and to many others are recorded in the text and notes, but I also very much appreciate their personal encouragement as I labored to get this book right. My most significant scholarly debt is, as always, to Phyllis Rackin—her intellect and imagination have inspired and guided me from the start.

Many of my colleagues in the English department at UAB have cheered me on, read my chapters, and offered me their professional and personal strength. For crucial assistance and administrative know-how, I thank my two great department chairs—Marilyn Kurata and Elaine Whitaker. I also thank Tracey Baker for her generosity and for conversations about administration and children's books. Randy Blythe and Bob Collins have been supermen when I needed them most. Dan Butcher has been a wonderful across-the-hall neighbor, and I much appreciate my conversations with Jody Stitt. Cassandra Ellis, Danielle Glassmeyer, Randa Graves, Sue Kim, Cynthia Ryan, Danny Siegel, and Gale Temple have been great friends and colleagues, and

I do not think I will ever pay my personal and professional debts to Alison. She has read every word that I have written (and improved every sentence); she has listened endlessly through bright and very dark days; she is the best colleague and friend I could imagine.

My students at UAB have listened patiently while I rehearsed all the ideas in this book in my classes. They have pushed me to think about texts in entirely new ways—I am very grateful. I need to thank especially my research assistant, Miranda Wade, and a group of quite remarkable students including, but by no means limited to, Monica Bland, Andy Blanks, Vic Camp, Lucy Dorn, Geoff Evans, Ron Guthrie, Heather Helms, Molly Hurley, Clay Isbell, Carolyn Lam, Natalie McCall, Josh Moore, Sarah Ray, Adrianne Roberts, Catherine Roth, Sarah Noel Sheffield, Jason Slatton, Monica Ssenkoloto, Madison Stubblefield, Adam Vines, and all of the students in my honors History of Sexuality course.

This book reached maturity during immensely challenging years. I thank my friends and family and Lee Ascherman so much for helping me through. I have thanked Beth above but never enough. I want to also thank Marni Bonnin and David Lee, Louise Cecil, Deborah Feingold, Vance Lehmkuhl, Carol Neuman, Nancy Sokolove, Marc Stein, and Cindy Way. Many thanks are due to Warren and Annie Weisberg, our loving Chicago family, and also to our amazing extended New York family, Steve and Carolyn Ellman, Delia and Eugene Mahon, and Lynne Rubin. I am grateful for the love and support of Brendan Helmuth, and Eric Helmuth and Judy Filc (my friend and now my sister-in-law as well). I owe so much to my beloved father and mother, Sheldon Bach and Phyllis Beren, and to my brother, Matthew. Julia Alison Bach is the most amazing girl in the world—Julia, this one is for you.

I thank Taylor and Francis, UK, for permission to publish a revised version of my article, "The Homosocial Imaginary of *A Woman Killed with Kindness*," *Textual Practice* 12.3 (1998): 503–524.

INTRODUCTION: BEFORE HETEROSEXUALITY

In 1928, Cole Porter wrote a song called "Let's Do It" that begins, "Birds do it, Bees do it, Even educated fleas do it; Let's do it; Let's fall in Love." More than 300 years earlier, William Shakespeare's King Lear cries out,

> ... the Wren goes too't, and the small gilded Fly
> Do's letcher in my sight. Let Copulation thrive ...
> Too't Luxury pell-mell, for I lacke Souldiers.
> Behold yond simpring Dame, whose face betweene her Forkes presages
>   Snow; that minces
> Vertue, & do's shake the head to heare of pleasures
>   name. The Fitchew, nor the soyled
> Horse goes too't with a more riotous appetite.
>   (TLN 2957–2576; 4.6.110–119)

At this point in the play Lear is mad, but his daughters' lust for Edmund confirms his belief in women's insatiable sexual appetite. Later, in the play's apocalyptic final scene, the eminently sane Edgar tells his bastard brother Edmund that "The darke and vitious place where thee he [our father] got, / Cost him his eyes" (TLN 3133–3134; 5.3.171–172). Edgar claims that their father, Gloucester, deserved to be brutally blinded because he begot Edmund with a woman who was not his wife, a woman whose genitals Edgar describes as a "darke and vitious place." And Edmund agrees. Unlike Shakespeare's lines, Porter's lyrics and the twentieth-century culture they participated in celebrate heterosexuality. Porter's song begs us to "do it," whereas Shakespeare's play despises those who go "too't." Although Porter himself was gay, his lyrics were anthems for a dominant culture that believed in the natural joy of love and sex between men and women: birds do it, and so do we, and we celebrate "it."[1] In Shakespeare's world, that same "it"—sexual intercourse between men and women done for the sake of pleasure—was viewed as polluting, a sign that men's reason had not triumphed over the disgusting urges of birds and insects; such joy in sex was the province and the curse of women and womanly men, whose appetites controlled their reason. This book charts the process by which Shakespeare's texts and Renaissance literature more generally have been made to reflect a heterosexualized world rather than to reveal their place in what I call "the homosocial imaginary" of Renaissance England (1550–1660). This book has two broad objectives: (1) to contribute to a developing genealogy of heterosexuality and (2) to rethink English Renaissance drama and culture in light of a worldview without heterosexuality.

I argue that we must separate out the ideology of "heterosexuality" (a word not coined until the late nineteenth century) from phenomena such as marriage and sexual activity between men and women. Though marriage and male-female sex are transhistorical phenomena, they have not always meant the same things to people, as the comparison between Porter's and Shakespeare's language suggests. A culture with what I call the "heterosexual imaginary" values heterosexual intercourse for pleasure, values men's sexual desire for women, and sees women as naturally less desirous than men. People living within that imaginary see male–female relations as central to male identity and see marriage and immediate family as more important for men than lineage and male–male (homosocial) bonds. In 1976, Michel Foucault argued that, "it is through sex—in fact, an imaginary point determined by the deployment of sexuality—that each individual has to pass in order to have access to . . . his identity. Through a reversal that doubtless had its surreptitious beginnings long ago . . . we have arrived at the point where we expect our intelligibility to come from what was for many centuries thought of as madness . . . our identity from what was perceived as an obscure and nameless urge" (155–156). In relation to the English Renaissance, Foucault's formulation would need to be amended; but if we amend "an obscure and nameless urge" to "identity-compromising lust and sin," it is an accurate description.[2] Foucault's commanding formulations have led to much productive work on Renaissance and early modern homoerotic relations by literary critics.[3] Historians and theorists of sexuality and gender have also pursued the implications of Foucault's claims, although primarily to investigate histories of homosexuality.[4] Jonathan Ned Katz has traced a genealogy of heterosexuality in the modern period (the nineteenth and twentieth centuries), but the history of its emergence in early modern representation is only beginning to be written.[5] This book will contribute to significant work by Renaissance scholars such as Phyllis Rackin and Valerie Traub, who have entertained Foucault's proposition that before the modern world heterosexuality did not exist.[6]

In the following chapters, I chart how Shakespeare's plays and other dramas from the English Renaissance were rewritten and shaped editorially in the Restoration and eighteenth century to make them conform to an emerging, but not yet fully formed, heterosexual imaginary. Shakespeare's plays and the Renaissance literary culture surrounding them are the sites of my primary investigations because for centuries those plays have been seen as displaying natural human behavior, including what has been considered natural in male–female sexual relations.[7] As Michael McKeon suggests, literature is "a singularly acute species of ideology" (*Origins* xxiii), and historical responses to literature show us ideology at work. As the homosocial imaginary began to lose its dominance in the long eighteenth century (1660–1800), Shakespeare's and other Renaissance plays were radically rewritten and edited. In that formative period for heterosexuality, authors and editors condemned the dominant, homosocial, aristocratic values of their immediate past as primitive.[8] Eighteenth- century editors and authors felt the need to rewrite Renaissance plays, and crucially Shakespeare's, to erase the traces of the homosocial past.[9]

Where eighteenth-century editors and writers sensed the differences between their views of male–female sex and Renaissance views, as Karma Lochrie suggests, the modern world has more fundamentally misread the past, misreading it as if that culture saw sex as modern culture sees it (*Heterosyncrasies*). By tracing the rewriting and editing processes of the long eighteenth century, and by pointing to misreadings of Renaissance plays by modern critics, I show how the heterosexual imaginary emerged in the realm of representation and how it has become dominant in the modern world. As the modern heterosexual imaginary has risen into dominance, Renaissance texts have been wrenched and adapted to make them share that imaginary's assumptions. In the chapters to come, I investigate that wrenching and adapting in order to see beyond or outside the heterosexual imaginary into a past that remains largely unfamiliar to us, despite, or even because of, the accretion of 400 years of commentary. Indeed, I show how that commentary helped to form the heterosexual imaginary. Contrary to the formulations of twentieth-century Shakespeare critics, Shakespeare was not our contemporary, nor did he invent "the human"; instead Shakespeare has been constructed over history as the contemporary of critics who live in a sex-positive world quite unlike the world that Shakespeare and his contemporaries knew.

The ascendance of the heterosexual imaginary was linked to English culture's gradual destratification; and this aspect of modernity has led us to underestimate profoundly the significance of rank when we look at sexual relations in Renaissance literary texts.[10] Thus, the Clowne in *As You Like It*, who wants to have sex with the goatherd, Audrey, without committing to marriage, can be taken by critics as representing a typical man even though he is clearly depicted as a clown, a social position miles away from nobility. As well as hoping to fake a marriage with Audrey so that she will have sex with him, *As You Like It*'s Clowne resigns himself to being cuckolded by any future wife. He tells the audience, "As [the cuckold's] hornes are odious, they are necessarie," and the horned "forehead of a married man [is] more honourable then the bare brow of a Batcheller" (TLN 1660–1661, 1667–1669; 3.3.42, 48–50). In his nonchalance about cuckoldry, *As You Like It*'s Clowne resembles the "clownish seruant" Launce in *The Two Gentlemen of Verona* as well as the Clowne in *Love's Labour's Lost*. Launce is in love with a milkmaid, but he cares nothing about controlling her sexuality. Speed, another "clownish seruant," reads Launce's "Cate-log of [the milkmaid's] Condition," and Launce responds to the items in the catalog:

> SPEED Item, She is too liberall.
> LAUNCE Of her tongue she cannot, for that's writ downe she is slow of:
> > of her purse,
> > shee shall not, for that ile keepe shut: Now, of another thing
> > shee may, and that
> > cannot I helpe. (TLN 1408–1412; 3.1.341–345)

"Another thing" here is the milkmaid's "thing," what the *Oxford English Dictionary* coyly calls "privy member, private parts," and, by implication, her sexual favors (*OED* "thing" 11c.). Launce says his milkmaid is stupid and slow to speak; he assures Speed that he will make sure that she does not spend money freely, but, like the Clowne, Launce cannot control his beloved's sexual longings and behavior. Likewise, The Clowne in *Love's Labour's Lost* tells the boy whose cuckold jokes delight him, "O & the heauens were so pleased, that thou wert but my Bastard; What a ioyfull father wouldst thou make mee" (TLN 1810–1812; 5.1.63–65). All of these clowns desire women sexually, but none cares much about controlling women's sexual desires since the issue of legitimate descent—the primary reason for highly ranked men to get close to a woman—can be no concern of theirs.

Modernity has discarded the idea that women naturally desire sexual variety; it has also discarded the idea that men of different ranks think and behave differently in relation to sex with women. Therefore, these clowns' attitudes toward male–female sex are generally not seen as marking their low status (see chapter 1). Critics, instead, can take Shakespearean clowns as models of male desire. Throughout Shakespeare's works and other drama of the early seventeenth century, clowns, servants, and other base men display rampant sexual desire for women. In modernity, this once-denigrated sexual behavior, associated with men of low status, has become a feature of a dominant masculinity associated with powerful men. If we take rank seriously, as people in Renaissance England unquestionably did, the sexual picture looks utterly different than it did in the eighteenth century: In Shakespeare's works and in the literary culture from his time, we cannot find a sexually desirous English nobleman who retains his nobility and masculine power. To find what we now deem natural, we need to descend to the ranks of clowns and the dispossessed.[11]

Literary critics and historians have tended to ignore essential rank differences between male characters, differences denoted in literary texts by these characters' attitudes toward male–female sex. Critics ignore these differences partly because they see men as having always been brim-full of sexual desire for women and partly because they implicitly see all men as psychological equals.[12] This psychological equivalence means that all men *de facto* desire sex. As Traub complains, "[i]t has become common to assert that northwestern Europe during the early modern period was what might be called a 'sex-positive culture' " (*Renaissance* 80). Traub rightly argues that this assertion must be qualified. As she notes, "[a] scatological disgust seethes from descriptions of the female genitals across the early modern period" (104). Just as significantly, scorn applied as well to men who neglected other men in order to involve themselves with women and sexual pleasure with women. In the following chapters, I will argue that the sex-positive picture of Renaissance England is fundamentally flawed. Not only does it underestimate the sex-negativity of the Reformation theology most significant to England, it also misrepresents a culture that saw common men as more like women than men, and as, therefore, sexually desirous and debased. In addition, historians who paint that sex-positive picture mistakenly homogenize a historical period that witnessed earth-shattering changes in attitudes toward male–female sex.[13] Even Anthony Fletcher's broad synthesis of work on gender and sexuality, which attends to changes in the realm of gender, sees no shift when it comes to male sexuality and sexual behavior. Rather than compressing the late sixteenth, seventeenth, and early eighteenth centuries into an undifferentiated whole, I will show how the progressive and uneven secularization and destratification of English culture over those centuries contributed to a new sexual world, a world in which all men might be expected to sexually desire women.

In the early seventeenth century, there was no single understanding of male sexual behavior, but women generally were believed to have less control over bodily desires, regardless of their status. Whereas aristocratic men were expected to control their desires, any woman might slip into her open-mouthed, sexually open nature. Although Renaissance culture constantly differentiated women from one another on the basis of rank, marital status, physical appearance, and other categories, assumptions about women's sexual nature and voracity of speech transcended these distinctions, enabling formulations such as John Donne's in *A Song*: "No where / Lives a woman [sexually] true, and faire."[14] The English Renaissance controversy about women, although it challenged these assumptions, still rested solidly upon them.[15] They were part of the ideological bedrock of the homosocial imaginary. In contrast, aside from having more perfect humoral bodies than women, men were radically differentiated from one another, largely on the basis of rank. Thus, a low-born man who served his social superiors in a household was represented as sharing more characteristics with women than he did with men. Certainly, his potentially voracious and undiscriminating sexual desire aligned him more with women and their unruly appetites than with the potentially controlled passions of dominant men.

Where the modern world believes fervently in bodily and psychological distinctions between men and women, the Renaissance, as so much important work has shown, saw gender as much more fluid. The humoral body connected as well as separated the sexes physically.[16] In addition, boys were seen as closer to women than they were to men.[17] Boys' propensity toward sexual license signalled their immaturity and femininity, not, as in the modern world, their affinity to men, and boys were viewed as potential erotic objects for women and debased men. Dominant men, however, were expected to distance themselves from their womanish boyhoods and from sexual desire. Thus, the sexual double standard familiar to us did not obtain in the Renaissance (see chapter 2). Likewise, male sexual honor (personal honor based on a wife's sexual fidelity) is a creation of modernity, not a natural feature of some ahistorical male personality (see chapter 4). As we will see, in the long eighteenth century, the gender continuum that connected men with women was displaced by a continuum of male identity that connected all men—libertine men with morally sound men. A modern world, which believes in natural and undeniable distinctions between men and women, tends to misread Renaissance gender categories. This misreading has serious consequences, causing critics to mistake the sex-negativity associated with portrayals of sexually desirous boys, base men, and women for sex-positivity.

Another reason for the mistaken picture of sex-positivity is the sheer number of depictions of sexual desire in Renaissance English literature. Its cornucopia of desire has led later generations to see sex-positivity in literature that continually makes such offhand comments as, "A man so resolute in valour as a Woman in desire, were an absolute Leader" and "soules are things to be trodden vnder our feete, when we daunce after loues Pipe."[18] The first comment is spoken by a debased knight in a Thomas Middleton play who is pursuing a lascivious jeweller's wife (a woman who sees her father's and husband's houses as "good for nothing else" but housing her lovers); the second comment is spoken by a courtesan in another Middleton play.[19] Both comments point to the English Renaissance imagination of women as eternally and essentially sexually desirous. Under the reign of the homosocial imaginary, women were (misogynistically) granted sexual desire, but only because of the alliance of sexual desire with irrationality and irreligion. Traub writes of "the cultural presumption in this period of women's erotic excess," and she argues that "[a]fter thirty years of feminist scholarship, this presumption is now a critical cliché" (*The Renaissance* 22). This presumption about women has massive consequences for male identity in relation to sex. As Rackin and Bruce Smith have shown, sexually desirous men are represented as acting like women in a culture that assumed "women's innate inferiority to men" (Kennedy 2).

For men who would be perceived as noble or gentle, male sexual desire for women was seen as a poor alternative to male–male bonds (homosociality). This negativity about male–female sex derived from Renaissance Christianity and the hierarchical structure of the English Renaissance social system; depictions of male–female sexual desire in English Renaissance literature reinforced Christianity and the hierarchical social system rather than challenging them. The modern ideological dominance of heterosexuality has misled some readers of that literature, prompting them to ignore the implications of the cultural belief in women's inherent, voracious sexual desire. That ideological dominance has also led some critics and readers to underestimate severely how often Renaissance literature stresses the relative safety and beauty of love relations between men. Where texts of the heterosexual imaginary encourage men to love their own sexual pleasure with wives and other women, Renaissance texts show us the debasement of the uxorious man, and they encourage men to love and support one another. Developed discourses of male beauty and of unashamed love between men are only two features of the homosocial imaginary that get refigured, displaced, or suppressed in the emerging heterosexual imaginary[20] (see chapters 5 and 3, respectively). Eve Kosofsky Sedgwick argues that "in any male-dominated society, there is a special relationship between male homosocial desire... and the structures for maintaining and transmitting patriarchal power" (*Between* 25). English Renaissance representation shows us a world in which male homosocial desire is primary rather than secondary or implicit (see chapters 1 and 4). When, in the folio final scene of Shakespeare's *2 Henry VI*, York tells Clifford, "With thy braue bearing should I be in loue, / But that thou art so fast mine enemie," he is not referring to the relatively limited realm of friendship between men that is licensed in the modern world; he is referring to a world of relations between men that the modern world has long misunderstood (TLN 3241–3242; 5.3.30.2–30.3). York is referring to the homosocial imaginary.

Alan Bray, Lorna Hutson, Jeffrey Masten, Lena Cowen Orlin, Laurie Shannon, Smith, and other fine critics have shown us that although male friendship was sometimes represented as a minefield in the English Renaissance, perfect friendship was idealized in the literature; indeed, male–male friendship was the most idealized of relations between people. In the Dekker and Middleton play *The Roaring Girle*, two plots involve gallants (young men about town) who betray citizens, and both plots are resolved with the men in question vowing love to one another. At the end of one plot, the betrayed tailor, Openwork, says to Goshawk, a gallant,

> I told you
> I kept a whoore, made you beleeue t'was true,
> Onely to feele how your pulse beate, but find,
> The world can hardly yeeld a perfect friend.
> Come, come, a tricke of youth, and 'tis forgiuen,
> This rub put by, our loue shall runne more euen. (I4; 4.2.210–215)

The "perfect friend" may be a fantasy, only "hardly yeeld[ed]," but men strive to retain their friendships above all; Goshawk's betrayal can be easily forgiven and Openwork's and Goshawk's love for one another easily reinforced. Just as modern literature explores the pitfalls of marriage but generally maintains the ideal, Renaissance literature shows particular friendships collapsing but maintains belief in male friendship's possibilities. It is not as optimistic about marriage in general.[21] Indeed, diverse texts use friendship as a trope to describe love between a man and a woman. When *Two Gentlemen*'s Valentine unites Proteus and Julia (the woman who has loved the faithless Proteus steadfastly), Valentine says, " 'Twere pitty two such friends should be long foes" (TLN 2242; 5.4.116). Julia and Proteus's love is best when it is thought of as friendship. One of Shakespeare's most passionate male–female sexual relationships, Queen Margaret's adulterous affair with Suffolk, ends when Margaret's husband, King Henry, banishes Suffolk. Margaret explicitly compares the lovers' reluctant leave-taking to the parting of two friends: "Euen thus, two Friends condemn'd, / Embrace, and kisse, and take ten thousand leaues, / Loather a hundred times to part then dye" (*2 Henry VI* TLN 2068–2070; 3.2.355–357). Male–male loving friendship provides Margaret with the most accurate trope for passionate male–female love.[22] Robert Burton, in *The Anatomy of Melancholy*, tells his readers that amongst "an heape of other Accidents causing Melancholy . . . losse and death of friends may challenge a first place" (356). In his subsequent discussion of loss and death of friends, Burton includes a woman grieving for her husband, a father for his son, and a man for his father. In English Renaissance texts, male–male friendship is the ur-category for personal relation, and friendship between equals is a far healthier relation for men than male–female sexual relations. As we will see, service relationships between socially unequal men were also frequently conceived as more reliable and durable than male–female sexual engagement (chapter 4).[23]

Under the reign of this imaginary, male–male relations had their inherent dangers. Servants could be unfaithful, men could attempt to rise in status, and men of equal status could betray one another.[24] However, literature in the English Renaissance represented those instances as not a natural condition of male–male competition (as they would be seen in modernity) but as motivated by demonized lust and greed. The most significant male–male relationship in the Renaissance was the all-important bond between man and God. Male–male relations more closely mimicked that bond, notwithstanding human flaws, than did male–female relations. As I will show, the homosocial imaginary only began to decay when the sins of lust and greed became relatively redeemed in the long eighteenth century. Greed, and the associated system of credit relations between men, emerged in the long eighteenth century as commonsensical and natural to men, rather than as a feature of hell. As significantly for the emergence of the heterosexual imaginary, adultery, which for many centuries had been seen as the inevitable result of a debased devotion to sexual pleasure, was also redeemed for a time (see chapter 2). This relative and uneven redemption of adultery meant that even moralistic men in the eighteenth century viewed adulterous desire as a feature of masculinity (see chapter 4). The following chapters will trace the redemptions of greed and of adultery/lust that accompanied the emerging ideology of heterosexuality.

Heterosexuality Is an Ideology

If an ideology is dominant, it is usually not labeled ideology. Thus, most people would call heterosexuality a natural feature of the human condition, not an ideology—this attitude is what Lochrie refers to as the "stubbornly intransigent notion of heterosexuality's transhistorical normativity" (*Heterosyncrasies* xiii). A dominant ideology expresses people's felt relations to their culture—it is how people imagine their world proceeds and/or should proceed. In fact, its collective felt truth is a mark of a dominant ideology. This collective, felt stature is what I mean when I refer to the ideology of heterosexuality or to the "homosocial imaginary" and the "heterosexual imaginary." Heterosexuality is an ideology, and, up until relatively recently in American culture, it was clearly a dominant ideology. Both of these points may be self-evident but, on the model of Sedgwick's vital elaboration of the point that "people are [sexually] different from each other," I am going to belabor them a bit in order to indicate their implications for readings of Renaissance English culture and literature.[25] Slavoj Žižek maps ideology on three axes: "ideology as a complex of ideas (theories, convictions, beliefs, argumentative procedures); . . . the materiality of ideology"; and "the 'spontaneous' ideology at work at the heart of social 'reality' itself" ("Spectre" 9). As a dominant ideology, a hegemony, heterosexuality lives as a complex of ideas, its materiality manifests in a wide variety of linked apparatuses, and it works as a spontaneous perception of social realities for people.[26] The ideas associated with heterosexuality include: the belief in the primacy and naturalness of the modern domestic family; the theory that men naturally desire as much sex with women as possible, and that women do not like sex as much as men do, but want love from men more than anything; the conviction that children are naturally programmed to be heterosexual—that is, girls naturally want boyfriends (love) from the cradle, whereas boys progress from the "girls are icky" stage to wanting as much sex with girls as possible; and the idea that men and women fall in love spontaneously (without taking into account upbringing, class, race, religion, etc.) and that this love is about wanting to have sex and to live with each other.[27] Heterosexuality as a complex of ideas is, of course, most deeply invested in the division of men and women into "normal" men and women (those who are heterosexual) and "deviant" men and women (those who are not). "The materiality" of heterosexuality includes, but is hardly limited to, schools, religious institutions, holidays, tax codes, films and television, advertising, fiction, fairy tales and other children's books, comic books, and magazines.[28] These apparatuses reinforce heterosexuality through ceremonies, authoritative approval and censure, economic benefits and costs, and relentless representations.

Žižek's third axis, "spontaneous" ideology, is its collective, felt truth, what Antonio Gramsci called "common sense": that which is unquestioned. Stuart Hall writes of the "practical as well as the theoretical knowledges which enable people to 'figure out' society, and within whose categories and discourses we 'live out' and 'experience' our objective positioning in social relations" ("Problem" 27). Žižek's third axis corresponds to that practical knowledge, which is not a body of expressible ideas like his first axis—which would correspond with Hall's "theoretical knowledges"—but is instead how we intuitively comprehend the world. As Hall has argued, "changing the terms of an argument is exceedingly difficult, since the dominant definition of the problem acquires, by repetition, and by the weight and credibility of those who propose or subscribe it, the warrant of 'common sense' " ("Rediscovery" 81). One example of heterosexuality's spontaneity is that so many people see a three-year-old boy and a three-year-old girl holding hands and start talking about "boyfriends" and "girlfriends" and couples and marriage, but people seldom speak that way when witnessing a same-sex three-year-old couple (and of course few people see the link between this practice and children's "natural" programming as described above). Heterosexuality is spontaneous in that it is unmarked in most cultural representations: so there is never an outcry about a television character coming out as a heterosexual. It is also spontaneous in that people in America today understand the world as if they were hetero-sexual even when they are not heterosexual; a homosexual or bisexual person's understanding of the world includes an understanding of the world as a heterosexual, whereas a heterosexual's understanding of the world need not include any understanding of the world as a homo-sexual or bisexual person. The homologous well-known example is that a black person needs to understand dominant white culture in order to operate in America today, whereas a white person need know nothing about black cultures.[29] Heterosexuality is spontaneous in that even birds and bees have heterosexuality; it is the story of "our" lives.[30]

However, heterosexuality is no longer so dominant that it is com-pletely invisible or unmarked in the way that, until quite recently, whiteness and dominion over animals were unmarked.[31] Itself one sign of heterosexuality's fall from hegemonic status, this book partcipates in a much larger seismic cultural shift taking place on all fronts: gay liberation, queer studies, same–sex unions, gay characters on TV and in films. This is not to say that heterosexuality is no longer "compulsory" in Adrienne Rich's sense or that other sexualities are not still heavily policed; America's dismal record on civil rights for gays and lesbians, the military's persecution of gays and lesbians, scapegoating of gays for the AIDS crisis, and daily baitings and beat-ings all attest to heterosexuality's dominance. Heterosexuality today is still dominant, but it has lost the total control it had when it was hegemonic; or, perhaps better, it is a currently embattled hegemony fighting for position in the same way that the nuclear family is currently embattled and fighting for position (and of course the two struggles are very much linked).[32]

Heterosexuality's hegemony until very recently accounts for its influence in studies of Renaissance English literature. Recent work that adds male–male sex and desire and, less frequently, female–female sex and desire to a heterosexual picture of the English Renaissance can assent to the dominance of heterosexuality if it assumes that wherever one finds marriage in early texts one finds heterosexuality. But marriage is not heterosexuality, and sex between a man and a woman is not heterosexuality. Men and women loved each other and had sex with each other under a homosocial imaginary that imagined the world in terms of the primacy of male–male relation-ships just as men and men and women and women love one another and have sex with one another under a heterosexual imaginary in whose dominant representations these experiences have, until recently, been almost invisible. Both the homosocial and the heterosexual imaginaries are only partial pictures of the world. But the homosocial imaginary structured the English Renaissance just as our heterosexual imaginary structures our texts, our critical visions, and our lives. The Renaissance literary texts that I discuss in this book were significant apparatuses of the homosocial imaginary: the public theater was immensely popular at the time, and the culture lacked many of the more developed and differentiated apparatuses of the modern world (films, television, novels, magazines). Literature reveals what the English Renaissance took for granted. As Hall suggests, "this movement—towards the winning of a universal validity and legitimacy for accounts of the world which are partial and particular, and towards the grounding of these particular constructions in the taken-for-grantedness of 'the real'—is indeed the characteristic and defining mechanism of 'the ideological' " ("Rediscovery" 65).

David Halperin's wonderful book *One Hundred Years of Homosexuality* shows clearly that marriage is not heterosexuality, for Halperin's argument, among his other crucial interventions in the history of sexuality, gives a detailed picture of sex and gender in classical Greece, a culture that had marriage but did not have heterosexuality.[33] And classical Greece is just one of many cultures in human history— including Renaissance England—that has had (or has) marriage without heterosexuality.[34] This may sound contradictory, but I think that if we look carefully at what we understand when we hear the term "heterosexuality" it becomes clear. Take, for example, two marriages in the early seventeenth century, one real, and one a representation: King James I's marriage to Anne of Denmark and Othello's marriage to Desdemona. Neither of these marriages partakes of heterosexuality's complex of ideas: neither validates the nuclear domestic family to the exclusion of the larger household; neither shows us that men want copious sex with a variety of women or that women are not so interested in sex; neither suggests that a man's masculinity is determined by his sexual interest in and prowess with women (in fact, rather the reverse is true); and neither marriage shows us that a man should love women exclusively.[35] Bray's analysis of James's letter exchange with Buckingham beautifully exposes how modern categories of friendship and marriage actually obscure relationships from the Renaissance (*Friend* 96–104); James and Buckingham's friendship had much more loving and more familial resonances than James's marriage with Anne. Bray's work shows that "in the past, marriage has been one, as it is not in modern society, among several forms of what one might call voluntary kinship: kinship created not by blood but by ritual or a promise" (*Friend* 316). This book will elaborate at length the argument that marriage is not heterosexuality (see chapter 4). The proposition that marriage is not heterosexuality means that we should amend Jonathan Goldberg's important formulation: "desire in the [early modern] period cannot be read as marriage and its syntax of compulsory heterosexuality" (*Sodometries* 41). We need to understand Renaissance England as a culture with compulsory marriage (for some, not for all) but without a syntax of compulsory heterosexuality. In Renaissance England, as so many critics have powerfully suggested,the social hierarchy was structured on the model of the patriarchal family.[36] God was conceived as an all-powerful father, and all fathers below him held power on that model. Men as well as women were subordinated to their biological and metaphorical fathers, although only men could become fathers in their turn. Under this cultural model, marriage was necessary in order to determine paternity, especially for the entitled men who had property and/or status to pass on; but under this model the heterosexual imaginary would have been actively dangerous, since (multiple) orgasm, a desideratum (for men) of the heterosexual imaginary, needed to be reserved for making more men.

Rather than signifying male power, as it does in the modern world, orgasm signified danger for men. One biographical story illustrates this point. Richard Boyle (1566–1643), an English yeoman's son who became the first earl of Cork in 1620, had fifteen children; eleven survived into adulthood, and Cork spent considerable money, time, and effort to marry them carefully so as to obtain prestigious connections for his newly ennobled family. Cork contracted early marriages for both boys and girls in his family, sometimes starting marriage negotiations before the child was five years old. In 1639, Cork married his son Francis to Elizabeth Killegrewe, one of Queen Henrietta's maids of honor; "the couple were then ritually bedded by the king and queen but, on Cork's insistence, the sixteen-year-old Francis, who was considered too young for the physical strains of marriage, was quickly separated from his wife and sent to travel in France with Robert his younger brother" (Canny 57). Unlike the proverbial twentieth-century father who takes his young son to a prostitute to initiate him into heterosexuality but guards his daughters from knowledge of and experience with sexual intercourse, Cork feared that early intercourse would kill his son but had no such concerns about his daughters' health. Cork was utterly uninterested in his son's having sexual experience with women and thus obtaining heterosexual masculinity; instead he wanted to shield him from such experience *even with his wife* in order to preserve his health so that he could maintain the prestigious kin tie and eventually make more men.

I am not arguing that no aspects of heterosexuality were emergent in the English Renaissance. Mary Beth Rose correctly sees some movement toward valuing sex within marriage and valuing men's love of their wives in her readings of seventeenth-century Protestant conduct manuals. Readers of these manuals and Protestant wedding sermons, however, may overlook how thoroughly the sex-negativity of the homosocial imaginary saturates these texts' rhetoric. William Gouge, in his 1622 manual, *Of Domesticall Dvties*, advocates marriage so "that men might auoid fornication" (209). He reasons that because "of that pronenesse which is in mans corrupt nature to lust" marriage is necessary and good (210). Gouge refers his readers to Christ's words about chastity in Matthew, "*all men receiue not this saying*," and he explicates Christ's argument, "Yea for those that haue not the gift of continency this [sex in marriage] is the only warrented and sanctified remedy" (210). Although Gouge is sure that "true *Eunuches*" are only one in a million, and, therefore, men must marry, his discourse frames sexual continency as a "gift." Sex between men and women, in contrast, is a feature of "mans corrupt nature." Gouge points us to a staple concept of the homosocial imaginary—male chastity—that will later disappear from sight except in specific settings cordoned off from general male culture (see chapters 1 and 4). In 1609, M.W. Perkins, another Protestant writer on marriage and family, advocated "moderation." "For," he says, "euen in wedlocke excesse in lusts is no better then plaine adulterie before God" (113). For Perkins, "immoderate desire euen betweene man and wife, is fornication" (114). Perkins's discourse shows us the imagined link between male–female sex and adultery that obtained under the homosocial imaginary (see chapter 2). If Perkins favors marriage for men and women, he writes about sex using a Christian vocabulary whose key-words are "lust," "adulterie," and "fornication." William Whately (1619) agrees with Perkins on the virtues, even the necessity, of sexual moderation in marriage: "It must further be temperate, I meane, sparing. Men and women are reasonable creatures, and therefore must remember, that God hath ordained matrimony, not for pleasures sake chiefly, but for the encrease of mankind, and not to enkindle lustfull desires, but to quench them" (18). Protestant writers used many of the same textual sources as Catholic thinkers on sex,and they shared with those thinkers a basically sex-negative vocabulary.[37] Before masculinity and sexual desire for women could become congruent in representation, English culture needed to shed much of the pejorative baggage attached to sex within Protestant conduct manuals. The redemption of male sexual pleasure was not, finally, a theological project; and, whereas the Reformation contributed to the emergence of the heterosexual imaginary, Protestant theology neither caused nor lauded that emergence.[38] As we will see, the conflation of marriage and some features of heterosexuality began to seem natural in the eighteenth century, but not without significant ideological shifts.

Just as marriage is not heterosexuality, sex between a woman and a man is not heterosexuality. Again, Halperin's work, *One Hundred Years*, is most helpful here, as it describes many cultures that have male–female sex but whose sexual practices might look alien to an average happily identified late-twentieth-century American heterosexual.[39] Indeed, since male–female sex is a relatively universal feature of human society (with a few exceptions such as the millenarian Shakers), one would have to see every culture everywhere as having had heterosexuality if this proposition was false. Of course, despite much evidence to the contrary, many critics and historians *have* seen every culture everywhere as having or having had heterosexuality. This phenomenon—seeing heterosexuality everywhere we see men and women having sex or everywhere we see marriage—is largely an ideological effect of heterosexuality's dominance, but not completely. The phenomenon is also an effect of the way hegemonies form and operate.

As Raymond Williams suggests, social formations such as the heterosexual imaginary do not appear out of nowhere.[40] Some of the beliefs and convictions of the heterosexual imaginary, or at least their building blocks, existed in the English Renaissance, although many of that imaginary's apparatuses had yet to be developed; the common sense aspect—heterosexuality's spontaneity—only came into place historically when the apparatuses and ideas cohered and gained power. So, although they were not dominant, or at least not the arrangements of the dominant group, nuclear families did exist in the English Renaissance, and some people focused their interests there.[41] There have always been men who desire lots of sex with women, and women who are not as interested in sex; there have always been men who want no sex at all, or sex only with men, or sex with lots of men and lots of women, or sex only with boys; and there have always been women who want sex with women only, or no sex, or sex with lots of different women or with only one man, or with many men—this short list by no means exhausts the possibilities for human erotic expression; the permutations are close to limitless.[42] However, different cultures place value on different permutations, and none of the central ideas of heterosexuality—that the husband–wife relationship (with its associated nuclear family) should be the focus of a man's life and duty, that a man's masculinity is tied to wanting and getting lots of sex with a woman or women, that women want love more than sex, that people are divided into hetero- and homosexuals— were features of Reniassance England's dominant structure of thinking, even though some people might have believed any combination of these ideas or acted as if they believed them.

Hall argues that "ideas only become effective if they do, in the end *connect* with a particular constellation of social forces . . . the effective coupling of dominant ideas *to* the historical bloc which has acquired hegemonic power in a particular period is what the process of ideological struggle is *intended to secure*" ("Problem" 43–44). In the English Renaissance, the historical bloc in power was the nobility and the gentry, and their imaginary, the homosocial imaginary, was the dominant ideology. Although that imaginary assumed that not all men would constitute their identities in relation to God and other men, it held this up as an ideal for all men, albeit an ideal certainly less reachable by those who were base and common. We should not mistake signs of ideological struggle for a modern worldview about sex, no matter how convenient or natural it is for us to believe that people have always been like us sexually. One, among many, of the significant differences between the homosocial imaginary and our own is that people under that reign generally believed that social superiors, members of the nobility and gentry should be morally superior to themselves, more Christian, and therefore more sex-negative.[43] In Samuel Daniel's play, *The Tragedie of Cleopatra* (1602), the chorus laments a world in which the sexual sins of the great have infected the masses:

> Kings small faults, be great offences.
> And this hath set the window open
> vnto licence, lust, and riot
> The wanton luxurie of Court,
> Did forme the people of like sort. (I4v)

Likewise, in *The Anatomy of Melancholy*, Robert Burton asserts that princes' "examples are soonest followed, vices entertained; if they be prophane, irreligious, lascivious, riotous, Epicures, factious, covetous, ambitious, illiterate, so will the Commons most part be idle, unthrifts, prone to lust, drunkards, and therefore poore and needy" (70). As Peter Lake suggests, people in the English Renaissance assumed that "when authority figures lapsed or fell they took many others down with them in a sort of domino effect" (128). This assumption weakened substantially after the English Revolution and was replaced, eventually, by the assumption that men of the middling sort might be moral models for those above them in rank; however, as we will see, when the men of the middling sort began to gain economic and political power, their sexual ideology had been formed in part by the sins of the great (see chapter 4).

Our modern ideology of heterosexuality was born in a massive historical conjunction. Figuring into its emergence were: the valorization of capitalistic relations between men;[44] the Reformation, the English Revolution, and the Glorious Revolution;[45] the philo- sophical innovations of the seventeenth century;[46] a series of libertine monarchs (see chapter 2);[47] the displacement of a monarchial embod- ied politics by possessive individualism;[48] the displacement of patri- archy by male dominance;[49] the consolidation of white male identity in relation to African slavery (see chapter 5); a New Science under- standing of the body and gender;[50] and the rise of women's voices into prominent visibility (see chapter 2). In addition, the reign of male physical power (personal military might) was ending, partly because of the Tudor centralization of political power.[51] Male physical power was eventually replaced by male sexual power. Such a replacement, however, was predicated on a new medical belief that sexual expres- sion did not effeminate and weaken a man. Economically, the differ- ence between overpopulation in late Tudor England and underpopulation in the early eighteenth century contributed to the move from the homosocial imaginary to the heterosexuality imaginary.[52] Of course, these changes were interrelated, but each put pressure on the homosocial imaginary and contributed to its decline. However, the heterosexual imaginary was not born fully formed, and it was born, as all ideologies are, in contest. In its early years (and even today), it contained the residue of the homosocial imaginary, although that residual imaginary had more power in the early years that are the subject of this book.

In this book, I trace a huge historical shift in dominant English ideas about sex between men and women. This book discusses a shift in ideas, not in the reality of people's daily lives, although it would be puerile to suggest that there is no relationship between a dominant ideological system and people's practices. Certainly what is hegemonic determines a great deal of practice, but it never determines everything, and some of what it determines is "unintended," that is, formulated in reaction to it.[53] The evidence for this shift in ideas about male–female sex is prodigious. Many more Shakespearean texts and many more texts by dramatists of Shakespeare's time were rewitten than I have space to deal with in this book; and, tellingly, every one of those rewritten texts shows the traces of the shift in sexual ideology that I am describing; this shift is apparent even though the texts were written by people of all political persuasions.[54] The shift is also apparent in nondramatic poetry and prose—I will look at some of these texts as the book proceeds. But the shift in sexual ideology is not the whole story of how men and women thought and wrote about male–female sex in Shakespeare's time or of how they have thought and written about this subject in the 400 or so years since Shakespeare died. Sedgwick felicitously warns us that, although the modern world divides people up into homosexuals, heterosexuals, and, less often, bisexuals, such categorization by no means accounts for what all people feel, think, or do.[55]

Although this book is about the shift in "The taken-for-grantedness of dominant sexuality," ideological shifts do not take everyone in a culture with them (Michael Warner 7). Ideological change is always uneven, and subcultures exist in every society.[56] Therefore, I have tried to suggest some of the unevenness of the shift in sexual ideology. Much more evidence exists for this unevenness, evidence apparent in contemporary everyday life, even within England and America. Certainly many English and American people in postmodern or late modern culture identify themselves as committed Christians fighting fornication and even believing that sex should be reserved for procreation. It is possible to find people today who fervently believe that women are sinks of sexual voracity (although it is also more than possible that such people might be categorized as disturbed). Whately argued in the early seventeenth century that women should be treated as individually as men treat horses: "Euen as he that is to ride a horse, must make his bridle fit for the mouth of the poore beast . . . for euery bridle will not agree to the mouth of euery beast.

In the like case it fareth with women" (130). In 1994, I taught Shakespeare's *The Taming of the Shrew* to a class of senior English majors at the University of Alabama at Birmingham. One of my female students, shocked by my feminist commentary on the play, said that "if a woman acts like a horse, she should be beaten like a horse." That student was quite unaware of Whately and of the prevalence of the woman-horse analogy in Shakespeare's time, but she shared many of Whately's assumptions.[57] Certain aspects of masculinity as constructed in twenty-first-century beer and truck commercials resemble, if they do not absolutely reiterate, appeals to masculinity in the early seventeenth century; they attempt, at times, to build male community against involvement with women.[58] However, the heterosexual imaginary is so established today that there are subtle but important differences between these stances and similar ones under the reign of the homosocial imaginary. Except in subcultures that utterly reject modernity and all of its apparatuses, most of heterosexuality's precepts are today's common sense. This was less true in the years of that imaginary's formation, the years this book discusses.

Methodology

Shakespeare and Renaissance Literature before Heterosexuality, as may be evident already, proceeds for the most part by comparing and contrasting texts from the late sixteenth and early seventeenth centuries (the later Renaissance) to texts from the Restoration and the eighteenth century (the long eighteenth century). Such comparisons and contrasts will, I hope, set into relief English Renaissance texts' devotion to the homosocial imaginary. In chapter 1, I dissect one play—*King Lear*—so as to show that imaginary's parameters *in situ*. In addition, I show how modern criticism, which takes the heterosexual imaginary's assumptions for granted, has made fundamental mistakes about the meanings of that play's misogyny and its attacks on greed. In chapter 4, as well, I discuss the pitfalls in readings of Renaissance household dramas that fail to appreciate those plays' devotion to homosocial relations. However, these displays of the homosocial imaginary's power in the English Renaissance would be less persuasive without the comparisons in chapters 2, 3, and 4, which allow me not only to show the homosocial imaginary's more general purchase on English Renaissance texts, but also to demonstrate its waning power over the course of the long eighteenth century. I hope that the comparisons will suggest just how alien the sexual sensibilities of the earlier texts are to modern thinking. The rewritten plays conform to assumptions about male–female sex much closer to those of the modern world. Those modern assumptions about sex, however, have governed reactions to the original plays since the eighteenth century (see chapter 5, as well as chapters 1 and 4). Shakespeareans over the last 200 years have generally reviled the Restoration and eighteenth-century rewrites of Shakespeare's plays and, at the very same time, reacted to Shakespeare's plays almost as if they were those rewrites, whose assumptions about sex and gender look more familiar to us. This critical irony is the best demonstration I can give of the power and ascendance of the heterosexual imaginary. That imaginary has made its own the very texts that, looked at without its blinders, reject its premises. We often, that is, read Shakespeare and his contemporaries as if they wrote in the late eighteenth or nineteenth centuries, thereby discounting what these plays say about male–female sex, male–male and female–female relations, and gender identity. The comparisons in chapters 2, 3, and 4, will, I hope, substantiate these arguments. Throughout the book, I read texts closely, examining small changes and revisions that reveal large ideological shifts. A history of sexuality, I argue, can be found in the details of close reading.

In addition to using close readings of plays and comparisons between texts from different centuries, this book shows the homosocial imaginary and its decline by investigating the histories of words; this is a method brilliantly employed in Masten's work on the history of sexuality. Traub says, "Jeffrey Masten has used the phrase 'queer philology' to describe 'a new historical philology that investigates the etymology, circulation, transformation, and constituitive power of "key words" within early modern discourses of sex and gender' " (*Renaissance* 15). Traub, Smith, and Patricia Parker have also shown how significant word histories can be to histories of sexuality and gender.[59] Niklas Luhmann, in his theoretical foray into the history of love, suggests that "word forms, set phrases, adages and precepts may very well continue to be handed down over the generations; however, their meaning changes and with it the way in which they pinpoint a specific referent, encapsulate particular experiences and open up new perspectives" (8). In this book, I look at the changing meanings of the words "mistress," "slave," and "knave" (chapter 2); "domestic," "harlot," "villain," and "liberal" (chapter 4); "wench" and "nice" (chapter 5). The *OED* is my main authority, but in my work on "knave," I show that great dictionary's limitations. These word histories by no means exhaust the possibilities for what histories of words can tell us about the history of ideas concerning male–female sexual relations. In fact, I investigate these particular words in the book because they happen to signify in important ways in the literary texts that I discuss. In the course of writing this book, I have come to believe that I could tell the same story solely through an investigation of word histories. The words I discuss, therefore, only hint at the rich history of (hetero)sexuality available through this method.

Another procedural aspect of the book that has probably already obtruded itself upon my reader's attention is my insistence on providing original spelling when I quote literary texts. Although scholars may be used to reading this old spelling, I want to alienate the texts for late modern eyes not used to reading unedited texts, quite the opposite effect than most editors have aimed at throughout literary history. If we struggle a bit to sound out Renaissance texts, we less easily, I think, read them as documents of our own times, feelings, and sexual arrangements. As those familiar with these texts know well, the original texts are far more alien to modern eyes than they look as I represent them on the page.[60] Certain textual features cannot be easily reproduced—for example, the long "s" (which can look like an "f" to modern readers) and the inconsistency between individual copies of books, since Renaissance books were corrected as they were printed. Those fascinating features, however, matter less for my argument than the unmodernized spelling and punctuation. English spelling and punctuation were standardized in the mid-eighteenth century. However, spelling and punctuation already look more modern and more standard in Restoration texts. The history of spelling and punctuation in English runs parallel to the history of sexuality that this book recounts. These histories are not causally linked; however, the lack of standardized spelling and the differences between modern and Renaissance punctuation do bear on the history of sexuality. The advantage of retaining nonstandard spelling in my quotations from Renaissance texts is that I can show that those texts belong to an earlier world generally, not to our own world.

A related, potentially strange procedural aspect of the book has already appeared in this introduction as well. An example of it is my calling the familiar character Touchstone "the Clowne." I call him "the Clowne" because that is how he is denominated in the speech prefixes and stage directions in the 1623 Shakespeare folio, from which I have chosen to quote speeches. That character's denomination as a clown without a name is not at all unusual in dramatic texts from the English Renaissance, which often give characters a rank or position title instead of a personal name. "Clowne" is, in the English Renaissance, not only a name for an entertainer but also (and more often) a name for a low-born man, one of a panoply of such names largely lost to modern usage. The character's name in *As You Like It* signifies his common birth, which, as I have argued, is also signalled by his sexual desire for women and his blithe acceptance of his future wife's sexual voracity. The advent of a more modern sexual system was, I will be arguing throughout this book, deeply linked to the notion that all men are, basically, the same and also, basically, different from all women. But the sexual system that preceded modernity adhered to the notion of essential differences between men, differences that meant that some men had personal names that signified and some did not. Whenever such differences are marked in original texts, I will retain the denominations given in those texts rather than giving personal names for the characters, as has been the custom since the eighteenth century. This custom is one more sign of the eighteenth century's project to make the texts show us men and women that eighteenth-century people recognized as like themselves, in this case, as devoted to individual, personal male identity.

My book's commitment to a critique and history of ideologies also means that I am forced to use imprecise and ugly terminology. Since our words have histories that are imbricated in the history of sexuality, when we analyze the ideological frontiers connected to sex, our tools, the words we use to describe those frontiers, are formed in the very ideology we examine. We are left with imprecision at best. "Heterosexuality," "homosexuality," "sex,"[61] "sexuality," and "gender" are all words whose histories make them very clumsy tools. Sedgwick describes one of her word choices in *Epistemology of the Closet* this way:

> My own loose usage in this book will be to denominate that problematized space of the sex/gender system, the whole package of physical and cultural distinctions between women and men, more simply under the rubric "gender." I do this in order to reduce the likelihood of confusion between "sex" in the sense of "the space of differences between male and female" (what I'll be grouping under "gender") and "sex" in the sense of sexuality. (29)

In this book, I follow Sedgwick's usages, using "gender" when I am writing about differences between men and women and using "sex" only when I am writing about physical acts and desires. The use of the words "sexual," "heterosexual," and "homosexual" is a much stickier matter for me, since I am writing about the construction of realms that were not yet in place. I am led to awkward formulations such as "male–female sex," "male–female sexual relations," and "male–female sexual engagement." These are far from elegant, but they are more accurate than terms that bring with them all the ideological baggage whose genealogies I am pursuing. They are the best way I have been able to figure out to avoid a problem Halperin notes in contemporary histories of sexuality: "Those historians who redescribe in modern conceptual terms the culturally specific phenomena they observe in the distant historical record . . . misrecognize the sexual features of the period they study as exotic versions of the already familiar" (*How to* 60). I am in another terminological bind when I write about literary and historical periods. Most of the recent work on sex and sexual relations in late-sixteenth and seventeenth-century England calls that historical period and place "early modern England." This, however, is also the name given to Restoration and eighteenth-century England in critical work focused on those periods. Since I need to distinguish these historical periods, I am calling one the English Renaissance and the other early modern England. Bray's phrase "traditional society" is perhaps a better way to encapsulate the values of what I am calling the English Renaissance (see *The Friend* generally). Both terms, "the English Renaissance" and "early modern England," as well as the term "modernity," bring problems with them; none of these terms are precise, and all carry baggage.[62]

Awkward and ugly terminology is a sign, I hope, of the cogency, even the necessity, of the project at hand. If we cannot find the language to describe the earlier world, then at least we are approaching its difference from our own. That sense of difference is crucial. For without that sense, we are destined to believe that our own world is inevitable and finally unchangeable. If this book is heavily indebted to the queer histories that have preceded it, if it is itself a sign of the cultural struggles over gender and sex that I have witnessed in my lifetime, it is also devoted to the struggles for equality in those realms. *Shakespeare and Renaissance Literature before Heterosexuality* shows us a world with a different misogyny than our own. It shows us a world where love between men was relatively valued and love between men and women relatively denigrated. The world before heterosexuality was not, in any universal sense, better than our own, nor was it worse, but in its ideas about male–female sex, it was truly different. I ask my readers, as they see how ways of thinking have changed, to imagine new worlds for themselves and for humanity.

THE HOMOSOCIAL *KING LEAR*: SEX, MEN, AND WOMEN BEFORE THE VALORIZATION OF LUST AND GREED

Wandering without his eyes, *King Lear*'s Earl of Gloucester stumbles upon his son, disguised as poor mad Tom, a Bedlam beggar. Gloucester asks Tom whether he knows the "way to Douer." By way of a reply, Tom complains that he has been "scarr'd out of his good wits" (TLN 2245–2247; 4.1.56–57). In the quarto version of the play, Tom elaborates, saying that he has been possessed by "Fiue fiends," the first of which is the fiend of "lust" (H3). In its quarto versions and in its folio version, Shakespeare's *King Lear* utterly rejects lust: both lust as male sexual interest in women and lust as female desire. As Margreta de Grazia suggests, the play does not laugh with Gloucester at the "good sport" he found in the extramarital sexual encounter that led to the conception of his bastard son, Edmund ("Ideology" 28–30; TLN 26; 1.1.21). Gloucester has wasted his seed, the bodily equivalent of his land, and his waste precipitates the stripping of his son Edgar's inheritance. In consequence, Gloucester loses his eyes; and even Edgar regards the loss as a fitting punishment for his father's lecherous crime (TLN 3131–3134; 5.3.171–172).

Shakespeare's *King Lear* espouses chastity as an ideal, perhaps the only ideal that remains unpolluted in the course of the play, although Kent's service relationship to Lear also, significantly, comes through the play untouched.[1] In *King Lear*, hell signifies as the sexual world and especially as female lust and male sexual desire for women. Thus, Regan's and Goneril's lust signifies their disregard of patriarchy, and the play resolutely removes Cordelia from any association with sexual desire. The play's hatred of male–female sex is pervasive: Edgar's story about becoming poor Tom is a story of sexual exhaustion; Lear's Fool makes bitter fun of men who engage themselves sexually with women; Lear (in)famously curses women's bodies and their sexual desire; and Gloucester's sexual exploits bear him the bastard who will destroy both his life and the grace still extant in the kingdom (if we see Cordelia as the symbol of that grace). Neither Kent nor Edgar has any interest in women; and Albany, like so many other characters within the homosocial imaginary, can only save himself by divesting himself of the profane woman who has blinded him through much of the play. However, homosocial bonds, by definition removed from male–female sex, offer comfort. Only Kent's loyalty, Edgar's filial piety (in the face of his father's ignorant renunciation of him), and Albany's rejection of his wife in favor of his bonds with men will save this world from destruction.

In the reading of *King Lear* that follows, I will second de Grazia's plea that, as we read Shakespeare's play, we resist making the "nascent dominant before history does" ("Ideology" 21). *King Lear*, I argue, far from anticipating the modern world, is a quintessential play of the homosocial imaginary. In texts from that imaginary—Renaissance texts—men's sexual desire for women is linked to other world-shattering desires: desires to break the essential bonds between masters and servants, between male friends, and between men and their male subjects. Renaissance texts display their allegiance to a Renaissance Christian[2] value system and reject the tendencies in men that they attribute to the devil, tendencies such as valuing bonds with women over bonds with men, valuing male sexual pleasure, and valuing profit rather than charity. Although those demonic tendencies resemble aspects of the modern sexual and economic world, they were, of course, already present in the Renaissance. Focused on condemning lust and greed (linked sins attributed to fallen men and women in the Renaissance), *King Lear* does not, as has been so often proclaimed, proleptically condemn a capitalist economy and/or ethos that the play could not dream of, at least in that economy's consolidated and dominant state. Rather, the play powerfully contributes to a prevailing, if always-challenged, discourse in which men's greed and lechery are soul-destroying sins.

I will suggest, as well, that my reading of *King Lear* goes a long way toward helping us to comprehend, and even perhaps to solder, a rift evident in late-twentieth-century *King Lear* criticism: the rift between Marxist and feminist readings of the play. This rift depends on a modern understanding of the play's energies. Thus the play's virulent misogyny—expressed on the levels of female character construction and male speech-making—has been read as a rejection of women as we know them or as we may believe they have always been conceived. In contrast, the play's leveling instincts—expressed in Lear's and Gloucester's comments on the gulf between rich and poor—have been read as a proto-Marxist analysis of capitalism's inequities and as a proleptic Marxist critique. Thus, feminists have largely rejected the play, and Marxist male critics have embraced it.[3] However, if the play does not anticipate capitalism, neither does it anticipate a misogyny that presumes a modern understanding of women as passive, weak, and distinct from men. When we read *King Lear* as a text of the homosocial imaginary, it is easy to see that " 'woman' is never an already accomplished, cold, hard, self-evident fact or category, but always a malleable cultural idea as well as a lived reality" (Callaghan, *Feminist* xii). In *King Lear* we see ideas about "woman" and also about relations between men that supported, described, and helped to sustain the homosocial imaginary.

King Lear on "Woman"

King Lear offers us three women, but its misogny is confined to what the play (and the English Renaissance) conceives of as women's potential fatal flaw: their lust. The play's portrayal of its three women may look to modern eyes as a division between a pure, idealized woman and two demonized whores; but what the play actually shows us is a world in which gender does not determine behavior. Cordelia sets the standards according to which women, and also men, might be expected to behave. She loves, honors, and obeys her father as her father and as the king (TLN 105; 1.1.97). Unlike her sisters (and unlike many women, according to the play), she has "no vicious blot, murther or foulenesse" to her name (TLN 249; 1.1.225). And she condemns her sisters' "vicious blot[s]" implacably. In the quarto, she tells the on- and off-stage audience that she will not marry like her sisters "to loue [their] father all," but the play cares not a whit about her as a loving wife (B2; 1.1.103). Her affection for her husband is insignificant to the play, as it distinctly was not when Cordelia was rewritten in the Restoration to conform to newly emerging ideals of women. *King Lear* also does not care about her as even a potential loving mother—the role that would make her an ideal Victorian woman. The ideals she performs and upholds are relatively non-gender-specific, at least if we compare them to ideals for women in later historical periods. Cordelia's loyalties are to her father the king and to her father's homosocial network, represented in the play most powerfully by Kent.[4]

As Kathleen McLuskie suggests, "Cordelia's saving love . . . works in the action less as a redemption for womankind than as an example of patriarchy restored" ("Patriarchal" 99).

In contrast, Cordelia's sisters are lust personified in its Medieval and Renaissance guise: not lust as it would come to be characterized in later centuries (as one of the more pleasant vices that is natural to men), but lust as overarching ambition, lust as greed, and lust as rampant feminine and feminizing sexual desire.[5] Thomas Aquinas, classifying lust as a contrary vice to temperance, explains that "lust applies chiefly to venereal pleasures, which more than anything else work the greatest havoc in a man's mind, yet secondarily it applies to any other matters pertaining to excess" (1804). Nothing if not excessive, Goneril and Regan's penchant for extremes characterizes them; it is expressed originally in their immoderate, (and therefore by definition) false, and intemperate professions of love for their father. As Cordelia points out, that love exceeds by far what is required for a daughter. Goneril claims that she loves her father "Deerer then eyesight, space and libertie . . . As much as Childe ere lou'd, or Father found" (TLN 61, 64; 1.1.54, 57). Goneril's claim might sound emotionally accurate or desirable in our post-Freudian world.[6] But in the pre-Freudian world, that claim—to love a parent or child without any reservation and, therefore, by implication, beyond God—is accurate only within the space of lust, the space Edgar calls the "indi[sti]nguish'd space of Womans will" (TLN 2764; 4.6.266).[7] Goneril's and Regan's unbridled tongues predict, presage, and synechdocally enact their sexual lust, their bloodlust, and their ambition.[8]

Goneril's and Regan's lust is distinctly premodern—a premodern marker of femininity. Edgar makes his comment on "Womans will" in relation to an intercepted letter from Goneril to Edmund in which she declares herself Edmund's "Affectionate servant." Like her sister, Regan is also Edmund's "servant" and the servant of her lust. The sisters' lust, which will inevitably lead to murder and oppression, rather than distinguishing them as unwomanly (as it might in the Victorian age), is a mark of femininity in the Renaissance. Significantly, however, Goneril's and Regan's desires do not bind them together as women. During America's twentieth-century sexual revolution, mass culture (re)discovered the clitoris and female sexual desire. In that revolution, activists (and then the mass media) claimed female desire as a liberating force—not a male fantasy, but a force that helped women to identify with one another.[9] This personally liberating and politically consolidating desire is not the desire that Shakespeare depicts in Goneril and Regan. Their sexual desire divides the sisters from one another. Or, more accurately to the play, in its earliest manifestations—as excess of tongue, and excess of ambition—it seems to bind them, only to later divide them horribly. Goneril says to her sister, "pray you, let vs sit together" (TLN 328; 1.1.301).[10] But the sisters' sexual and political ambition knows no bounds, as ambition frequently does not in Renaissance texts, especially when found in women or other subordinated people, such as servants and bastards; and, ultimately, their lust will divide them to the point of reciprocal murder plans.

Goneril's and Regan's horrific lust accompanies the play's general commentary on women as essentially whores, commentary that comes from trustworthy characters as well as from the arguably mad Lear and other characters who might be less credible. The Fool, in particular, mouths this terrible "truth" about women's sexual desires, but his critique of lustful women echoes in Kent's and Lear's discourse. The play's continual commentary on women's debased sexual natures has angered and disappointed feminist critics, and our ire is surely justified. Indeed, readers and audiences should be angry with this language if we are not to bypass, and then perhaps to naturalize, this hateful discourse; we ignore it at our peril. The feminist critique of the play's misogyny points to the continuities between misogynies that belong to different historical eras. Traces of revulsion at women's sexual desire can still be found in American mass culture, a culture that generally celebrates sexual desire in men especially but also in women and that uses desire to sell products.[11] But continuity between ideologies and cultures is not identity. Whereas the Victorians assumed that women had or should have no sexual desire and that men had plenty, the English Renaissance assumed that women had more sexual desire than did men. *King Lear* is not dedicated to the hatred of women, but it is dedicated to the hatred of lust; it is this second hatred that we as modern readers have confused with modern misogyny.[12] Seeing the distinctions as well as the continuities between misogynies is crucial to the task of tracing the early genealogy of heterosexuality.

King Lear for "Tender Minded" Men

What the feminist critique of *King Lear*'s misogyny has missed is the play's pervasive disgust with lust on the part of both men and women. Also missed in that critique are the play's mixed messages on femininity. Both *King Lear*'s disgust with male lust and the play's mixed messages point to a world in which gender was not essentially linked to bodies. In *King Lear* we are not yet in the world that would be created over the course of the long eighteenth century: a world that would be more divided according to gendered bodies, gendered spaces, gendered professions, and less divided according to rank.[13] This more modern sexual/social/political world is also a world that would begin to value in its core ideologies (and for men only) the lust and greed that *King Lear* is so concerned to denigrate. Over the course of the English long eighteenth century, the sin of greed would be tranformed into, on the one hand, the positively valued pursuit of profit by most white men and, on the other hand, the negatively valued (but necessary to the economy) pursuit of luxury goods by white women.[14] Over that same period, the sin of lust would be transformed into, on the one hand, the positively valued pursuit of sexual pleasure with women by most white men, and the negatively valued pursuit of sexual pleasure with men by a small group of women (whores). These profound and profoundly linked ideological shifts were uneven and sometimes contradictory, and they intersect with the formation of racial discourse and of discourses of lesbianism and homosexuality.[15] What is significant at this point in my overall argument is that *King Lear* does not anticipate those shifts any more than medieval morality plays anticipated those shifts. If we look carefully at the play's misogyny, we can see the shape of its critique of lust and greed as they had been imagined in Christian discourse for many centuries.

When *King Lear* talks about femininity in other than sexual terms, its references are less consistently hateful and more contradictory than might be immediately apparent. The play applauds as often as it degrades what belongs to femininity in the play, aside from sexual desire. Likewise, *King Lear* does not approve men's actions just because they are gendered masculine. Edmund asks the unnamed captain to kill Lear and Cordelia in jail, commenting that "to be tender minded / Do's not become a Sword" (TLN 2974–2975), and in the quarto the captain replies that "If it bee mans worke" he'll "do't" (K4v; 5.3.32–33, 40).[16] But unlike Edmund, *King Lear* does not unambiguously condemn tender-mindedness. The captain would certainly have done better "to be tender minded." The play's approval of tender-mindedness is reiterated, and tender-mindedness is, simultaneously, explicitly feminized in the series of insults that Goneril flings at her husband, Albany. Goneril accuses Albany of "milky gentlenesse," and she calls him her "mild husband" (TLN 865, 2268; 1.4.320, 4.2.1). She also tells Oswald that "the Cowish terror of [Albany's] spirit" is responsible for his critical attitude toward her plans (TLN 2280; 4.2.12). As soon as this disdainful Albany appears on stage, Goneril calls him "Milke-Liver'd man"; and, in the quarto, when Albany tells her that she is shielded from any physically violent response by her "womans shape," Goneril taunts him with "Marry your manhood now" (H4; 4.2.51, 68–69). Goneril also tells Edmund that since Albany is "Cowish" she "must change names at home, and giue the Distaffe / Into [her] Husbands hands" (TLN 2285–2286; 4.2.17–18).[17] Whereas Goneril intends these references to womanliness as insults, the play, not surprisingly given her characterization, may not. Albany's femininity may be the source of his strength.

The play seemingly offers Albany's "milky gentlenesse" as a contrast to and as a corrective for the brutality of the sisters' lust and greed. In this play, Albany's efforts to restore connections between men and between men and women seem to be valued over war. Constance Jordan suggests,

> [b]y representing woman as a type in whom are incarnate virtues specifically associated with femininity—mercy, patience, temperance, and so forth—[Renaissance] feminists began to argue not only for the worth of woman but also for the feminization of society as a whole. Correspondingly, they spoke of a degenerate kind of masculinity—the cruelty (typically gratuitous) of the bully and the tyrant—and its deleterious effects on the family and the state. (137)

King Lear seems to value Albany's womanly gentleness above his wife's and her sister's tyrannous and masculine war-making. Thus, although the play contributes to misogyny in its representation of the sisters, its representation of a feminized Albany may contribute to Renaissance proto-feminism.

Unlike the sisters who would destroy their father's kingdom, Albany would like to reknit the bonds that originally constituted it, the bonds Kent calls "the holy cords . . . Which are t'intrince t'vnloose" (TLN 1148; 2.2.66–67). Kent's usage of the word "intrince" is the sole usage the *OED* can find (apart from Henry Howard Furness, the Shakespeare editor who picked up the word from this *King Lear* usage and used "intrinse to unloose" in his introduction to *A Midsummer Night's Dream*). The *OED* defines "intrince" as "intricate, entangled, involved"; however it is as likely that Shakespeare was reaching for a meaning closer to the modern meaning of "intrinsic."[18]

Kent speaks in this scene of the bonds between men that tie them to godliness in one another, bonds that do not loosen even when people disregard them. Albany's milky, nutritive nature connects him to these "holy cords." Goneril is insulting Albany by feminizing him, but the play endorses a feminized milky kindness at the same time that it rejects lust and greed. Though critics have read Albany's actions in the play as weak and have connected Goneril's gendered insults to the play's misogyny, those insults can be read as inadvertent compliments about Albany's attempts to maintain the play-world's "holy cords."[19] Perhaps we should not so quickly accept Goneril's judgments of her husband; rather we should see the compliments that Shakespeare imbeds in those judgments.

Like Goneril's gendered insults, Lear's references to feminine weakness and sickness have customarily been read as part of his (and the play's) misogyny. However, it is also possible to read them as participating in the play's valuation of certain aspects of what was seen as femininity at the time. Lear asks the gods to give him anger, which will drive his revenge on his daughters, rather than tears, which he describes as "womens weapons, water drops, / [that] Staine [his] mans cheekes" (TLN 1577–1578; 2.4.272–273). His speech contrasts devalued feminine tears to valuable masculine revenge. It is far from clear, however, that the play assents to Lear's hierarchical valuation of emotion. Revenge in the play is atavistic, the emotion that motivates the play's villains — the bastard Edmund wants revenge for his inability to inherit under primogeniture, the sisters take revenge on each other for what they see as sexual transgressions, and, tellingly, Regan and Cornwall exact one of the most horrific stage revenges in the period when they stamp out Gloucester's eyes on stage. In contrast, *King Lear* highly values pity that inspires tears. Lear's tears, which he rejects as feminine, connect him to Cordelia, whose understanding of her father's dire situation and of her duty as a child, provokes "an ample teare" (in the quarto) (H4v; 4.3.11). When he begins to pity the mad Lear, Edgar almost loses his role as poor Tom: "My teares begin to take his part so much, They marre my counterfetting" (TLN 2018–2019; 3.6.55–56). Here tears lead to truth: they are a mark of authenticity, and they are also (or in consequence) a sign of goodness and purity.[20] If we can read Lear's reference to the "Mother," the "*Hystorica passio*," that he orders "downe" in act two as a piece of the play's misogyny, we can also read that reference as connected to the play's affection for the milk of human kindness.[21] Lear says that his sorrow is a wandering womb, a "Mother," and that its "Element [is] below" (TLN 1328–1329; 2.4.54–56). Again, Lear invokes a hierarchy, one that connects what is feminine to the bottom, the "below" that in his later speech becomes the "sulphurous pit" of women's genitals (TLN 2570; 4.6.125). Again, however, Lear's hierarchical understanding of gender apart from sexual desire may be a piece of his deeply mistaken (in the play's terms) worldview. Shakespeare may well invoke "the Mother" in this point as a corrective to Lear's vengefulness. Lear might have listened productively to what is below rather than dismissing it and trying to soldier on, relying on his vengeful masculinity.

The "Virus of the Precursor" and Male Chastity

King Lear certainly shows us horrible women, but its misogyny is distinctly not modern misogyny. While the play overwhelmingly sees women as monstrously sexually loose, in the quarto, Cornwall's servant asserts that if Regan "live[s] long, & in the end meet[s] the old course of death, women will all turne monsters" (H2; 3.7.104–106). The servant is commenting, however, not on Regan's sexual desires but on her inordinate violence, a violence that Cornwall shares and for which the play condemns him. According to the servant, women are not yet monstrously violent (and, of course, Regan does not "live long" or die of old age). There are significant continuities between the misogyny in the play and today's misogyny as well as significant continuities between Renaissance and today's (American and English) ideologies of masculinity and femininity. Tears, gentleness, cowardice, and milkiness are still largely gendered feminine; however these continuities or similiarities do not mean that the respective culture's gender ideologies are the same. Furthermore, they do not mean that gender held the same place within the social order in different historical eras. Arguably, rank was a more meaningful category than gender within Shakespeare's culture.[22] Also, passion has been gendered male during different historical eras.[23] And, as Jean Howard and Phyllis Rackin suggest, femininity has at times been associated with taking up arms and at other times been radically disassociated from fighting.

When we, as critics and readers of the play, insist that the play's disgust with female desire is the same thing as the play's disgust with women as a category, we reduce women to the same thing that the play's sexual misogyny attempts to reduce women to—sexual desire. This insistence that these disgusts are the same may be a feature of the modern era, a feature of what Arnold Davidson calls "the psychiatric style of reasoning" (23). In that style of reasoning, sex is believed to determine, to a large extent, "the shape of ourselves as subjects" (18). Under the influence of that style of reasoning, we read and see the play's disgust with sexual desire (which the play often links to women in general and to the evil sisters in particular) as its disgust with women when, in reality, the play is as disgusted with men's desire for women as it is with women's desire for men. Since we, under the influence of "the psychiatric style of reasoning" see sex and sexual desire as central to identity, our revulsion at how the play treats sexualized women can hardly be ameliorated when it is pointed out that the play approves of the desexualized Cordelia and of expressions of "femininity" in men. This pattern of disgust and approval would mean, to a late-twentieth-century critic like myself, that women cannot be approved of if they have sexual desire. This is hardly a boon if we believe, as most post-Freudian people do, that sex is at the core of subjectivity. Nevertheless, I want to insist, with Davidson, that "Chastity and virginity," the categories under the auspices of which *King Lear* and Shakespeare's culture understood sex,

> are moral categories denoting a relation between the will and the flesh; they are not categories of sexuality. Although we tend to read back our own categories of sexuality into older moral categories, partly because it is so difficult to distinguish them precisely, it is crucial . . . that we separate the two. Blurring the two kinds of categories leads to epistemological and conceptual lack of differentiation, and results in the historiographical infection that the great French historian of science Georges Canguilhem has called the "virus of the precursor." We perpetually look for precursors to our categories of sexuality in essentially different domains, producing anachronisms at best and unintelligibility at worst. (37)

We risk making the play's attitude toward sex unintelligible when we collapse its representation of women's and men's horrific lust into our own understanding of misogyny. One consequence of this particular "virus of the precursor" is our neglect of the category of male chastity, a category of behavior essential to the play and to Renaissance understandings of lust but largely absent from a modern map of sexuality.

Saint Paul (who modeled his male chastity after Christ), Augustine, Thomas Aquinas, and the Renaissance Christian thinkers, Catholic and Protestant, who followed their lead saw women as particularly susceptible to lust because lust was a besetting sin of humankind initiated in the Fall (frequently blamed largely on Eve) and because women, naturally weaker than men, were naturally more prone to sin.

John Donne, reflecting on the problem "Why Hath the Common Opinion Afforded Women Souls?"—distinctly not a twentieth-century problem—suggests that "we have given women souls only to make them capable of damnation" (*John Donne* 142). In contrast, twentieth-century thinkers, conditioned by "the psychiatric style of reasoning," see sexuality as the essence of human personality. To mistake the Renaissance Christian understanding of lust besetting the soul for the modern understanding of sexual desire as forming gender and personality is to misread fundamentally the history of sexuality and, therefore, to misread sex as it is represented in earlier eras. In the case of *King Lear*, this misreading has caused critics to see the play's thoroughgoing critique of lust as modern misogyny rather than the critique of lust in men and women that it is. That misreading has also caused critics to misunderstand the relationship between the play's critique of lust and its critique of greed.

If *King Lear* despises sexual desire in women, it equally, and even perhaps more strongly, despises men's sexual desire for women. Gloucester's lecherous laughter at his sexual "good sport" is the first critical mistake by a man in the play (TLN 26; 1.1.21–22), and this mistake initiates a series of men's blunders in *King Lear*. The play's central villain, Edmund, called just "Bastard" in many speech prefixes, personifies his father's sexual desire and his mother's whoredom.[24] Kent's own goodness is partially signified by his disdain for sexual involvement with women. Disguised as Caius, he tells Lear that he is "not so young, Sir, to loue a woman for singing, nor so old to dote on her for any thing" (TLN 568–569; 1.4.34–35). Modern texts render "any thing" as the compound word "anything"; thus they lose the sexual connotation in Kent's clause. However, the word "thing" throughout Shakespeare's plays, as we have seen, can signify as sexual organ, sometimes male and sometimes female.[25] Kent is not so old that he would be interested in a woman for her "thing." Sexual interest in women belongs to young fools and old dotards. Although boys are heavily sexualized in many of Shakespeare's plays, confirming his culture's belief in the sexual heedlessness (and the femininity) of boyhood, the only boy in *King Lear*, the Fool, derides male sexual desire as much as he derides the whores who participate in lust.

The Fool teaches Lear "a speech" that tells him to "Leaue [his] drinke and [his] whore" (TLN 654; 1.4.107). If the connection between female speech and female unchastity is a commonplace in Renaissance England, so is the more familiar connection between male drunkenness and male unchastity. However, with notable exceptions, the late-twentieth-century American and English publics approve of both drinking and sex (with women) for men.[26] Masculinity, men having (or desiring) sex with women, and drinking, even to excess, go together—a cultural common sense relied upon in some American beer commercials.[27] In contrast, Shakespeare's England praised abstemious behavior in noble men, whatever that abstemious behavior might have meant in a world in which alcoholic beverages were drunk as a matter of course throughout the day.[28] The early-seventeenth-century link between men's drinking and men's sexual interest in women (both of which feminize a man) shows up in *Hamlet*'s first act, when Hamlet criticizes Claudius's "wassels" (TLN 613; 1.4.10). Claudius has enslaved his soul to his lust for Gertrude, and his lust appears as well in his alcoholic debauchery. In *King Lear*, Goneril tells her father that he cannot keep his hundred knights and squires in her house any longer because his men are

> so disorder'd, so debosh'd and bold,
> That this our Court infected with their manners,
> Shewes like a riotous Inne; Epicurisme and Lust
> Makes it more like a Tauerne, or a Brothell,
> Then a grac'd Pallace. (TLN 751–755; 1.4.217–221)

Coming from a queen of excess, this criticism is surely meant to seem hypocritical, but the complaint has its roots in the same linked critique of drinking and male–female sex that informs the Fool's lesson for Lear and Hamlet's criticism of Claudius. Taverns resemble brothels, and both are opposed to grace.

The opposition between sex and reason for men appears in another ironic speech during *Lear*'s storm. The Fool begs the king to take shelter from the storm, saying, "He that has a house to put's head in, has a good Head-peece." Then he chants a little piece of doggerel, which begins "The Codpiece that will house, before the head has any; The Head, and he shall Lowse: so Beggers marry many" (TLN 1680–1683; 3.2.24–29). Stupid men neglect preparing for life, according to the Fool, because of their propensity to "house" their codpieces in women's vaginas. In Renaissance sexual slang, the codpiece, the item of clothing that simultaneously covered and displayed the penis, often functions as a metonym for the penis.[29] The Fool praises the intelligence of men who ignore housing their penises in favor of housing their bodies and feeding themselves. He also invokes the social cost of male–female sex, which produces "Beggers." England's food shortages at the time of *Lear*'s first performances may well have made the beggars produced by such sex seem excessive. Moments later, Kent comes on scene and asks in the storm's melee, "Who's there?" The Fool answers, "Marry here's Grace, and a Codpiece, that's a Wiseman and a Foole" (1691–1693; 3.2.37–38). The Fool's answer is a complex piece of rhetoric. He states that the king, who represents God's grace on earth, is on the stage with the Fool, who may have worn an outsized codpiece as part of his Fool's regalia. The king should be wise by the nature of his office and person, and the boy Fool, by his nature, should be foolish. In fact, since the king refuses shelter, he is foolish, and the Fool, seeking to get both people out of the storm, is wise. The Fool's irony works, nevertheless, only because of the cultural commonplace that associates wisdom and grace with kingship, and the penis and sexual pleasure with foolishness. Male sexual pleasure with women is foolish and naturally opposed to grace.

We can see the association of male sexual pleasure and fools very clearly in Shakespeare's comedy *As You Like It*. That play's Clowne, as we have seen, pursues Audrey for his sexual satisfaction, willing to be falsely married so that he may leave her thereafter to pursue other women. Audrey is not his first sexual experience; he recalls his wooing of *"Jane Smile,"* to whom he offered two "cods" (peas, but also testicles in Renaissance slang) (TLN 830–834; 2.4.43, 46). Testicles were seen in the Renaissance as the home of the seed that was responsible for making boys who would grow up to inherit property.[30] They were, therefore, highly valued. Noble men protected them and displayed them in codpieces as symbols of power and property. This power did not reside, as sexual power may in modern men, in the ability to take pleasure in ejaculation with multiple women; rather this power inhered in conservation of the seed and very discriminate ejaculation, within marriage, and only for the "making" as Gloucester puts it, of legitimate male heirs. Only a clown, without property or concern for status, would give away his "cods." Unlike *As You Like It*'s Clowne, *King Lear*'s fool speaks of the foolishness of men who house their codpieces rather than themselves, men who divest themselves of their rightful places in society. *King Lear* is deeply invested in maintaining sexual/rank distinctions between men, just as it is invested in male chastity.[31]

When Kent, the Fool, and Lear enter the hovel to escape the storm, they run into Edgar, disguised as poor Tom, a Bedlam beggar. True to the Fool's wisdom about sex and beggary, Edgar blames his madness and his descent into poverty, in his faux-lucid moments, on his sexual exploits.[32] Two of his pieces of advice to the men around him concern their propensities for sex with women. He warns, "commit not with mans sworne Spouse" and "Keepe thy foote out of Brothels, thy hand out of Plackets" (TLN 1861–1862, 1876–1877; 3.4.77, 89–90). Echoing the play's preoccupation with adultery—the natural partner of male–female desire, as I will argue in chapter 2—Edgar, as poor Tom, tells men not to violate marriage oaths, as his father Gloucester might have. Edgar, also, like the Fool, admonishes men against whorehouses. He goes beyond illicit sexual activities, however, and advises against sex with women altogether, which would entail men putting their hands in "plackets," "the opening or slit at the top of a skirt or a petticoat" (*OED* "placket" 3). When Lear asks what kind of a man poor Tom was before his transformation to Bedlam beggar, Edgar tells the story of his origins. He says,

> A Seruing man? Proud in heart, and minde; that curl'd my haire, wore Gloues in my cap; seru'd the Lust of my Mistris heart, and did the acte of darknesse with her . . . One, that slept in the contriuing of Lust, and wak'd to doe it. Wine lou'd I deerely, Dice deerely; and in Woman, out-Paramour'd the Turke.[33]

Again, we see the connection between the excessive consumption of alcohol—"Wine lou'd I deerely"—and sexual desire for women. Edgar's story also alludes to another Renaissance story surrounding male–female sex, the fantasy of the Turkish harem. As I will show in chapter 5, that fantasy informed English Renaissance attitudes toward exotic and alien men, shoring up English masculinity against the projected effeminate sexual looseness of those men. Edgar's story is yet another manifestation of *King Lear*'s concern with male chastity. Although the story notes "the Lust of [Tom's] Mistris heart" and thus contributes to the play's sexual misogyny, it is as much or more a story that admonishes men for their own lust for women. Tom did not only serve his mistress' lust, he served his own. The "Gloues in [his] cap" represent the trinkets given him by the women he has wooed, and he boasts of having collected a harem, outdoing the famously lustful (and effeminate) Sultan. Of course, in the play's reality, Edgar, like Kent, has no interest in women at all. Both virtuous characters represent, instead, male chastity.

Greed and Lust

King Lear censures male unchastity as much as it does female lust. And its condemnation of male–female sexual desire on the part of both men and women is not separable from its condemnation of the abuses suffered by the poor at the hands of the rich. As de Grazia notes, in the twentieth century, *Lear* has often been read as somehow straddling or negotiating an ideological divide between emerging capitalism and what James Kavanagh, for example, terms "the hierarchical ideology of fealty, faith and restraint, which lives the world as a field of reciprocal obligation" (157).[34] However, as Judy Kronenfeld has demonstrated so comprehensively, what might look like radical or modern ideas about the perfidy of the rich or of capitalism are actually premodern Christian concepts, political and social ideas that "turn up as much or more in the traditional Christian culture as in revolutionary discourse" (Kronenfeld 224). If we attend to the imbrication of the play's economic messages in its critique of lust, what we see is a play deeply embedded in the Renaissance Christian homosocial imaginary, which is constituted in ties between men and which is continually under threat from men's own lust and greed.

Both feminist and Marxist readings of the play, though immensely productive, have had to read the play partially, in both senses of the word partial. As all readings must do, they have attended to what looks like pertinent language: feminists reading the play's misogyny, and Marxists reading its economic language and its grasping characters. Therefore, both feminists and Marxists have read *King Lear* as if the play's obsessive focus on adultery and lust and its consequent disgust with female bodies and female desires are somehow divorced from its discussion of men's economic and political interests. Jean Howard and Scott Cutler Shershow ask why "the present relationship of Marxism to feminism [is] imagined as an unhappy marriage where the wife loses control of her property?" (9). *King Lear* has certainly been a case in point. Marxist readings of the play have proliferated, and feminists have largely given up on the play. However, a less fragmented reading of the play may help to us to see the homosocial imaginary in the play that both feminists and Marxists have missed.

Let me begin this segment of my argument with my own use of evidence in this chapter so far. In order to divorce the play's critique of male–female sex from its critique of greed, I have had to either quote the play partially (of course all quotation is always partial) or to attend to only one of a quotation's valences. For example, in my discussion of poor Tom's origins, I left lines out of the middle and the end of Edgar's story. After Edgar says that he did "the act of darkness" with his mistress, he says that he "Swore as many Oathes as [he] spake words, & broke them in the sweet face of Heauen" (TLN 1868–1869; 3.4.82–83). After he talks about "out-Paramour[ing] the Turke," he says that he was "False of heart, light of eare, bloody of hand; Hog in sloth, Foxe in stealth, Wolfe in greedinesse, Dog in madnes, [and] Lyon in prey," and he warns his auditor, the king, to "Let not the creaking of shooes, Nor the rustling of Silkes, betray [his] poore heart to woman" (TLN 1872–1876; 3.4.86–89). These comments add to the misogynistic valence of poor Tom's story: women are out to steal men's hearts. Those comments also embed the story's misogyny and its antisex rhetoric within a broader discourse that connects women's perfidy and men's inclination to lust to other sins against "the sweet face of Heauen."

The references to sex in *Lear* come packaged with a general critique of sin that had been central to Christian doctrine since that doctrine was codified by Saint Paul, and that has its roots in the Hebrew bible. Thus, the lust that the imagined poor Tom served in his mistress and in himself is intimately related to the "Oathes" that he "spake" and "broke . . . in the sweet face of Heauen." And heaven's "sweet face" is utterly opposed to his lust, his drinking, his greed, and the litany of other bestial sins that Tom recounts. Lust is primary, because, as Aquinas says, "it works the greatest havoc in a man's mind" (1804), but oaths, lies, bloodiness, sloth, and stealth come in the package, and lust's partner, greed, is prominently displayed in Tom's regretted behavior. His greed manifested in his gambling, his wolvish avarice, and his penchant for women's "creaking" shoes and "rustling" silks. This penchant is part of the play's ongoing demonization of luxury.[35] *King Lear* continually associates sex with either the greed of the man involved in sex with women or the greed of men who surround men who enjoy sex with women and (like the whores who prey on men) take pecuniary advantage of those sex-loving men's weakness. Poor Tom warns Lear to keep his "hand out of Plackets, [his] pen from Lenders Books, and [also to] defye the foule Fiend" (TLN 1776–1778; 3.4.90–91).

The Fool's discourse, and then the king's, on women's and men's sexual crimes (that is, their penchant for male–female sex) also refers to greed and to economic disparity. According to the Fool, Fortune is not just an "arrant whore" but, specifically an "arrant whore, / [who] nere turns the key to th'poore" (TLN 1325; 2.4.50–51). Just as the play depicts Goneril and Regan as lustful and also negligent toward England's people, the Fool links Fortune's notorious sexual looseness to her disregard for the impoverished. The prophecy about Merlin that the fool speaks in the folio version of the play also links greed and lust. He predicts a time when "Vsurers tell their Gold i'th'Field / And

Baudes, and whores, do Churches build" (TLN 1744–1745; 3.2.87–88). This never-never land of generous, open moneylenders and church-supporting sexual criminals is the magical solution to the play's reality, in which greed and lust temporarily triumph together, as Renaissance Christian doctrine predicts they will when men and women succumb to their sinful natures. Lear's own mad discourse becomes an echo of the Fool's critique of this "natural" pair, lust and greed. He cries out,

> Thou, Rascall Beadle, hold thy bloody hand: why dost thou lash that Whore? Strip thyne owne backe, thou hotly lusts to vse her in that kind, for which thou whips't her. The Vsurer hangs the Cozener. Through tatter'd cloathes [small]³⁶ Vices do appeare: Robes, and furr'd gownes hide all. (TLN 2603–2608; 4.6.154–159)

In this mad speech, even Lear (whose words for the most part focus on women's desire and women's debased bodies) concentrates on male lust. It is the "Rascall Beadle," the representative of male moral authority, who suffers from the lust that destroys the social world. In the speech, Lear makes an analogy between the degraded desires of the beadle, who should represent the church (and male chastity), and the sins of the usurer, the greedy moneylender who, in the guise of authority (the "Robes, and furr'd gownes" of the rich), punishes the lesser vices of the poor.

Most modern critics have failed to see how central the play's concern with lust is to its concern with poverty: the focal spectacle displayed in *King Lear*, the Bedlam beggar, is a man destroyed by his own lust on the level of his fictional story and destroyed by his father's lust on the level of Edgar's "real" story. The play does not separate the spiritual and social problems of lust and greed. So, in Gloucester's famous moment of repentance, he not only gives his remaining fortune to his disguised son (who, of course, is its proper recipient), he also begs the Heavens,

> Let the superfluous, and Lust-dieted man,
> That slaues your ordinance, that will not see
> Because he dos not feele, feele your powre quickly:
> So distribution should vndoo excesse,
> And each man have enough. (TLN 2252–2256; 4.1.67–71)

This appeal explicitly links lust and greed and connects their punishment to a social vision in which all will be able to eat—the vision that opposes Goneril and Regan's voracious, sexualized grasping world, the world that Gloucester embraced at the beginning of the play.

In the two plots of the play, Gloucester's lust creates his youngest son's greed, which in turn creates his eldest son's beggary, and Lear's greed (his penchant for measuring everything in economic terms) provokes his eldest daughters' lusts and causes him to reject his youngest daughter, a rejection that symbolically makes her into a beggar by depriving her of her dowry. Both fathers repent by rejecting lust and greed in themselves and in the world: both beg the rich to "feele what wretches feele, / That [they] maist shake the superflux to them, / And shew the Heauens more iust" (TLN 1815–1817; 3.4.35–37). Though the play offers neither Lear nor Gloucester any unqualified redemption in this world, it does show both men lifted up, literally and figuratively, by their fellow men. *King Lear* was performed at court on St. Stephen's Day, the day of the year on which "the poor were entitled to the hospitality and charity of the rich" (de Grazia, "Ideology" 32); and Kent's speech about the "holy cords" sounds remarkably like verse 12 of Ecclesiastes 4 (one of the texts in the Saint Stephen's Day liturgy):[37] "And if one ouercome him, two shal stande against him: and a threfolde coard is not easely broken." Like the Saint Stephen's Day liturgy, the play offers homosocial bonding as the best possibility for living men. The bonds that hold men to their masters and most importantly to God's word are "the holy cords . . . Which are t'intrince t'vnloose" (TLN 1148; 2.2.66–67). These bonds define the comfort the play offers, and, tellingly, they are not marital or sexual bonds. They are the bonds that at the play's end hold Kent, Albany, and Edgar together, in at least a temporary "threfolde coard" that will not be broken.

King Lear opens with two social problems, two problems that I have been arguing are deeply linked in its culture's imaginary: Gloucester's unrepentant lust and Lear's unrepentant greed. As Peter Holbrook brilliantly notes, that greed manifests in the play's first scene (as does Gloucester's lust). Greed is Lear's sin when he sells his land for love, believing that love has a price. Sales like this have a hoary literary history. And scholars of English literature need not go as far toward modernity as Shakespeare to find characters for whom everything is salable. In the late fourteenth century, William Langland's dreamer, Will, sees a pardoner preaching to the unlearned and vowing to redeem them of their sins. He says, "Thus ye gyue youre gold glotons to helpe / And leneth hit lorelles that lecherye haunten" (*Piers Plowman*, Prologue 74–75).[38] This pardoner offers

God's grace for his parishoner's gold, and he is a lecher and a glutton as well as a human representation of avarice. Langland's dreamer watches while Simonye (the sale of chuch appointments) and Syuile (the corrupt civil law) proclaim the marriage of Mede (profit) to Fals[e]. Their marriage charter enables them to be "pr[inces] in pruyde and pouert to dispice." It grants them "vsurye and Auaryce . . . With al the lordschip of leccherye" (Passus II, 87, 94, 96). Langland and Shakespeare envision a world in which greed (the profit motive) and lechery walk hand in hand. They envision that world, but they do not approve of it, even when they make their greedy characters charismatic and fascinating. Throughout the medieval and Renaissance worlds, authors acknowledge the attraction of sin, an acknowledgment that is by no means an endorsement. As McKeon suggests, "[c]apitalist ideology entails, most fundamentally, the attribution of value to capitalist activity: minimally, as valuable in its own right; finally, even as value-creating" (*Origins* 201). Critics who fail to see that *Lear* does not satisfy this most minimal criterion of capitalist ideology risk ignoring how this text imagines the correct relation of people to their conditions of sexual and economic existence.

I would argue that *Lear*'s premodernity is signalled particularly in the way it links its critique of greed to its critique of lust. As Langland's marriage of Meed to Fals[e] suggests, lechery, avarice, and the prideful dismissal of poverty are demonized together in the world before modernity. Avarice and Lechery ride next to one another in Spenser's House of Pride (*Faerie Queene*, book 1), and they are similarly linked in *King Lear*, where they are also defeated as a twosome. Thus Lear's revelation in the storm that "houselesse pouertie" deserves shelter and that he has "tane [taken] / Too little care" of the plight of "Poore naked wretches" (TLN 1807–1814) and Gloucester's plea that "distribution should vndoo excesse, / And each man haue enough" (TLN 2555–2556) are linked in the play to Goneril's and Regan's lustful self-destruction and to greedy Edmund's downfall.

Just as feminist readings of the play miss its criticism of lust in men as well as in women and miss its approval of "milky gentleness" because they read the play's misogyny as modern misogyny, Marxist readings of the play misread its Renaissance critique of avarice as a criticism of modern or proto-modern economic relations; they are also succumbing to "the virus of the precursor." Thus neither types of readings have seen the relationship between the play's sexual misogyny and its criticism of economic disparity. Likewise, neither feminist nor Marxist readings have spent much time wondering about the relevance of multivalent Renaissance Christianities to either of their focal points—the play's misogyny or its criticism of inequitable economic relations.[39] I am not suggesting that attending to the play's Christian context somehow magically heals the split between feminist and Marxist readings of the play or that it will solve the problems the play raises. I am suggesting, however, that the play's and Shakespeare's world's sexual misogyny and especially its disgust with lust in men as well as women is founded in Christian doctrine. That doctrine took up the ubiquitous classical beliefs that women were less reasonable than men and that, therefore, they were more sexually interested than men and colored those beliefs with a rejection of the carnal in men and women. As Kronenfeld shows, the play's beliefs that the rich are no better than the poor in the eyes of God, but that the disparity between the rich and the poor will only be erased in heaven—that on earth charity is the solution for this disparity—are also founded in Renaissance Christian doctrine. Should feminists and Marxists—or for that matter Marxist feminists (materialist feminists)—be satisfied with Renaissance Christian doctrine as somehow offering the solution to either their problems with the play or the solution to the suffering the play exposes? No way. The sexual misogyny in the play certainly fed hatred of women's bodies and that hatred must have had real consequences in Shakespeare's world. Unremarked, that hatred could confirm misogyny today. Nevertheless, those two misogynies are not the same; and the differences between them are significant. The play's hope for a charitable solution to the problem of poverty— in charitable giving by people who are naturally better off in this world than other people—must also have confirmed oppressive economic structures in Shakespeare's world even as today the insistence that poverty is a problem only to be ameliorated by private charity confirms today's oppressive structures. Despite their resemblances to one another, however, the two solutions and the two economic structures are not the same. And the differences between them are significant.

If Fredric Jameson is right that great works of art are always both complicit with "privilege and class domination" and simultaneously "Utopian," then both aspects of *King Lear* are linked to the play's Renaissance Christian worldview (299, 296). On the one hand, the solution that Lear and Gloucester and the play propose to the problems of the poor is based on "violence and exploitation." That solution depends upon and advocates natural distinctions between people, distinctions that guarantee that some people will have a lot and many will have (at best) only enough. That solution "effaces the less comfortable real inequality of place that it assumes and confirms" (Kavanagh 159). As de Grazia notes, Edgar finally inherits all: "There is nothing 'handy-dandy' or 'pell-mell' about the shaking of the superflux, the undoing of excess: it follows the precise course of primogeniture and succession" ("Ideology" 31). On the other hand, this solution is at the same time one of the play's Utopian impulses. Seventeenth-century England could only imagine Christian charity truly manifest on earth in a Utopia; any work of art that strives to show the poor having enough as a real and viable possibility is Utopian. Of course the term "Utopia" comes from Thomas More's sixteenth-century imaginary land, founded on Christian communal principles, a land in which there are natural distinctions between people but in which everyone has enough. In addition, on the one hand, the solution to lust that the play proposes is a world without women or at least without the male lust that women inspire and feed. Clearly this is a solution based on "violence and exploitation." On the other hand, it is a Utopian solution in a Renaissance Christian context in which lust is an aspect of people's original sin. The early Christian thinkers such as Aquinas and Augustine whose thought was still so powerful in Shakespeare's England were eager to imagine a world without lust, in which the sexual organs would act for propagation only and then only under the control of men's reasonable minds and wholly without lust. And in this Utopian world there would be less poverty since men's and women's indiscriminate sex would not lead to beggars.[40] The Utopian desires for the defeat of greed and lust give *King Lear* its vital energy, and those Utopian desires are inseparable from the play's vested interests in a world that requires human suffering.

The New Sexual World

King Lear suggests that we do not get to a new sexual world until, to use Marx's words, we see Plutus pulled "by the hair of his head from the bowels of the earth" and greeted "as the glittering incarnation of the very principle" of English life (*Capital* 149); that new world is also not present until white male sexual pleasure is a principle of English life and female sexual pleasure is buried in the earth's bowels—this would entail men no longer being imagined as naturally belonging forever to different categories based on rank. It would also require that in men's imaginations women become securely placed either in the home or in the brothel, and that in people's common sense, homes would not be always potentially brothels because they have women in them. This reading of *King Lear* also suggests that a new sexual world is not present until the male and the female are more securely defined as essentially separate and distinct, and until personality rather than the soul defines people. The process of these distinctions, reimaginations, unearthings, and burials was long and complex, and it involves several partial, tentative, and rejected distinctions, reimaginations, reburials, and rebirths; but one massive birth occured, as the coming chapters will suggest, in Restoration England. And we can see its signs, its tracks, in Restoration rewritings of Shakespeare's plays.

In *King Lear*, Edgar declares that his father Gloucester's sexual pleasure "Cost him his eyes," and the Bastard replies, "Th'hast spoken right, 'tis true" (TLN 3134–3135; 5.3.172).[41] Edmund might appear to anticipate a new sexual world; but he is conceived firmly within the homosocial imaginary, an imaginary whose precepts he, in his death throes, approves. When Nahum Tate rewrote *King Lear* in the Restoration, it made much less common sense to blame Edmund's villainy on Gloucester's adulterous sexual pleasure. Tate has Edgar elaborate on the charge that Gloucester's act "cost him his eyes," so as to explain how exactly such an act might have such a result. Tate's Edgar says to Edmund, "from thy licentious Mother / Thou draw'st thy Villany" (60). Although Tate's Edgar calls Edmund "Thy Father's Sin," he cannot see Edmund as the natural and naturally villainous Bastard that in Shakespeare's play is the result of that sin. Instead, Tate attributes Edmund's villainy to his "licentious Mother." In Shakespeare's play, Gloucester claims that "there was good sport at [Edmund's] making, and the [w]horeson must be acknowledged" (TLN 26–27; 1.1.21–22). Tate's revision assumes that Edmund's villainy comes from his "licentious Mother," not from his father's "good sport." His villainy becomes an inherited characteristic rather than the natural result of male–female extramarital sex. In fact, Tate's Gloucester sees Edgar too as the result of sexual pleasure. Tate's play opens after Edmund has convinced Gloucester of Edgar's disobedience, and early in the first scene, Tate's Gloucester complains that *Edgar* "draws plagues on [his] white head that urge [him] still / To curse in Age the pleasure of [his] Youth" (2). In this Restoration tragedy, both Edgar and Edmund are the results of their father's natural sexual pleasure. Tate's *Lear* does not automatically link sexual pleasure with bastardy and evil. As male sexual expression became commonsensical and not naturally degraded in the Restoration, Shakespeare's early-seventeenth-century motivations had to be modified. No longer could a noble man's sexual exploits with women automatically pervert his progeny and his estate. Lust and greed together were embarking on their voyage to the modern sexual world.[42]

CHAPTER 2

RESTORATION SHAKESPEARE 1: ADULTERY AND THE BIRTH OF HETEROSEXUALITY

Renaissance plays such as *King Lear* imagine male–female sexual desire as adulterous, an understanding of desire predicted by the Renaissance's Biblical, classical, and courtly love heritage.[1] This understanding of desire anticipated devastating consequences for male–female sexual appetite. In a primary Biblical example, Samuel's King David falls in love with Uriah the Hittite's wife, Bathsheba, and manages his adulterous affair by having Uriah killed in battle; thus David violates his duty to his male subject and to his God for the sake of his own debased desire. Burton comments, "So *David* knew the filthinesse of his fact, what a loathsome, foule, crying sinne Adultery was, yet notwithstanding he would commit murther, and take away another mans wife, enforced against Reason, Religion, to follow his Appetite" (161).[2] The most significant classical texts echoed Samuel's connection between male–female "appetite" and adultery. Throughout the Middle Ages and the Renaissance, poets retold *The Illiad*'s story of Helen and Paris's adultery and the resultant waste of Troy. Like David's story and Gloucester's in *Lear*, *The Illiad* links adultery, male–female sexual desire, and destruction. Similarly, Plato's *Symposium*, another seminal text for Renaissance humanism, features Aristophanes's linkage of adultery and male–female desire.[3] In a story often retold these days in sexuality studies, Aristophanes asserts that humans were originally globular beings, born male, female, or hermaphrodite, with "four arms and four legs, and two faces." Zeus punished their ambitions by slicing these creatures in half, and the hermaphrodites became men and women who desire members of the opposite sex. Aristophanes claims, "The man who is a slice of the hermaphrodite sex, as it was called, will naturally be attracted by women—the adulterer,[4] for instance—and women who run after men are of similar descent—as for instance the unfaithful wife." For Aristophanes, these creatures are far less noble than the creatures who were originally male and who "show their masculinity throughout their boyhood by the way they make friends with men, and the delight they take in lying beside them and being taken in their arms" (544).[5]

Imagining male–female sexual desire through adultery emphasized the destructive character of such desire and its debased and debasing effects upon both the men and the women involved. As does *King Lear*, classical, Biblical, and courtly love texts suggest that male–female sexual desire and its adulterous consequences threaten male friendship and homosocial relations. David's adulterous desire violates the most significant of these relations, the relation of a king to his God.[6] The early-sixteenth-century poet Thomas Wyatt frames his translation of David's penitential psalms with a poem about his affair. Wyatt calls Bathsheba "her" "Whom more than god or hymsellff [David] myndyth" (l. 25). In the poem, Nathan reminds David of "The gret offence, outrage, and Iniurye, / That he hath done to god as in this Case, / By murder for to clok Adulterye" (ll.35–37). The English Renaissance could easily read male sexual passion (directed toward women) as adultery, as a story of the destruction of the male–male world.

In the English and American imaginations, adultery has not lost its links with immorality; however, adultery now signifies different problems.[7] By the nineteenth century, fictions of adultery focus on the adulterous woman as "an unassimilable conflation of what society insists should be separate categories and functions": "wife and mother" and "mistress and lover" (Tanner 12–13). Since Renaissance texts took women's sexual desire for granted, a wife's desire could not be a central problem of adultery. Rather, Renaissance dramas of adultery criticize the male lover's susceptibility to effeminating sexual desire, his violation of his crucial homosocial bonds, and the female lover's violation of patriarchal inheritance. Sedgwick rightly suggests that adultery always signifies the relationship between the men triangularly involved. What differentiates Renaissance texts from later representations of adultery is that in Renaissance texts this homosocial component is primary.

In contrast, Restoration drama hinted at the nineteenth-century distinction between wife and sexually desirous woman, and it helped to produce a masculinity defined, at least in part, by sexual desire for women. Dramatists wrote Restoration plays under the influence of

Louis XIV's and Charles II's courts, courts that openly displayed and tolerated adulterous relations.[8] In the Restoration's Shakespeare adaptations, we can glimpse a moment in the rewriting of possible sexual positions for both men and women. In these adaptations, male sexual desire, even adulterous desire, is valued. Men with sexual desire for women become masculine; in fact such sexual desire becomes a condition of masculinity. As well as rewriting codes of masculinity, these Restoration adaptations create two novel English identities for women: the "mistress true" and the essentially desexualized wife. Although these identities became a bedrock upon which the novel's fictions of adultery rested, in the English Restoration they were newly established and not yet fully formed. However, even in their infancy, these female positions, as we will see, helped to make male sexual desire for women normative and even elevating, rather than debased.

We can see these new sexual positions in Restoration revisions of a famous story of adulterous love, the story of Antony and Cleopatra. Shakespeare's *Antony and Cleopatra* clearly states the terms of adultery under the homosocial imaginary: male–female sexual engagement threatens masculine identity; and women, who always risk being identified as whores, confirm their whorish identity in adulterous liaisons. These terms are shared among the other literary accounts connected to Antony and Cleopatra in Shakespeare's time: Robert Garnier's play *M. Antonie*, translated by Mary Sidney, the Countess of Pembroke; Samuel Brandon's play *The Tragicomoedi of the Vertuous Octauia*, and the two verse letters, *Octauia to Antonius* and *Antonius to Octauia*, that Brandon published with that play; Samuel Daniel's two works about the Cleopatra story: the long epistolary poem, *A Letter from Octauia to Marcus Antonius*, and the play, *The Tragedie of Cleopatra*; John Fletcher and Philip Massinger's *The False One*; and Thomas May's *The Tragedie of Cleopatra*.[9] These literary works agree with Francis Bacon in his essay "Of Love": "Marcus Antonius . . . was indeed a voluptuous man, and inordinate" (358). During the Restoration, the ideological ground that these earlier works share shifted, and that shift is visible in many Restoration adaptations. Thus, John Dryden's *All for Love, or the World Well Lost* and Sir Charles Sedley's *Antony and Cleopatra*, both Restoration Antony and Cleopatra plays, as well as Thomas Shadwell's *Timon of Athens*, show crucial aspects of the emerging heterosexual imaginary. These texts, collectively, show continuities in sexual ideologies as well as differences, and they also suggest that Restoration adaptations of Shakespeare may have answered, if obliquely, concerns about female sexual identity raised in earlier texts.

Written for female patrons, Daniel's and Brandon's texts about Cleopatra criticize the presumption that women are naturally sexually "loose." These texts take women's sexual desire for granted; however, unlike the Cleopatra stories that surround them, they call for an acknowledgment of women's ability to control that desire. The Restoration answered that call obliquely, in a way that helped to produce the essentially desexualized woman, a construct that would become increasingly powerful and also damaging to women in later centuries. Thus, alongside the influences of Louis and Charles's courts, the proto-feminism aired in writings for and by women seems to have played a part in producing new conceptions of male–female sexual relations. Perhaps then, to use William B. Warner's formulation, this "historical change motivated by the effort to arrive at a certain destination . . . comes to bear systemic effects that have a 'paradoxical' relation to original intentions" (72). These proto-feminist texts were surely not intended to produce what Ellen Pollak calls "passive womanhood," but they appear to have had the inadvertent paradoxical effect of assisting in its production.

In order for male sexual desire for women to achieve legitimacy, adultery seems to have needed to gain temporary legitimate status. In the differences between Renaissance and Restoration texts, we can see as well other crucial aspects of emerging heterosexuality. We can see male honor being defined as dependant on women rather than men, and we can see reason and passion being redefined as compatible. Significantly as well, the contrasts between these texts make visible a genealogy of the modern sexual double standard. These texts show that the double standard as we understand it today did not exist in the Renaissance, but that it was beginning to assume its modern form at the time Shakespeare's texts were being rewritten for the Restoration stage. Restoration Shakespeare texts reconfigured sexual morality almost entirely. They thus laid the ground for emerging heterosexuality. As we will see, this reconfigured moral ground was shortlived, but it left a legacy that remains with us today.

Masculinity and (Hetero) Sexual Desire

Late-sixteenth- and early-seventeenth-century Cleopatra stories explore Antony's and (in the case of *The False One*) Julius Caesar's devotion to sinful pleasure, and they anatomize Antony's and Caesar's consequent debasement.[10] They never assume that all men are bound and devoted to sexual pleasure with women. These earlier stories offer multiple models for masculinity, linking elite masculinity with national identity, service, friendship, and warrior power. In the earlier texts, men are not defined as men because they love and desire women. Between early-seventeenth- and late-seventeenth-century texts, we can see the movement away from this paradigm. In Sedley's *Antony and Cleopatra* and Dryden's *All for Love*, all men are in love with women; that love may be adulterous, but adulterous love does not humiliate men. Love for women defines the male condition in these Restoration plays: it is an ennobling and essential aspect of masculinity. In Shadwell's *Timon*, in fact, only devoted love of his mistress could have saved Timon from his degraded death. In this newly defined masculinity, we can see one root of the ideology of heterosexuality.

Sedley's play's fundamental belief in the motivating power of men's desire for women is signaled in Caesar's opening complaint to his men about Antony: "And more than drunk with *Cleopatra*'s charms, / He scorns both *Roman*-Love [Roman women] and *Roman*-Arms" (2). Although Shakespeare's Caesar complains about Antony's neglect of Octavia, he is overwhelmingly concerned with Antony's political missteps. Perhaps modeled on Shakespeare's Caesar, Sedley's Caesar also uses the complaint about Antony's sexual behavior as a mask for his political agenda;[11] however, in order to appeal to his Roman soldiers, Sedley's Caesar complains about Antony's scorn of "*Roman*-Love." In this play's world, such a complaint in front of such an audience makes sense, because in this play, unlike in Shakespeare's, all Roman men are lovers of women. Dryden's *All for Love* lacks Sedley's play's atrocious couplets, but it is equally devoted to male–female coupling and to the inevitability of male sexual desire for females. In *All for Love*, Antony's dear friend Dolabella loves Cleopatra as deeply as Antony does. In an exchange with his general, Dolabella admits his love: "Thus I discovered, / And blamed, the love of ruined Antony, / Yet wish that I were he, to be so ruined" (4.50–52). Like Antony, Dolabella believes that the world would be "well lost" for a woman. Sexual desire for women is the condition of masculinity in this play as it is in Sedley's *Antony and Cleopatra*. Even *All for Love*'s Ventidius, who speaks constantly in the homosocial imaginary's terms, secretly lusts after women.

In Dryden's adaptations and transformations of Shakespeare's lines and characters, we can see how sexual desire for women has become essential to the construction of male character in the

Restoration. Ventidius exposes Dolabella's alleged sexual involvement with Cleopatra to Antony with a speech that echoes the words of *Much Ado about Nothing*'s villain, Don John, when he frames the virtuous Hero for a sexual crime.[12] Don John claims that Claudio's beloved is "*Leonatos Hero*, your *Hero*, euery mans *Hero*" (TLN 1302–1303; 3.2.88–89). Ventidius tells Antony that his mistress is, "Your Cleopatra; / Dolabella's Cleopatra; / Every man's Cleopatra" (4.297–299). Unlike Ventidius, however, but like so many of Shakespeare's men, Shakespeare's Don John shows no sign of interest in women; he is motivated by his hatred for his brother (Claudio's patron) and for Claudio. Don John does not want Hero himself; he shares the distrust of women that pervades *Much Ado*. When his man Borachio comes to him with news of Claudio and Hero's engagement, he says, "what is hee for a foole that betrothes himselfe to vnquietnesse?" (TLN 386–387; 1.3.38). Women are the "vnquietnesse" of the cuckolded man and the analogous "vnquietnesse" of loose tongues.[13] Ventidius resembles Don John with a (hetero)sexual twist, and he also resembles Shakespeare's Enobarbus, although unlike Enobarbus, Ventidius desires women. Within his misogynist diatribes, Ventidius's commitment to women is clear. Ventidius (in his homosocial mode) distrusts women for Don John's reasons, but (in his Restoration mode) he "naturally" desires them as well. If anything, Ventidius is more devoted to Antony than is Enobarbus, but Dryden adds the following lines to Ventidius's echo of Enobarbus's praise of Cleopatra: "Ev'n I, who hate her, / With a malignant joy behold such beauty, / And while I curse, desire it" (4.242–244). Cleopatra inspires personal sexual desire in all men in these Restoration plays.

She can inspire such desire because, in these plays, masculinity and masculine honor are being redefined as directly related to desire for women. Since Dryden himself discussed the conflict between love and honor as a central concern of tragedy, critics have focused on how his plays address or resolve that conflict.[14] Lynn F. Kloesel suggests that "the military victory celebrated in the opening of Act III occurs not because Ventidius has been able to divide Antony from his passion but because Antony has been able to harness passion in the service of honor" (233). In the earlier Cleopatra stories, passion and honor would be a barely conceivable horse and rider, since in these earlier stories sexual passion is almost impossible to harness, and honor and sexual passion are generally incompatible. In *All for Love*, however, the team of honor and passion is not only conceivable but is easily conceived by the play's men and women.

This results from the play's construction of Antony's honor as personal and sexual as well as military and political. In fact, the political aspect of honor, preeminent in Shakespeare's *Antony and Cleopatra*, is almost absent in Dryden's text. Dryden's Antony resists Cleopatra's pleas to take her back with the following lines: "I have a fool within me takes your part / But honor stops my ears" (4.561–562). If Shakespeare's Antony spoke these lines, the word "honor" would necessarily refer to Roman military and political honor. Shakespeare's play brilliantly exposes how men in Caesar's Rome behave dishonorably, but the play does not challenge military and political honor as ideals.[15] Despite the dishonorable behavior of Caesar and the other Romans, political and military honor are still such desired objects that they necessitate and motivate Antony's and Cleopatra's suicides.

Dryden has redefined that honor as sexual. In Dryden's play, Antony says that "honor stops" his ears in a scene in which he has rejected Cleopatra because he believes Ventidius's story that she loves Dolabella. The honor Antony cites here is his honor as a sexual man who has been betrayed, his reputation as a sexual man. Its violation by Cleopatra's transgression leaves him emasculated, struggling to "recollect what's left / Of man within" (4.403–404). As Sedgwick suggests, like adultery, male sexual honor as we understand it today is a homosocial construct. Cleopatra's supposed sexual transgression humiliates Antony in front of men and particularly in terms of his relationship with Dolabella. Again, however, the historical dimension of the homosocial continuum is pertinent here. Shakespeare's Antony's military and political honor is primary in his play, a play in which homosocial bonds are the primary bonds for men. Dryden's Antony's sexual honor, more familiar to us today, points toward a society in which male–female bonds are primary. Those bonds always have homosocial components, but in this Antony's sexual honor we can see that homosocial component retreating from primacy.

Of course, the earlier concept of male honor did not exclude women entirely. In Renaissance literary texts, male military valor could win women, and women could be occasions for demonstrations of male courage and military prowess; but even in romance texts such as Spenser's *Faerie Queene* that celebrate quests to save and protect women, military courage and sexual expression are antithetical. Spenser's knights ride with women and fight for women's honor, but those knights whose interest is sexual or who express their sexual desire for women are loose and disempowered. The earlier Cleopatra stories view Cleopatra's sexual charms as interfering with Antony's military identity. Sidney's Antony complains that he is

> Falne from a souldier to a Chamberer.
> Careles of vertue, careles of all praise.
> Nay as the fatted swine in filthy mire
> With glutted heart [he] wallow'd in delights,
> All thoughts of honor troden under foote. (1153–1157)

A "Chamberer," a man devoted to the bedchamber, is a pig, wallowing in the mud, without regard for "vertue" or the "praise" of other men.

In the Restoration plays, the pleasures of the chamber, in contrast, enliven Antony's courage. The lines Dryden's Antony uses to describe military victory would be unlikely in the earlier texts. Antony recalls, "I thought how those white arms would fold me in, / And strain me close, and melt me into love: / So pleased with that sweet image, I sprung forwards, /And added all my strength to every blow" (3.1–4). The vocabulary surrounding the sexual act in this speech comes directly from earlier sexual vocabulary; however, when that sexual vocabulary in used in late-sixteenth- and early-seventeenth-century texts, it describes a process in which a man becomes like a woman because his essential male self has melted. In the earlier texts, a man enfolded in a woman's "white arms" is a man disempowered—captured by a woman.[16] Likewise a man who "melt[s]" is a man without any power.[17] In contrast, as Kloesel suggests, thoughts of sexual congress strengthen Dryden's Antony.

Actium is the nadir of Antony's masculinity in Shakespeare's play and the contemporary Cleopatra texts surrounding it. Antony flees that battle to follow Cleopatra, and he, like the men around him, sees his masculinity diminished in that flight. In contrast, Sedley's Antony feels shame after Actium, but he is ashamed in front of his mistress. He tells Cleopatra,

> Love gives short courage to the meanest soul,
> The creeping things he arms, and winged fowl.
> Yet overcharg'd with love, I lost the day,
> And in my Mistress presence ran away.
> Cover'd with shame, I fear to meet those eyes. (8)

Sedley's Antony claims that he "lost the day" because he was "overcharg'd with love." This claim sounds like earlier Antonys' despairs that they followed Cleopatra from battle because of their sexual ties to her. However, Sedley's Antony's lament is new and different in that he is ashamed to meet Cleopatra's eyes because, rather than being physically and mentally empowered by love, he "ran away." Sedley reaches into the world of animals to describe proper action inspired by male–female love: Antony should have had the courage that "creeping things" and "winged fowl" have when powered by love. Earlier antisex discourse separated noble men from the world of animals. Male sexual self-control was a sign of male transcendence.[18] In Sedley's trope, we can see the world of sexual ideology moving closer to the world Cole Porter's song "Let's do it" celebrates.

In *All for Love*, Dryden picks up the tropes and images of the earlier Cleopatra stories—tropes that describe male disempowerment and emasculation because of (hetero)sexual desire—and rewrites them to describe a new male–female sexual field, a field in which that desire inspires greatness in men and in which the same features of masculinity that Cleopatra had threatened are now endangered by her loss. The earlier texts rely on a theory of lust that sounds proleptically Lacanian in its insistence on perpetual dissatisfaction and lack. Enobarbus's famous speech about Cleopatra—in which he claims that, while other women "cloy / The appetites they feede," Cleopatra "makes hungry, / Where most she satisfies" (TLN 952–954; 2.2.241–243)—is one version of this vision of perpetual lust. Dryden's Restoration version of this claim comes from Antony's mouth and sounds quite different. He says to Cleopatra, "Enjoyed, thou still art new; perpetual spring / Is in thy arms; the ripened fruit but falls, / And blossoms rise to fill its empty place, / And I grow rich by giving" (3.25–28). In this speech, the men made perpetually hungry by Enobarbus's Cleopatra are replaced by an Antony who finds his youth—"perpetual spring"—in Cleopatra's arms. A starving Antony is replaced by an Antony who in giving himself to Cleopatra "grow[s] rich." Just as Dryden rewrites the vision of lust as lack, he also rewrites the distinction between reason and passion that was so central to Renaissance sexual ideology. His Antony claims, "Since I have heard of Cleopatra's death / My reason bears no rule upon my tongue" (5.313–314). In *All for Love*, Cleopatra renews rather than threatens Antony's life spirit, and his life work is her love. Likewise, in this play, Antony's "reason" depends on his physical involvement with Cleopatra. This alliance of reason, life, and Cleopatra is a Restoration development, virtually impossible in the earlier world in which sexual involvement with a woman can destroy male reason.

"The Mistress True" and the Slave

To found Antony's lover identity in its necessary female counterpart, Dryden abandons the glorious false Cleopatras of Shakespeare, Daniel, and May, creating a female sexual partner who is not a wife but is an honest woman. Dryden's Antony can safely anchor his manhood in Cleopatra because his Cleopatra occupies a sexual identity that the homosocial imaginary, for the most part, did not recognize. Dryden's Cleopatra, as Dryden claims in his prologue, is a "mistress true," very like other female characters in the Restoration and eighteenth century but quite unlike earlier Cleopatras (l.18). "Mistress" in this Restoration usage designates a woman in a sexual relationship with a man (usually a married man), a sexual relationship that often displays his virility. The *OED* offers a relevant definition: "a woman who illicitly occupies the place of wife" (*OED* "mistress" 11). In this definition, the *OED* attempts to describe an "illicit" sexual position for a woman that is distinguished from a prostitute. Embedded in the *OED*'s entries for "mistress" is the story of the construction over the seventeenth and eighteenth centuries of new gender/sexual positions for both men and women. Dryden's *All for Love* and other Restoration Shakespeare adaptations participate in that story, helping to break ground for the emerging heterosexual imaginary.[19] "Mistress" becomes increasingly unlikely to signify a position of power as the seventeenth century unfolds, but this semantic diminishment is not a story of women's fall from power, although it may be related to that story.[20] Rather it points to the new sexual/gender positions possible for men and women in a world with emerging heterosexuality.

As it is used in late-sixteenth- and early-seventeenth-century English texts, "mistress" designates a woman in power. For example, Shakespeare generally uses "mistress" in four senses: to denote "the female head of a household" (*OED* "mistress" 2), to signify a wife, to name the position of "a woman with a household servant or servants" (*OED* "mistress" 1), or to designate a female beloved, such as a sonnet mistress. This latter usage corresponds to the *OED*'s tenth definition: "A woman who has command over a man's heart; a woman who is loved and courted by a man; a sweetheart, lady-love (Now avoided in ordinary use exc[ept] in unequivocal contexts)" (*OED* "mistress" 10). Four definitions current in the Renaissance are now obsolete: "The female governor of a territory, state or people" (*OED* "mistress" 5); "A woman, a goddess, or something personified as a woman . . . having dominion over a person or regarded as a protecting or guiding influence"

(*OED* "mistress" 6); "A woman, or something personified as a woman, regarded as the authoress, creatress, or patroness of an art, religion, a state of life, etc." (*OED* "mistress" 7); and "A female possessor or owner" (*OED* "mistress" 8). In addition, the *OED* classifies definition 4, "a woman who has the power to control or dispose *of* something," as "now rare." According to the *OED*, each of these usages became obsolete by approximately the end of the eighteenth century.[21] Taken together, these obsolete meanings and the still residually active tenth definition describe the homosocial world depicted in late-sixteenth- and early-seventeenth-century Cleopatra stories — stories in which men who succumb to women sexually are enslaved and disempowered.

Shakespeare uses the word "mistress" frequently in *Antony and Cleopatra* but never to signify Cleopatra's sexual alliance with Antony.[22] Rather, Cleopatra's household servants refer to her as "mistress." The one usage of "mistress" in *Antony and Cleopatra* that implicitly names a relationship between Antony and Cleopatra rather than a relationship between Cleopatra and her servants occurs when Alexas gives Cleopatra Antony's message:

> Say the firme Roman to great Egypt sends
> This treasure of an Oyster: at whose foote
> To mend the petty present, I will peece
> Her opulent Throne, with Kingdomes. All the East,
> (Say thou) shall call her Mistris. (TLN 573–577; 1.5.42–46)

Antony's message implies that just as Antony will be political master of the East, Cleopatra will be the East's political mistress. Shakespeare's use of "mistris" reveals that his play is "a notorious story about politics on every level" (Charnes 138).[23] "Mistris" in this speech designates Cleopatra's political domination.

Although Shakespeare seldom uses the word "mistress" in its sexual register, in texts of the homosocial imaginary, "mistress" could be a word for a woman who was sexually related to a man outside of his marriage. In those usages, it could be another word for whore. Shakespeare uses "mistress" this way in *Timon of Athens* when the play's fool talks about his "mistress" who entertains multiple men in her house (22.93–96). As Tanner's analysis of adultery shows, by the nineteenth century the line between wives and whores was so distinct as to constitute a category crisis when it was crossed. Shakespeare's England, in contrast, was a world with a vast panoply of words that designated sexually false women, a world in which the word "queen" could signify as its homonymic double "quean," a prostitute.[24] In addition, this panoply of Renaissance words did not indicate a variety of possible sexual positions with variable moral valences. Unlike Italian literature, which could refer to an established tradition of upper-rank courtesans who garnered respect despite their sexual position, Renaissance English texts, strikingly, for the most part do not differentiate categorically among the women they call by all the words for "whore." This lack of differentiation allowed for a slippage between categories such as wife and whore that would be less possible in another sexual system; thus, the possible debased sexual significa-tion of "mistress" in the Renaissance coexisted with its more domi-nant denotations, denotations of power for the women in question.[25]

Perhaps because of its derivation from the French "*maitresse*," "mistress" in the early seventeenth century could also signify a for-eign sexual system in which men might have more than one sexual partner. The pre-Restoration usages that the *OED* gathers under its eleventh definition, "A woman who illicitly occupies the place of wife," attest to this foreign significance.[26] The dictionary finds the word in Robert Johnson's collection of travel narratives, where it is used to describe alien sexual practices. Donne's usage of the word this way in the sermon on the Psalms in which he discusses David's sin with Bathsheba also indicates its exotic resonance. Donne does not use "mistress" to describe Bathsheba; rather he validates Bathsheba's bathing practices by claiming that in the Bible, "We see that even those women, whom the Kings were to take for their Wives, and not for Mistresses, (which is but a later name for Concubines) had a certaine . . . time assigned to be prepared by these aromaticall unctions, and liniments for beauty" (*LXXX, Sermons* LXIV, 642). That Donne feels compelled to define "mistress" for this usage testifies to its relative rarity.

Though the usage of "mistress" as sexual partner (*OED* definition 11) was relatively rare in late-sixteenth- and early-seventeenth-century English texts, by the time the *OED* was collecting meanings in Victorian England, it had become the immediately available meaning of "mistress." Therefore, the *OED*'s editors feel compelled to add the parenthetical caveat to the tenth definition: "A woman who has com-mand over a man's heart; a woman who is loved and courted by a man; a sweetheart, lady-love (Now avoided in ordinary use exc[ept] in unequivocal contexts)."[27] The parenthetical caveat in the *OED* is nec-essary because by the Victorian age, "mistress"'s primary significance had shifted. Dryden's *All for Love* and Thomas Shadwell's *Timon of*

Athens participate in that redefinition of "mistress," constructing a sexualized, nonmarital female identity, separate from the category whore and without connotations of female dominance, that corresponds to and supports a sexualized male identity newly available to elite men. Dryden's Restoration Cleopatra is both a proudly sexual and a proudly faithful "mistress."

Although Dryden's text dates from well before the "great gender shift" described by twentieth-century scholars, *All for Love* begins to outline some of that shift's terms.[28] The common sense that called women "by nature . . . wau'ring" was under pressure well before the long eighteenth century, as all ideological positions are, even when they help to constitute the system in dominance (Sidney 145).[29] In fact, some of the earlier Cleopatra stories were helping to put it under pressure, significantly Daniel's *Letter from Octauia*, dedicated to Lady Margaret, Countess of Cumberland, and Brandon's *Tragecomedi of the Vertuous Octauia*, dedicated to Lady Lucia Audelay. However, none of the earlier Cleopatra stories reveal that common sense under pressure in their portrayals of Cleopatra. In all of these earlier stories, the most available word to describe her is "whore."[30] In contrast, *All for Love*'s Cleopatra, Sedley's Cleopatra, and Shadwell's Evandra (Timon's mistress) challenge the common sense that "by nature women wau'ring are." But unlike Renaissance proto-feminist texts that challenge that common sense by creating chaste married women, these Restoration texts challenge it by creating chaste mistresses.

In *All for Love*, Cleopatra is openly sexually desirous. This alone would make her a whore/woman in early-seventeenth-century terms; however Dryden's Cleopatra is absolutely devoted to one man, which would make her chaste in the terms of pre-Restoration ideals. Since in the early seventeenth century that definition of chastity was generally linked to marriage, however, Dryden's Cleopatra is an oddity in earlier terms, a creature hardly imaginable in early-seventeenth-century representation: a chaste mistress. Dryden's Cleopatra, like Shakespeare's, owns her sexual power, and she defines her position as "mistress" as the cause and effect of that power. She exclaims, "Respect is for a wife: am I that thing, / That dull, insipid lump, without desires, / And without pow'r to give 'em?" (2.82–84). In comparison with all of the earlier Cleopatras, Cleopatra here sounds recognizably modern, defining the position of wife as a position for a woman "without desires, / And without pow'r to give 'em." This is not the dominant vision of a wife in the homosocial imaginary.[31]

The newly born mistress referred to in this speech of Cleopatra's not only divides women into two categories—desexualized wives and sexualized mistresses—it also constructs men as creatures who need sexual satisfaction and must resort to mistresses to receive such satisfaction. And that newly born mistress was a feature of Restoration representation generally. Restoration plays, including Shakespeare adaptations, are chock-full of men with mistresses. Much of the action of Restoration comedy involves the negotiations men must make to juggle mistresses and wives and to satisfy discarded mistresses.[32] The prologues and epilogues of Restoration Shakespeare often assume an audience made up of men with mistresses and women who will become mistresses. Wives in these texts, as Dryden's Cleopatra indicates, have begun to be emptied of sexual desire and sexual prowess. Both the desexualized wife and the sexually desirous elite man—two new gender positions that entailed sexual identities— were only under construction in the Restoration, although their eventual ascendance to dominance would have enduring consequences. The chaste mistress, as personified by Dryden's Cleopatra, was a temporary building block in the emerging edifice of the heterosexual imaginary.

Dryden's Antony embraces the new gender/sexual identity for men, the male, more enduring, companion to mistress—lover. He loves Cleopatra as his mistress, which in turn means that he defines himself as a man who proudly possesses a mistress. In an attempt to win Antony back for Cleopatra, Cleopatra's eunuch, Alexas, presents him with a ruby bracelet from Cleopatra, whom he calls "Your slave, the queen"; but Antony corrects him, accepting it only from "My mistress" (2.196). Although Antony uses "mistress" here in contrast to Alexas's word "slave," he does not use that contrast to indicate his own enslavement. Rather Cleopatra is Antony's "mistress," which makes him her lover. The word "mistress" is used at least eleven times in *All for Love*, and its various usages reflect the shift in sexual identities that Dryden was helping to effect.

Dryden's Cleopatra is a "mistress" in the *OED*'s eleventh definition sense—"A woman who illicitly occupies the place of wife"—and also distinctly not a whore; she is also not a dominatrix, as much as her eunuch, Alexas, would like her to be one. As Cleopatra's proud ownership of her "mistress" identity suggests, Dryden uses "mistress" in a manner that approaches the modern common usage, the "illicit" meaning of the word that a twentieth-century audience would immediately understand. But if the familiarly understood meaning of "mistress" was shifting in the Restoration, what we now see as its customary meaning was not yet so common as to be immediately understood, and Dryden's characters come close to debating its usage. When his Antony proudly calls Cleopatra "my mistress," Alexas, a servant whose character derives from the homosocial imaginary, answers sardonically, "Then your mistress" (2.196). The import of Alexas's agreement becomes clear later in the play when Alexas tries to woo Antony back from Octavia with a message from "The queen, my mistress, sir, and yours" (3.373). Alexas understands mistress as a term of dominance, the term that signifies Cleopatra's relationship to him, her eunuch servant. Dryden's characters also use "mistress" as a term denoting a sexual woman in the only way that the word could have signified earlier in the century, when a sexual woman outside of a marriage was by definition a whore. Thus Ventidius attempts to convince Antony that Cleopatra has betrayed him by arguing, "Should mistresses be left, / And not provide against a time of change? / You know she's not much used to lonely nights" (4.301–303). For Ventidius, a woman who is a mistress is a woman who needs a man—any man—sexually at all times. Dryden's Cleopatra, herself, not long after her proud ownership of the identity, calls that same identity "the branded name of mistress" (3.464). This is the same understanding that leads her to claim the title of Antony's "wife" at the end of the play (5.413). However, as her earlier proud "respect is for a wife" speech indicates, the play has almost discarded the presumption that a woman who loves a man sexually outside of marriage is categorically a whore.

The position that Dryden's Cleopatra assumes, the position of "mistress true" signals the new Restoration sexual world. For Cleopatra claims that she is a mistress only out of "true love." Dryden's Cleopatra has always been true to Antony. She declares that her love affair with Julius Caesar was not only inferior to her affair with Antony but annulled by her prior love for Antony.[33] Antony also contends that he loved Cleopatra before Caesar ever saw her (2.262–359). These claims support each other, and they are also linked. In them we can see the full-blown modern ideology of "true love." Even Shakespeare's *Romeo and Juliet*, which deals with love between very young people, depicts Romeo's earlier passion for another woman—a fact of the play that embarrassed the emerging and established heterosexual imaginaries for centuries. Dryden's *Antony and Cleopatra or The World Well Lost*, a play about older "true lovers," is distinctly unembarrassing for modernity. It confirms and establishes a newly born "truth," a "truth" that will become a tenet of the heterosexual imaginary—the "truth" of a love that in the earlier world could be defined as sin.[34] Where earlier Cleopatras attracted men with their devastating physical and psychologically manipulative (rhetorical) charms, charms that turned men into women, *All for Love*'s Antony loves her because she loves him and because she is the "true mistress" who confirms his masculine lover identity; he claims, "she has truth / Beyond her beauty" (3.233–234).[35]

Although critics have seen this innovation as Dryden's and analyzed it as a feature of Dryden's artistic identity, Sedley's Cleopatra is just as "true" and just as dedicated to truth. The "mistress true" is a feature of Restoration sexual ideology, a harbinger of the heterosexual imaginary. Dryden's literary rival Thomas Shadwell published his adaptation of *Timon of Athens* the same year that Dryden published *All for Love*.[36] Shadwell and Dryden were bitter enemies, but Shadwell is as dedicated to the "mistress true" as is Dryden. Shadwell's *Timon of Athens* even more emphatically distinguishes the true mistress from the wife. Shadwell gives Timon a mistress, Evandra, who is unconditionally loyal and loving. Their relationship is challenged when Timon plans to marry the most chaste and most beautiful young woman in Athens, Melissa. In her effort to persuade Timon to keep her as his mistress, Evandra advances arguments against marriage itself. She calls marriage a commercial arrangement and claims that her own love, made of "truth and constancy," is more valuable than married love that, by definition, is mixed "With other aims" (16).[37]

Shadwell's elevation of the mistress over the wife deconstructs the premise of Renaissance elite marriage. If married women are always potentially suspect in earlier drama, this is because women were always sexually suspect, not because marriage itself was suspect. When Renaissance texts challenge marriage as an institution, they focus on corrupt or ambitious fathers or father figures who arrange marriages for their own gain. Thus, these texts focus on abuses of patriarchal marriage. The exchange of women is a given of marriage in earlier texts; in itself, that principle of exchange does not predict women's perfidy.[38] In Evandra's analysis, the economic aspect of marriage for women, not for fathers, becomes its taint; and women who seek marriage rather than freely giving themselves to the men they love are whores. This essentially antifeminist argument sees men's sexual "liberty" as the ultimate good, a good that would be constrained in marriage, a system in which only women gain. Such an argument is only barely possible within the homosocial imaginary, which takes the morality of marriage for granted and which puts no value on a man's sexual liberty.

In his mistress Evandra, Timon finds "The truest and the tenderest Love that e'r / Woman yet bore to Man" (33). And the play agrees with Timon. Early in the play, before his friends abandon him, Timon complains about his own behavior:

> Gods! Why should I not love this Woman best?
> She has deserv'd beyond all measure from me;
> She's beautiful and good as Angels are;
> But I have had her Love already. (33)

Together, Timon's praise and his conundrum signal the new sexual world that *All for Love* and Shadwell's *Timon* explore. Evandra, in giving herself sexually to Timon without marrying him, would have already violated Renaissance moral codes so completely as to deserve extreme punishment. In Shadwell's *Timon*, in contrast, she is depicted as "beautiful and good as Angels are." Timon, however, cannot continue to love her because he has "had her Love already." Evandra is a Restoration chaste mistress, that paradox in earlier terms, and Timon is the Restoration man as understood by Nahum Tate, Dryden, and so many other Restoration playwrights, the man never satisfied with one sexual conquest.

The contrast the play pursues between Evandra, Timon's chaste mistress, and Melissa, Timon's fiancée, explodes the conventions that linked chastity, truth, and marriage so closely in the earlier world. Melissa is indeed what in American slang could be called a "gold-digger." She cares only for her own appearance and advancement. She wants to sell herself to the highest bidder, and she eagerly discards Timon when he loses his fortune. She also prides herself on her chastity. Similarly corrupt women in Shakespeare's plays, ambitious women such as Goneril and Regan, and Joan (in 1 *Henry VI*), manifest their ambition in sexual openness. Melissa, in contrast, flaunts her chaste sexual behavior. But Timon recognizes Melissa eventually as a woman with "a vile / Corrupted filthy mind" who acts "As if the Body made one honest" (71). Of course, it is exactly the body that does make a woman honest in late-sixteenth- and early-seventeenth-century sexual ideology. But not in this play.

Shadwell's *Timon* does not celebrate all women who have sex with men outside of marriage. Timon rails against "whores" in his misanthropic rages, and Alcibiades, as he does in Shakespeare's *Timon of Athens*, appears in the forest accompanied by a group of whores, whom the play characterizes as money-hungry and dishonest. Demonstrating the redefinition of the sexualized mistress in the Restoration, one of Alcibiades's whores tries to claim the new identity to save herself from Timon's railing: "Hang thee Monster; we are not Whores, we are Mistresses to *Alcibiades*" (76). However, the play claims that even these women are better than the chaste Melissa. Alcibiades argues that "one / Kind, faithful, loving Whore, [is] better than / A thousand base, ill-natur'd honest Women" (83). And, in its depiction of Melissa, the play goes some way to proving this modern point. If even a "kind, faithful, loving Whore" is better than a base woman who is bodily "honest," Shadwell's *Timon* argues that best of all is a chaste mistress, extramaritally sexually available, but only to one man, constant and true till death.

As Dryden's Cleopatra becomes a constant yet disempowered "mistress," Antony is empowered as a man. In his dialogue with Antony, Cleopatra's Alexas uses the word "slave" as the counterpart to the word "mistress," and in late-sixteenth- and early-seventeenth-century Cleopatra stories, Antony is Cleopatra's "slave." When "mistress" indicated a woman's dominance, "slave" indicated a man's subservience, his debasement in relation to her.[39] May's Agrippa describes Cleopatra as having "so long . . . sway'd / A soveraignty ore [over] half the Roman world, / Trod on the necks of humbled Kings, and rul'd / *Antonius* as her slave" (C10; 3.2.72–75). "Slave" was used generally in sonnets and other Renaissance literature to describe male lovers. As with the fortunes of its companion word "mistress," the shift in "slave"'s usage from the early seventeenth century to the Restoration points to the emergence of the (hetero)sexually desirous male as masculine. In *All for Love*, Cleopatra describes her condition after she believes she has lost Antony: "I'm fit to be a captive: Antony / Has taught my mind the fortune of a slave" (2.14–15). Later in the play, she compares herself to a discarded slave: "Would you cast off a slave who followed you, / Who crouched beneath your spurn?" (4.563–564). Sedley's Cleopatra also embraces the comparison between her position and slavery (30). Because of their imperial settings, all of the Cleopatra stories abound with references to slavery; however the usage of the term shifts over the seventeenth century. All of the early texts refer to Antony as Cleopatra's "slave," but none of the early texts uses "slave" to describe Cleopatra's sexual position, whereas both of the Restoration texts use "slave" for Cleopatra.

England's increasing involvement in the trade in African slaves may have figured into the transition in sexual terminology that I am describing here. During the late sixteenth and early-seventeenth centuries, the word "slave" would have had multiple real-life referents in England apart from the African slave trade. Many early-seventeenth-century English travel texts worried that English merchants and other travelers would become slaves of Eastern potentates, especially of the Turks, and colonists such as Captain John Smith in Virginia advertised their histories of slavery and escapes from slavery. Although slavery was by definition debasing, it was also a possible subject position for English men and even a piece of a potential English male adventure story. The word "slave" was also widely employed in English texts as a word for a despised or denigrated man and even as a synonym for "rascal," without any connotation of actual slavery.[40] By the time that Dryden, Sedley, and Shadwell were adapting Shakespeare, England was heavily involved in the African slave trade. If, in the Restoration, women were becoming "slaves" and simultaneously "chaste mistresses," elite men were no longer so easily termed "slaves." Perhaps as slavery became linked in the real world with degraded blackness at the same time that elite men were coming to believe that sexual love was no longer degrading, "slave" could less easily denote elite men in love.[41]

The shifts indicated by the fortunes of "mistress" and "slave," shifts that divorced both sexual appetite and inconstancy from most women and that associated masculinity with (hetero)sexual appetite, happened slowly and unevenly over the course of the long eighteenth century. However, late-eighteenth- century reactions to Shakespearean and Fletcherian characters are a good indication of the power of that shift. As we will see in chapter 5, Dryden's constant Cleopatra was so influential over Shakespeare editors that some began to read Shakespeare's Cleopatra as if she were Dryden's Cleopatra. We can see the power of that shift as well in George Colman's notes in his 1778 edition of *The False One*. When Cleopatra's servant Eros enters that play and rejects Septimius, the play's villain, Colman comments,

> We have not made a variation here, but cannot suppose the Poets intended *Eros, Cleopatra's waiting woman*, to enter here as the *loose companion* of Septimius, and to profess herself *a strumpet*. The error, most probably, originated from the players, who making one person perform both *Eros* and this *courtezan*, confounded the characters together ... The Poets most probably meant another woman, but

they seem to have intended (perhaps from inadvertence) to name this character *Eros*. (124n.)

Colman's comment indicates that, for him, by 1778, Cleopatra in anyone's play has taken on Dryden's character's constancy. For Colman, Cleopatra's respectability extends to her serving women, so he finds it outrageous that Cleopatra's waiting woman Eros could profess herself a whore. Following general eighteenth-century editorial practice, initiated by Alexander Pope, Colman attributes what he sees as *The False One*'s distasteful portrait of Cleopatra's woman to the players, actors who import theatrical garbage into previously pure authorial text. Contrary to Colman's wishes, however, Fletcher and Massinger's Eros is a sexually active woman as well as being Cleopatra's waiting woman. Later in the play when the populace has rebelled against Cleopatra and ransacked the court, Eros comments, "They rifled me: / But that I could endure, and tire 'em too, / Would they proceed no further" (158–159). This Eros can "endure" some sexual handling, and she can beat the sexual aggressors at their own game due to her superior sexual power. Colman, in contrast, can only endure this Eros if he can pretend she does not belong to Cleopatra. Shakespeare's Cleopatra would welcome her to her court; indeed, her waiting women are at least equally bawdy. But this Eros could not belong to Dryden's Cleopatra. And, by the end of the eighteenth century, Dryden's constant Cleopatra was the "true mistress" available even for most readers of Shakespeare's and Fletcher and Massinger's texts.[42]

Octavia's "Vertue" and the Sexual Double Standard

Throughout the period during which the line between woman and whore was indistinct, men and women produced texts that tried to claim that women are naturally faithful—we often read these texts as feminist or proto-feminist.[43] Brandon's and Daniels's proto-feminist texts solicit such an understanding of women as, if not sexually undesirous, sexually bound to only their husbands. Brandon's Octavia replies to her brother's praise of her exceptional virtue,

> I know not what you thinke of woman kinde,
> That they are faithlesse and vnconstant euer:
> For me, I thinke all women striue to finde
> The perfect good, and therein to perseuer. (D3v)

As sexual ideology shifted, the Restoration answered the plea implicit in Octavia's argument by creating its Cleopatras and its Evandra, chaste mistresses, sexualized but faithful, in whom men could found their identities. If history answered this plea, however, it answered it with a vengeance, slowly, and as if inexorably, removing the possibility of sexual desire from virtuous women. Dryden's and Sedley's Restoration Cleopatras and Shadwell's Evandra can be seen as transitional figures in this historical process. Dryden's Cleopatra retreats from her claim that a wife is a "dull, insipid lump, without desires, / And without pow'r to give 'em" (2.83–84); but the emerging history of heterosexuality was moving her way.

Octavias across the early modern period can also be a window into this process. If the words used to describe Cleopatras changed radically in the Restoration, the word "virtue," often spelled "vertue" in the earlier texts, is attached to Octavia in all the Cleopatra texts in which she appears; however, the parameters of Octavia's virtue change radically over the course of the seventeenth century. If Shakespeare shows little interest in Octavia, Brandon and Daniel, male authors with female patrons, tell Octavia's story as much as they tell Cleopatra's. Brandon writes his play about the "vertuous Octauia," and he appends imaginary letters between Octavia and Antony. If we can trust publication dates, Daniel wrote his letter from Octavia to Antony before he wrote his tragedy of Cleopatra. In their texts, Brandon and Daniel see Octavia as a primary player in the Cleopatra story, and they see her virtue, which they define as her sexual commitment to her husband, as the moral barometer of that story. Both authors work to establish Octavia's virtue as exemplary and even representative of women's behavior, but they do not represent her as desexualized. Dryden's and Sedley's Restoration Cleopatra plays agree that Octavia represents an exemplary married woman; however, they define that virtue as a complete lack of interest in sex. The shift in representations of virtuous Octavias is significant for what it reveals about the shift in gender ideology about women; in addition, that shift in representation indicates a genealogical history for the sexual double standard.

Both Daniel's and Brandon's Octavias take for granted a world in which even virtuous women are naturally sexually desirous, a world that seems to have disappeared as early as Dryden's version of the Cleopatra story. Daniel's Octavia explains that she will not behave like Antony: "Although my youth, his absence, and this wrong / Might draw my bloud to forfeit vnto shame; / Nor neede I frustrate my delights so long, / That haue such meanes to carry so the same" (*Letter* 125, stanza 12). This Octavia has "bloud," "delights," and sexual frustration, but she will not sink to her husband's depravity. Unlike Antony, she will not succumb to her "will" because, she argues, "Greatnesse must make it great incontinence: / Chambers are false, the bed and all will tell, / No doore keepes in their shame that doe not well" (125, stanza 13). Would Octavia follow her "will" and her "bloud," she argues, she might allay her frustration, but she understands that "will" as sinful, and besides, sin is impossible to hide. Octavia's argument, that, although a lack of sex is frustrating, she will avoid sexual escapades both because they are sinful and because they cannot be hidden, characterizes her as virtuous in the Renaissance; in the Restoration, and especially in the eighteenth century, it would characterize her as immodest. In *All for Love*, Octavia castigates Cleopatra for having charms that "a modest wife" should not even recognize: "Shame of our sex, / Dost thou not blush to own those black endearments / That make sin pleasing?" (3.442–444).

In eighteenth-century terms, Brandon's virtuous Octavia is as immodest as Daniel's Octavia. Like Daniel's, Brandon's Octavia does not deny that she can and will supply sexual pleasure. She claims that she has "true delights" and "wanton sports" (*Octauia to Antonius* G5–G5v).[44] In Daniel's *Letter*, Octavia harangues Antony:

> What? are there barres for vs, no bounds for you?
> Must Leuitie stand sure, though Firmnesse fall?
> And are you priuiledg'd to be vntrue,
> And we no grant to be dispens'd withall?
> Must we inuiolable keepe your due,
> Both to your loue, and to your falshood thrall?
> Whilst you haue stretch't your lust vpon your will,
> As if your strength were licenc'd to doe ill. (*Letter* 127, stanza 20)

Octavia argues that Antony, who as a nobleman should embody "Firmnesse," has no business succumbing to his will if she who, by definition as a woman, embodies "Leuitie," is capable of standing firm (*OED* "levity" 3b).[45]

Octavia's speech resembles a modern critique of the sexual double standard, but its differences from that modern critique are crucial because they show both that the sexual double standard has a genealogy and that that genealogy is intimately related to a genealogy of heterosexuality. What separates Octavia's Renaissance proto-feminist attack on a double standard for male and female sexual behavior from modern attacks on a double standard is her earlier attack's birth in a system in which gender is fluid and sexual desire is still seen in largely negative terms. The modern attack on the sexual double standard assumes that all men have sexual desires and indulge them and, therefore, that men should not deny women the indulgence of their sexual desires. Daniel's and Brandon's Renaissance challenges to a sexual double standard assume that all *women* have sexual desires that are inherently debasing, but that supremely virtuous women control their desire; therefore, men above the lowest rank, who should naturally have more self-control than "weak" women, should, in turn, have more control over their debasing sexual desires. Although the modern and the Renaissance challenges to the sexual double standard resemble one another, they are not the same.

Again, as in the case of premodern and modern misogyny, the distinctions between these attacks and the ideologies that generated them can seem fine, but we must understand those distinctions if we are to see how the attacks and the ideological systems that generated them are genealogically related but ideologically opposed. Brandon's Octavia writes to Antony,

> More then a man thou wouldst be thought,
> And shouldst indeed be so:
> But let thy deeds more manly bee,
> Or els that name forgoe.
> The man which seemes a man in shew,
> And is not such a one:
> Deserues another name by right,
> For he by right is none. (H–Hv)

In these lines, Octavia argues that, given Antony's position as ruler of half the world, he not only would like to be seen as "more than a man," he should be a higher-order man. However, his sexual debauchery with Cleopatra is not "manly"; in fact, it means that he is not a man at all. Writing back to Octavia, Antony tries to justify his behavior. He admits that he is acting against reason: "I know the safe, and perfect way, / Which reason saith is best: / Yet willingly I follow that, / Which wisdom liketh least" (H2v). Brandon's diction here follows the terms of the Christian argument about sex that we have seen in chapter 1. Antony has abandoned perfection, "reason," and "wisdom" for his own will; and, damning himself further, he has abandoned them "willingly." Antony then attempts to nullify his own transgression by reading Octavia through the homosocial imaginary's dominant lens on female sexuality. He argues that Octavia has surely fallen sexually herself: she must have "consent[ed], / To *Venus* sweet delights": "No, no," he claims, women "are not alwaies true, / Which doe most truely speake: / If it were so, how then am I, / More than a woman weake?" (H7). Octavia must be lying about her own chastity, for, if she were really as chaste as she professed, how could he be weaker, less able to be chaste, than a woman?

These verse letters and Brandon's play are proto-feminist in that they insist on the possibility, even the likelihood, of women's virtue. These texts attack a double standard for male and female sexual behavior, but they do not attack it as a modern text might. Brandon's debased Antony, in his self-serving slippery defensiveness, speaks what could look like a modern attack on the sexual double standard: Antony argues that he likes sexual pleasure and, therefore, should follow his will, and that his desires and satisfactions are justified by what he imagines are Octavia's desires and satisfactions.[46] Octavia's attack on Antony's behavior is an essentially earlier attack, and the text is clearly on Octavia's side. She argues that devotion to sexual pleasure is debasing: that type of devotion turns a man into a woman. Antony should give up his illicit desires if he wants to be a noble man.

What makes the distinctions between these arguments seem so fine is that Octavia is complaining about Antony's adultery, behavior that, although it is foundational for modern heterosexuality, is always nominally disapproved by dominant ideologies. However, if we look carefully at Octavia's complaint, we can see that it is phrased in a way that makes it foreign to even modern complaints about adultery. For it is Antony's devotion to pleasure that effeminates him. Octavia is asking Antony to be faithful to patriarchy and Rome, and she defines what we might call his (sexual) virility as antithetical to his manliness. Her acknowledgment of her own sexual desire and proficiency is not a complaint about his sexual transgression in modern terms. That is, she does not complain that he has violated their sexual bond. Rather she must acknowledge her sexual desire because that is part of what makes her a woman. Antony, who should not be a woman, is acting like a woman, even more like a woman than she is; his sexually desirous effeminacy is the problem.[47]

Brandon's and Daniel's texts, dedicated to noble women, attempt to extend the exceptional woman's definition as virtuous to encompass most women. Genealogically, this attempt seems related to the production of Dryden's and Sedley's Octavias, neither of whom ever acknowledge their own sexual desire. Sedley's Octavia, supremely virtuous in Restoration terms, and anticipating eighteenth-century norms, argues, "Wives (like good Subjects, who to Tyrants bow) / To Husbands though unjust, long patience owe: / They were for Freedom made, Obedience We, / Courage their vertue, ours is Chastity" (33–34). Octavias from the late-sixteenth and early-seventeenth centuries do not agree that husbands are made "for Freedom"; they define that "freedom" as emasculating. And they define chastity as a virtue for men as well as for women. Restoration and eighteenth-century texts, in contrast, are invested in the chaste wife and the sexually free man.

In a challenged but still-influential article, the great historian Keith Thomas describes and critiques the sexual double standard that he says "has been deeply rooted in England for many centuries" (195). Thomas argues that Christianity advanced "the idea that unchastity was as much a sin for the one sex as for the other"; however, he calls Christianity a "current of opinion" that did not essentially disturb the sexual double standard's deep roots (203). Rejecting a Freudian explanation for the double standard's persistence because of that explanation's roots in Victorian sexual ideology, Thomas cites Kinsey in support of a possible biological explanation for differences in sexual desire between men and women (215). Throughout this book, I am arguing that these differences are constructed and only seem natural to us after and because of their construction. Indeed, Thomas gets the bulk of his evidence for an explicit modern double standard—which says that male unchastity is natural whereas female unchastity is unforgivable—from the Restoration, the eighteenth century, and the nineteenth century. As my comparison of Octavias suggests, it is in the Restoration that the Christian devotion to male chastity becomes less viable in theatrical representation. In "Sex and Consequences," James Grantham Turner examines eighteenth-century attacks on the double standard. Turner summarizes some of these attacks as examining "the painful experience of being condemned, irreversibly and without reference to any other moral criteria, for errors on which men would be congratulated" (158). In texts of the homosocial imaginary, as we have seen, elite men are seldom "congratulated" for these "errors."

Despite evidence that challenges its premises, Thomas's article has been foundational for historians writing about male–female sexual relations in the English Renaissance. For example, in her important work on sexual slander, Laura Gowing depends upon Thomas's contention that the sexual double standard has always existed, even though the evidence she cites from conduct literature, sermons, and criminal prosecution of men could make her question this contention (2). Gowing argues that in early-seventeenth-century London, there was little or no language for men's sexual misconduct, although in the church court records she finds men called "whore-master" and "whoremonger," and although "whoremaster" occurs pervasively in English Renaissance literature as a sexual insult for a man.[48] As Bernard Capp observes, when men were slandered with these words "they were clearly being condemned for their own promiscuity" (*When Gossips* 255). Gowing says men were often slandered "with non-sexual words like knave" (62–63). Her evidence, however, points to "knave" meaning, among other things, male sexual criminal: Discussing references to venereal disease, Gowing says, "Men were called 'pocky knave,' with occasional graphic details such as 'he . . . had lost halfe his yard' " ([penis] 90); Gowing finds Jane Davis, in 1575, saying to Katherine Brisley, "Thow art a drabbe and a harlott and the evell favoured knave thy landlord keepeth thee" (Gowing 104); and in 1629, Henry Wiltshire said to Elizabeth Stott, "Thou art a privat queane and a base queane and . . . thou keepest privat knaves in thy house or els thy bed would not goe jigge and jogge so often as it doth" (Gowing 71).

As it does in Wiltshire's accusation, "knave" functions as the male equivalent of whore in Thomas Heywood's *A Woman Killed with Kindness* (see chapter 4). In that play, Wendoll plays cards with his friend Frankford and Frankford's wife Anne, with whom he is conducting a scandalous adulterous affair; meanwhile, Frankford's loyal servant, Nicholas, watches. In the context of the card game, Anne asks Wendoll, "what are you" (i.e., what card have you picked up). Wendoll says "I am a knaue," and Nicholas, in an aside, says "Ile sweare it." Anne picks a card and says "I a Queene?"; and her betrayed husband comments, in another aside, "A queane thou shouldst say . . . They are the grosest paire that ere I felt" (E; 8.169–171).[49] Earlier in the play, Nicholas tells the audience that, if the two conduct their affair, "*Wendols* a knaue, [and Nicholas's] Mistris is a &c" (D; 6.183). Though it is certainly true that today, under the dominance of the heterosexual imaginary, there is no word for male sexual criminal equivalent to the word "whore," Gowing's evidence and the evidence from this play among others suggest that Renaissance England had such words, and that "knave" was among them.[50]

Other fine recent historical work is similarly indebted to Thomas's argument at the same time that its evidence challenges an understanding of the double standard as transhistorical.[51] Peter Lake reads play texts and pamphlets in which, he says "[t]he sexual double standard is caricatured, indeed reduced to a sinister absurdity" (121). Likewise, Capp remarks that a "few women even introduced sexual reputation into disputes with men that had broken out over entirely different issues. Remarkably bold in the context of the double standard, their behavior confirms the potency of sexual defamation as a weapon against both sexes" (*When Gossips* 258). The evidence these historians cite points directly away from Thomas's transhistorical double standard. Capp argues that his evidence "suggests that the contrasts between male and female honour have been exaggerated" ("The Double Standard" 98). Perhaps his careful revision of Thomas's seminal work does not go far enough. Perhaps in Renaissance English texts what looks like a caricature of the modern double standard is, instead, an insistence on another standard of sexual behavior for men. Likewise, perhaps what looks like "remarkably bold" behavior is in fact behavior predictable in a society whose standard for sexual behavior is not familiar to us. Restoration revisions of Renaissance literary texts suggest that the modern sexual double standard was newly born in the Restoration. In the early seventeenth century, as Capp's, Gowing's, and Lake's evidence and the evidence of the earlier Octavias suggest, the standard for women *and* for elite men was chastity, and it is women who were thought of as less likely to achieve that standard.

The Moral Response and Emerging Heterosexuality

Thomas Shadwell's critique of marriage in his *Timon of Athens* has conventionally been understood as a satiric response to, or perhaps a reflection of, a debased moment in English court culture.[52] In the context of a history of emerging heterosexuality, however, it might better be seen as a newly possible, and a temporarily necessary, ennoblement of adultery between a man and a woman.[53] In Shadwell's *Timon*, the previously debased category of (hetero)sexual love is elevated over marriage, formerly the institution that made male–female sexual expression potentially moral, if still quite dangerous for men. Unlike Shakespeare's *Timon of Athens*, which does not partner its Timon with a woman, Shadwell's *Timon*, like Dryden's *All for Love*, argues that men can depend on sexual women; constant "mistresses" will confirm their identities as men. Michael Warner notes that in late-twentieth-century America, "We live with sex norms that survive from the Stone Age, including prohibitions against autoeroticism, sodomy, extramarital sex, and (for those who still take the Vatican seriously) birth control" (5). A look at Restoration Shakespeare adaptations shows that we need to modify that claim if we are to understand how the sexual system that is dominant today (which does indeed include ancient prohibitions) came into being. For the temporary validation of extramarital sex was a condition of emerging heterosexuality. Warner suggests that in contemporary America, "those who advocate sexual shaming usually believe, or claim to believe, that sex (theoretically) is good" (74). The claim "that sex (theoretically) is good" undergirds our dominant sexual system, but it was newly born in Restoration England, born in the temporary celebration of adultery in (among other discourses and practices) the Shakespeare plays rewritten to make Restoration sexual sense.

Any story of the fate of English drama over the long eighteenth century must include the "moral" reaction to Restoration drama's flaunting of sexual license. That story usually starts with Jeremy Collier, a Cambridge-educated Jacobite clergyman who in 1698 published an influential, although not the first, attack on Restoration plays. Collier's *A Short View of the Immorality, and Profaneness of the English Stage, Together with the Sense of Antiquity upon This Argument* and the polemics and social movements associated with it are generally regarded as having had a profound effect on eighteenth-century drama, reducing it to sentimentalism.[54] Even the dramatists who fought with Collier are said to have accepted Collier's premises, and modified their craft accordingly.[55] This account of the controversy and the allied phenomena of the Societies for the Reformation of Manners and the Licensing Act of 1737 (which provided for censorship of plays) is certainly true on one level; but in relation to emerging heterosexuality, the story of English dramatic history might be told differently.

Collier attacked the stage for displaying profanity and libertinism, and for disrespecting the clergy. He certainly understood the stakes of the controversy he helped to incite over theatrical representation, at least in terms of the patriarchal world that was crumbling before his eyes. That is, Collier understood that to celebrate adultery (among other sins) meant the beginning of the end of an order that condemned pleasure on earth in favor of eternal happiness with God.[56] He rightly saw Restoration drama as manifesting the new antipatriarchalist philosophies that justified the act he most despised, the deposition of James II.[57] And Collier also understood that the older worldview for which he yearned, like all worldviews, was created in and dependent on language.

In the introduction to *A Short View*, Collier tries to rescue the words "mistress" and "lover" from their newly emerging definitions. He declares that he will not accept these dangerous usages when he writes about Restoration plays:

> I have Ventured to change the Terms of Mistress and Lover, for others some what more Plain, but much more Proper . . . As Good and Evil are different in Themselves, so they ought to be differently Mark'd. To confound them in Speech, is the way to confound them in Practise. Ill Qualities ought to have ill Names, to prevent their being Catching. Indeed Things are in a great measure Govern'd by Words: To Guild over a foul Character, serves only to perplex the Idea, to encourage the Bad, and mislead the Unwary. To treat Honour, and Infamy alike, is an injury to Virtue, and a sort of Levelling in Morality. I confess I have no Ceremony for Debauchery. For to Complement Vice, is but one Remove from worshipping the Devil. (A4v–A5v)

Collier would like to cleanse the words "mistress" and "lover" from the redefinitions to which they had been subjected in texts such as *All for Love* and Shadwell's *Timon*. He wants to reserve "mistress" for the usages that would have been generally familiar to Shakespeare and his contemporaries, especially for the meaning that would correspond to sexually pure "beloved" woman. To call Cleopatra his "mistress" and himself a "lover," as Antony does in *All for Love*, is, for Collier, to give an "ill quality" a good name, to "Complement Vice." And in *A Short View*, Collier does indeed reserve the word "mistress" for what he sees as its honorable and true meanings. He uses "mistress" only for those women who have not strayed or been active sexually and who are beloved by men. Thus, when he interprets Ovid's *Art of Love*, Collier avoids the word, saying that Ovid describes the playhouse as a place of sexual activity: "Nothing being more common than to see Beauty surpriz'd, Women debauch'd, and Wenches Pick'd up at these Diversions" (238). If Collier succeeded in prompting playwrights to write more "moral" plays, however, he was fighting a losing battle on the level of language, as the history of the word "mistress" shows.

The critic and failed playwright John Dennis was quick to respond to Collier's *Short View* with the 1698 pamphlet, *The Usefulness of the Stage, To the Happiness of Mankind. To Government, and To Religion*. Dennis answers Collier, "tho some people go to the Theatre to meet their Mistresses, yet it is evident that most go to see the Play" (30). Dennis takes for granted that Collier is talking about both "mistresses" and men with "mistresses"; Collier would like to discuss "wenches," a word that for him can and should signify sexual looseness. "Wench," as we will see in chapter 5, was another of that panoply of words for women that could, but did not necessarily, signify sexually in Shakespeare's time. Collier would like a world in which "wenches" are sexually available and "mistresses" are not. Dennis, however, is already living (as was Collier) in a world in which when one calls a woman a man's "mistress," one is understood to mean his "illicit" sexual partner.[58]

Dennis's response to Dryden's *All for Love* indicates the power of the "moral" critique that Collier advocated. In a fit of pique over the displacement of his adaptation of *Coriolanus* from the stage in favor of a revival of *All for Love*, Dennis writes to Richard Steele in 1719 that, unlike his own Shakespeare adaptation, Dryden's is a sinkhole of immorality. He translates the "Title and the two last Lines" of *All for Love; or the World Well Lost* into what he calls "plain *English*":

> that if any Person of Quality or other shall turn away his Wife, his young, affectionate, virtuous, charming Wife (for all these *Octavia* was) to take to his Bed a loose abandon'd Prostitute, and shall in her Arms exhaust his Patrimony, destroy his Health, emasculate his Mind, and lose his Reputation and all his Friends, why all this is well and greatly done, his Ruine is his Commendation. (*Critical* II 163)

Dennis castigates Steele for letting his players "preach up Adultery to a Town which stands so little in need of their Doctrine" (II 163). The anti-Jacobite Dennis was Collier's political and religious, as well as his literary, enemy; but he accepted Collier's premise that the stage, by representing adultery favorably, was propagating sin. Dennis here sounds as if he has swallowed whole the homosocial imaginary's interpretations of the Antony and Cleopatra story—interpretations that Collier would, to some extent, approve.[59]

However, Dennis also accepts a premise that Collier would have immediately rejected. Dennis, like Dryden and Shadwell, knows the Restoration truth about men: Men will inevitably succumb to their natural sexual desires. When Dennis voices his acceptance of that truth, he comes close to outlining a position that would not become commonsensical for at least another hundred years: a position in which natural heterosexual desire is opposed to unnatural homosexual desire. In *The Usefullness of the Stage*, Dennis considers drama's influence upon what he calls the four chief "moral vices": "1. The Love of Women. 2. Drinking. 3. Gaming. 4. Unnatural Sins." According to Dennis, "Unnatural Sins," which include men associating sexually with men, are never "encourag'd by the Stage." Men's sexual desire for women is another story:

> And now, lastly, for the Love of Women, fomented by the Corruption, and not by the genuine Art of the Stage; tho the augmenting and nourishing of it cannot be defended, yet it may be in some measure excus'd.
>
> 1. Because it has more of Nature, and consequently more Temptation, and consequently less Malice . . .
> 2. Because it has a check upon the other Vices, and peculiarly upon that unnatural sin, in the restraining of which, the happiness of mankind is in so evident a manner concern'd. (26–27)

Dennis argues that only corrupt plays (like Dryden's *All for Love*) actually augment and nourish illicit (hetero)sexual desire. However, even those plays' encouragement of desire can be excused because such desire is more natural, more tempting, and less malicious than other sins. In addition, male sexual desire for women "check"s "other Vices," particularly male sexual desire for men. In a 1726 pamphlet, *The Stage Defended*, Dennis elaborates on these caveats, using Saint Paul's strictures on both male–male sex and female–female sex to excuse the incitement of male–female desire.

Dennis's distinction between men's natural desire for women and male–male sexual expression hints at modern heterosexuality, but it by no means predicts it. Dennis sees adultery as a venial sin, which at least keeps men from seeking their sexual pleasure with other men and women from seeking their sexual pleasure with other women. Although he sees male–female sex as more natural, he openly describes male–male and female–female sex as possibilities for people—possibilities that must be headed off. For Dennis, scenes in plays that incite male desire for women "might be of some Use to the reducing Mens minds to the natural Desire of Women" (II 314). In dominant twentieth-century heterosexuality, there was no general category of Men whose minds needed to be reduced into heterosexuality. In that ideological understanding of the world, homosexual men are irreducibly different than "normal" heterosexual men. To produce modern heterosexuality, men had first to be defined as sexual animals, and then further to be differentiated into categories on the basis of sexual object choice. This process would be long, slow, and uneven. In chapter 3, I will discuss further Restoration Shakespeare's place in the process of defining men as (hetero)sexual animals.

Unlike Dryden, Shadwell, and other Restoration dramatists, Dennis does not validate adultery; however, he does admit it as a lesser sin than "unnatural Affections." As we will see in chapter 4, the "moral" sentimental rewritings of late-sixteenth- and early-seventeenth-century domestic tragedy believe fervently that male sexual desire for women is natural and good. Although they reject Restoration drama's "license," they admit the premise that such drama helped to establish. The temporary validation of adultery was necessary for the installation of male (hetero)sexual expression as both good and natural. In late-sixteenth-century and early-seventeenth-century England, this was by no means a foregone conclusion. Actually, representations in that period argued against male sexual desire for women. But, by the end of the seventeenth century, that celebration of male sexual desire for women had become natural for Dennis and his contemporary authors and their audiences.

Dennis and Collier were both deeply committed Christians, but Collier was committed to a Christianity allied with a patriarchalism that was dying at the moment that it was being most firmly articulated in the work of Robert Filmer.[60] Dennis, in contrast, was indebted to the philosophical innovations of the seventeenth century. Collier looks backward to a patriarchal past that distrusts individualism; Dennis looks forward to Romanticism.[61] Dennis refers to Pascal's philosophy to justify his theory of poetry, a theory in which great poetry induces passion, which in turn produces pleasure (I 149–50). This theory, which is a child of Locke's philosophy as much as it is of Pascal's, is close to a definition of sin in the homosocial imaginary's terms.[62] That is, it resembles the discourse of debased characters in drama from the previous century—only the craven Antony of Brandon's play tries, unsuccessfully, to defend this kind of pleasure. Given this resemblance, it is perhaps not surprising that the sin of greed is missing from Dennis's list of "moral vices." In the "moral" response to Restoration dramas of adultery, we can see a bit of the linked valorizations of lust and greed that were to assist in producing modern heterosexuality.

CHAPTER 3

RESTORATION SHAKESPEARE 2: FRIENDS AND LIBERTINES

Restoration Shakespeare adaptations participated in rewriting manhood in terms very different than those that prevailed in texts of the homosocial imaginary. For a short but crucial period of time, possession of a mistress became a possibility for elite men and even, temporarily, a condition of masculinity. Despite the efforts of men such as Collier, this new (hetero)sexually desirous masculinity became so dominant that Alexander Pope wrote in its terms. In his private correspondence, Pope complains about his muse, whom he characterizes as "an old stale wife" and as "that Jade whom every body thinks I love, as a Mistress, but whom in reality I hate as a Wife" (*Correspondence* 292–293). As James Grantham Turner shows, by the beginning of the eighteenth century even a small deformed man like Pope could style himself as a man with an adored mistress and a wife.[1] Such a lustful man would look clownish, debased, and ludicrous in texts of the homosocial imaginary, and a man grasping for literary and social status would reject such a style. By Pope's time, the clown's position has become a possible position for a real man, a position to which Pope aspired. The recategorizations of "mistress" and "wife" articulated tentatively by Dryden's Cleopatra have become so compelling by the early eighteenth century as to seem a truth of masculinity.

If Pope considered himself a poet with a muse that behaved more as a boring wife than as a desired mistress, he also considered himself a loving friend to men as well as women. In a typical letter to John Caryll, Pope writes on June 25, 1711, "you have been beforehand with me in the proofs of friendship you speak of, and my heart is a debt, not a present" (*Correspondence* 120). Pope's loving language to his friend indicates that, as George Haggerty suggests, the wall between a man loving a male friend and a man loving a woman was by no means fully constructed in eighteenth-century England.[2] When rewriting Shakespeare's plays, Restoration playwrights confronted numerous eroticized male friendships. They did not reject those friendships, but they treated them cautiously, no longer completely comfortable with representations in which a man's friendship with another man defined his character. Ventidius may love Antony dearly in *All for Love*, but he must, at least, also express sexual interest in a woman. In Restoration Shakespeare adaptations, we can see playwrights struggling to define Shakespearean male friendships in ways that would make sense to their audiences. Their struggles, but also their relative comfort with eroticized male friendship, tell us much about the only partially constructed edifice of modern heterosexuality.

Equally revealing and fascinating are the ways in which Restoration playwrights recategorized so many of Shakespeare's male characters as libertines. Many of Shakespeare's male characters apparently made little sense to Restoration and early-eighteenth-century dramatists and their audiences. Those dramatists rewrote as libertines male characters who in their original Shakespearean incarnations might have had little or no sexual interest in women. In this chapter, I will discuss these rewritten male characters from adaptations such as Nahum Tate's *The History of King Lear*, William D'Avenant's *The Law against Lovers* (a combination of *Much Ado about Nothing* and *Measure for Measure*), Thomas Otway's *The History and Fall of Caius Marius* (an adaptation of *Romeo and Juliet*), Edward Ravenscroft's *Titus Andronicus*, Thomas D'Urfey's *The Injured Princess* (an adaptation of *Cymbeline*), and Shadwell's *Timon*. These Restoration rewritings are a window into radical transformations in male identity. When the Restoration made sense of Shakespearean villains and Shakespearean protagonists by rewriting them as libertines, it fundamentally changed the way these characters were seen, even by later critics who returned to the Shakespearean texts. Today, Restoration Shakespearean libertines can set into relief Shakespeare's male characters, letting us see them as Shakespeare represented them, as compromised by sexual desire for women.

Restoration Shakespearean libertines contributed to a leveling of the sexual playing field for men. A world in which men had been differentiated from one another partially on the basis of relative sexual desire for women (relative propensity for sin) was slowly becoming a world in which (white) men could be imagined as more equal. We can witness that world's construction even in Restoration Shakespearean rewritings that do not turn men into libertines, such as John Lacey's *Taming of the Shrew: Sauny the Scott: or, the Taming of the Shrew* (1698). D'Avenant's *The Law against Lovers*, which makes *Measure for Measure*'s

Lucio the best friend of *Much Ado about Nothing*'s Benedick, is equally evidence of that construction. If at the end of the Restoration white men in England were actually divided from one another politically and economically, they were beginning to be imagined as connected in their sexual desire for women.

Friendship, Homoeroticism, and Hetero Desire

As Haggerty argues, eroticized male friendship is another area in which *All for Love* shows the continuity between Restoration sexual ideology and what I am calling the homosocial imaginary (27–31). *All for Love* participates in the process of constructing the newly masculine sexually desirous man, but it is not interested in cordoning off adult masculinity from either a discourse of male beauty or from homoerotic friendship. Men are still permitted to love men, to speak of their love for men, and to invest themselves in other men in ways that are very consistent with the representations of the homosocial imaginary. Yet even in this area of continuity, subtle differences between Renaissance and Restoration representations indicate a world to come. In Renaissance representations, as in Montaigne's discussion of friendship, "sex between women and men (both within and outside marriage) lies below male friendship" in the hierarchy of human relationships (Masten 36). Although male friendship is still an ideal and still idealized in *All for Love*, it is no longer permissibly, or even preferentially, the sole focus of elite men. Ventidius and Dolabella are both lovers of Antony, but they also desire women.

When we look at late-sixteenth- and early-seventeenth-century English representations of male friendship, we often see pairs of male friends, such as Kent and Lear in *King Lear*, Enobarbus and Antony in *Antony and Cleopatra*, and Horatio and Hamlet in *Hamlet*, in which one of the friends (Kent, Enobarbus, Horatio) has no desire for women and no marital or sexual relationship with any woman. These texts expend no energy linking these men with women. Friendship and marriage may coexist, or they may conflict with one another in these texts and in Restoration representations. However, friendship in the earlier texts is as likely to be the focal point of the representation as is male–female love; and men who love men do not need to demonstrate any interest in women to make them viable male characters. *Timon of Athens* depicts a man devoted completely to his friends, self-serving men who shatter Timon's dream of ideal friendship. Even then, Shakespeare's *Timon* lauds one true man, Timon's steward

Flavius, who remains loyal to his master.³ When Shadwell rewrites *Timon*, he replaces the world of friendship and service with the world of male–female love. Shadwell's Timon has false friends, but his heart is broken more deeply by his false fiancée; and he dies having found only one true *woman*, his mistress Evandra. In *All for Love*, *The History of Timon of Athens*, and other Restoration Shakespeare adaptations, men love men but they must love women as well. The realm of male friendship is as copious in Restoration representation, but it is no longer as powerful; it can no longer completely define men.

As Haggerty indicates, *All for Love* is replete with love language spoken by men toward men, language that is as loving as that spoken between men in Shakespeare's plays. Robert McHenry Jr. also notes that "Antony greets [Dolabella] with extremely affectionate, sexually charged language" (452). Antony's loving greeting—"Let me not live, If the young bridegroom, longing for his night, / Was ever half so fond"— intimately resembles Aufidius's address to Coriolanus in Shakespeare's tragedy, when Coriolanus appears in Antium: *Aufidius* "But that I see thee heere / Thou Noble thing, more dances my rapt heart, / Then when I first my wedded Mistris saw / Bestride my Threshold" (TLN 2773–2776; 4.5.114–117).⁴ Both warriors favorably compare seeing their friend/competitor again with their first night of wedded bliss, and in neither case do these comparisons reflect badly on the characters' masculinity.⁵ In *All for Love*, Ventidius sees Antony's attachment to Dolabella as a sign that he can be redeemed as a man from his feminizing engagement with Cleopatra. Ventidius, with the homosocial imaginary's eyes, sees Antony and Dolabella's loving friendship as an enduring marker of Antony's masculinity. In fact, if we read *All for Love* as a competition between Cleopatra and Ventidius for Antony, it looks very like numerous plays from the homosocial imaginary (see chapter 4's readings of *A Woman Killed with Kindness* and *Arden of Faversham*). Ventidius, that imaginary's representative, is deeply in love with Antony; he loves him just as so many men in Shakespeare's plays love other men. Ventidius's love for Antony leads him to try to sabotage Antony and Cleopatra's relationship in the name of Antony's Roman identity. Structurally, his part resembles Antonio's in *The Merchant of Venice*. The difference is that we are never led to believe that Shakespeare's Antonio also loves Portia or any other woman; but Ventidius reveals his desire for Cleopatra.

Throughout Shakespearean and other Renaissance representations, a fully male world, divorced from the love of women, hovers as a possibility, sometimes incomplete but also sometimes redemptive, depending on the play. If we conceive of Shakespeare's career as *The Norton Shakespeare* does, as framed by *The Two Gentlemen of Verona* on one side and *The Two Noble Kinsmen* on the other, then Shakespeare started his theatrical career writing a play that in the end elevates male friendship over even a marital bond and ended his career cowriting a play in which "[h]eterosexual desire is rendered . . . unappealing . . . by the extended representation of what it destroys." In *The Two Noble Kinsman* the "positive alternative [to male–female desire] is same-sex attachment, whether understood as the Renaissance ideal of male friendship, as girlish intimacy, or as homoerotic attraction" (Cohen 3199).[6] In Renaissance representations, the ideal world of male friendship can redeem characters, providing them a refuge from the greed and lust that can be stimulated by and embodied in women. Late-sixteenth- and early-seventeenth-century English representation argued that a friend was far superior to the kind of a woman who would be a mistress, and even that a friend might well be far superior to a wife. According to May's *Tragedie of Cleopatra*, a man devoted to a woman like Cleopatra, "knows not what true friendship means, / But makes his friends . . . / Slaves to his lusts and vices" (B7; 1.2.175–177).

As Alan Bray's, Jeffrey Masten's, and Laurie Shannon's work so powerfully shows, this piece of wisdom about men and the priority of male friendship is confirmed throughout Renaissance representation. By the Restoration, however, received wisdom no longer claims that male friendship is vastly more important than male–female sexual engagement. Male friendship loses priority over male–female sex slowly and unevenly over the course of the long eighteenth century, but we can glimpse the beginning of that loss in Restoration texts. If in Renaissance English representation, as the introduction demonstrates, friendship is a trope used to positively describe the love of women, by the Restoration, love of women has assumed a centrality that enables this trope to be reversed. In *All for Love*, Antony describes Dolabella to Ventidius:

> Yet I had [a friend], the bravest youth of Rome,
> Whom Caesar loves beyond the love of women;
> He could resolve his mind as fire does wax,
> From that hard, rugged image melt him down,
> And mold him in what softer form he pleased. (3.84–88)

In the earlier Cleopatra stories, the "love of women" was always potentially debased and degrading; love between a man and a woman could seldom if ever match the love of male friends. In *All for Love*, Caesar's love for his friend Dolabella is surpassingly great because it can be compared to male love of women, which is now the essential love. The image of a man melted by love in these earlier texts was an image of a man weakened into formless chaos by an engulfing woman. In Antony's description of Dolabella, this same weakness is valorized as the beautiful effect of a perfect male friendship, so perfect that it surpasses the love of women—a love that, in turn, Antony, the play as a whole, and Restoration sexual ideology take for granted.

In 1662, D'Avenant staged *The Law against Lovers*, a play that combines and rewrites Shakespeare's *Measure for Measure* and *Much Ado about Nothing*, two plays that continually stage how dangerous sexual engagement with women can be for men. The rewritten play celebrates male–female sexual love and sees friendship as relatively impoverished. Its Beatrice and Benedick use "friendship" as a euphemism for male–female sexual engagement. D'Avenant's Beatrice, preparing to visit her cousin, Juliet (jailed for an affair), muses: "*Juliet*, I cannot but/Pity thy private friendship" (309). Angelo's brother, Benedick, enters the scene, and Beatrice and Benedick discuss men's "friendship" with women. This Benedick, as we will see, assumes that all men should naturally pursue women, and when Beatrice protests that Juliet got into her terrible trouble because she listened to Claudio's "sighs," Benedick proposes that women should listen to men's "Platonick" whispers. Arguing that her cousin "has Plato'd it / Profoundly," Beatrice calls for a "new" course of action for men, a course of action that Benedick rejects:

> *Beatrice* Make friendship with your selves, and not with us.
> Let ev'ry *Damon* of you, chuse his *Pitheas*,
> And tattle Romantick Philosophy
> Together, like bearded Gossips.
> *Benedick* Though such conversation might breed peace in
> A Palace, yet 'twould make but a thin Court. (309)

In Shakespeare's play, Benedick is initially famously resistant to male–female love. When his friends fool him into believing both that Beatrice is in love with him and that the world scorns him for rejecting her, he pretends to resign himself to marriage, saying "the world must be peopled" (TLN 1063–1064; 2.3.213–214). At the end of the *Much Ado*, he is still making nervous cuckold jokes. D'Avenant's Benedick searches for arguments in favor of male–female love instead of making those arguments as rationalizations for ignoring the foolishness of such love.

Beatrice offers Benedick the choice between sexualized "friendship" with women and feminized friendship with men. The classical story of Damon and Pythias, one of the staple stories that supported the elevated concept of male friendship in the Renaissance, becomes a barren, degraded existence for men.[7] In this projected world, men will love each other like "bearded Gossips." This vision of male friendship calls men who exclusively love other men effeminate, and it also criticizes male friendship as unproductive. According to D'Avenant's Benedick, the male–male world might be more peaceful than a world in which men naturally pursue and fight over women; however, " 'twould make but a thin Court." Shakespeare writes plays with courts full of men in no way connected with women. In those courts, the female connection is generally more dangerous than the realm of male friendship.

In Shadwell's *Timon of Athens*, the satirical Apemantus shares a world in which male–female love transcends male friendship. Watching Timon's false friends praise him, Apemantus comments, "They hate and scorn each other, yet they kiss/As if they were of different Sexes" (12). In this emerging world, men may kiss and love their friends, but that love is envisioned as an imitation of sexual love between men and women. Men display their love for one another "as if they were of different Sexes," that is, as if it were the real thing, which, in this definition, it is not. As Haggerty suggests, male friendship in the Restoration and the eighteenth century has by no means been cordoned off from homoerotic behavior. But it is losing its meaning as the thing that by itself would make a man's life worth living. In the twentieth century, *All for Love*'s depiction of male friendship inspires homophobic criticism.[8] In the Restoration, it was *All for Love*'s elevation of the mistress to the level of the friend that might have shocked earlier eyes.

In Restoration Shakespeare, this elevation is the rule. Dryden's adaptation of *Troilus and Cressida*, which he subtitled *Truth Found Too Late* (1679), stages a debate on the relative worth of a mistress and a friend. Shakespeare's Troilus rather blithely accepts that his Trojans will transfer Cressida to the Greek camp in exchange for a Trojan prisoner. Dryden's Troilus, in contrast, fights desperately to save his mistress. The Trojans know that Troilus will resist the exchange, so they send his brother Hector to persuade him, since Troilus loves Hector with "more than a Brothers love" (32). Hector is Troilus's friend as well as his brother. As his friend, he is finally able to convince Troilus that he must bow to the wills of his father, brother, and the Trojan council, but Troilus consents only after a protracted struggle that airs and finally reveals the new stakes of male friendship. Although Troilus vows that "there can be nothing" that could make him hate Hector, whom he loves "with that awful love /[he] bear[s] to Heav'n," Hector's news that he must give up Cressida to the enemy camp tests that vow to its limits (35). Troilus immediately refuses to give up Cressida, arguing that it is enough that he has borne the news of her exchange and "yet live[s]" (36). When Hector insists, Troilus declares that he is "no more [his] friend," that Hector has betrayed and even "prostitute[d]" the "Sacred name" of friend, "which none but brave and honest men shou'd wear" (37). Hector challenges Troilus to fight over Cressida, whom he says is hardly worth the quarrel, but the two men do not actually physically engage until Troilus insults Hector's wife, Andromache's, chastity. At this point, Hector declares that Troilus can "use the name . . . of friend no more" (38). This announcement decides Cressida's fate. For at this point, Troilus cannot bear to lose his friend as well as his mistress: "For I have lost (oh what have I not lost!) / The fairest dearest, kindest of her Sex, / . . . And if I had a joy beyond that love, / A friend, have lost him too" (39).

Friendship would seem to have trumped male–female bonds as it so often does in pre-Restoration representation: friendship is "a joy beyond . . . love." Yet, in this scene, friendship's victory is pyrrhic. For the primacy of friendship lies bleeding after this exchange. Although Hector refuses to countenance the idea that his brother and friend would sell "his Country for a womans love," he is embedded in a world in which male–female love finally transcends all other bonds. Hector himself believes that the news that Troilus must lose his mistress is "nearer" "more close" and "more yours" than would be the news of the death of his father or mother (35). Indeed, if we can believe his protestations at the end of the dialogue, Hector is finally willing to shift his allegiance in favor of Troilus and Cressida's love, which he pities and with which he identifies. This Hector, unlike Shakespeare's, loves his wife more than he loves any man. Shakespeare gives his Hector only one short scene with his wife, and in that scene he summarily dismisses her as well as her fears that he will die in battle, whereas Dryden's Hector loves his wife so much that he comes close to remaining at home to quell her anxiety. Dryden's focus on that love as well as on the love between Troilus and Cressida is a signpost for emerging heterosexuality's reversed priorities.

Restoration Shakespearean Libertines

When Restoration dramatists came to Shakespeare's canon, they found many male characters who did not fit into any mode of masculinity and sexual engagement that appealed to them and their audiences. In addition to portraying the appeal and priority of eroticized male friendship, Shakespeare's plays are full of what must have looked like inappropriately asexually motivated men: villains who have no interest in illicit sex and whose only determinant of their villainy is their birth on the wrong side of the bed, and men who fear marriage because it attaches them to women, not because it restrains their own sexual freedom. One solution the Restoration found to this dilemma was to recreate these male characters in the mold of a newly available character type, the libertine. Although critics disagree about what the profusion of libertine characters and libertine discourse on the Restoration stage meant for Restoration drama and culture, the libertine presence in Restoration plays is undeniable.[9] In Shakespeare's plays, the male characters that the Restoration rewrote as libertines do not display the propensity for sex with many different women that helped to define Restoration male characters as libertines; nonetheless, many of them do resemble Restoration libertines in their distrust of women's virtue. This distrust may have prompted their reconstructions as libertines by Restoration dramatists. These libertine characters could then serve as the wild version of the plays' ordinary men who could have sexual desire for women that looked comparatively benevolent. Thus, the reconstructions of Shakespeare characters as Restoration libertines, perhaps paradoxically, helped to produce non-libertine heterosexuality. Like the temporary elevation of adultery, libertinism served as a way station for heterosexuality.

Restoration dramatists classified Shakespearean male characters as libertines because in the original plays they showed an interest in sex with women while simultaneously despising them or because, according to new sexual codes, they should show such an interest. Villains who seemed sexually interested, like *King Lear*'s Edmund and *Cymbeline*'s Cloten, made particular sense as libertines because libertinism could signify as pervasive immorality. It therefore accorded with and helped to motivate villainous behavior. Ambiguously villainous male characters, such as *Coriolanus*'s Aufidius and *Cymbeline*'s Iachimo, also made Restoration sense as libertines, notwithstanding that in Shakespeare's plays Aufidius lacks sexual desire for women and Iachimo condemns his own sexual misdeed. James Grantham Turner argues that the "most important movement within libertinism [was] the attempt to locate sublimity . . . *within* sexuality *itself*" ("Culture" 10; his emphasis). What links these diverse characters as the Restoration conceived them is their devotion to sexual pleasure and their deification of inconstancy. However, since in Shakespeare's plays none of these characters located sublimity in sexuality, each of them had to be significantly altered to make them conform to the libertine creed.

The word "libertine" and the associated vocabulary of male identity, including "rake" and "fop," appear throughout Restoration drama.[10] Shakespeare, in contrast, uses "libertine" sparingly, and never with its Restoration connotations. In *Much Ado about Nothing*, Beatrice uses it as an insult that lacks a sexual reference (TLN 544–549; 2.1.118–122). When Shakespeare's usages of "libertine" do imply sexual engagement, as they do in *As You Like It*, *Hamlet*, and *Antony and Cleopatra*, they do not denote sublimity. In *As You Like It*, Duke Senior accuses Jacques of having led a libertine life, one in which he has used his "license" to travel among women and acquire diseases. According to the Duke, Jacques would now spread these diseases throughout the world in the guise of decrying sin (TLN 1039–1043; 2.7.64–69). Jacques replies that were he to criticize women for wearing fancy clothes, presumably acquired through sexual sin, and men for their pride and acquisitiveness, they could not defend themselves. This vision of the indiscriminately libidinous and diseased libertine is entirely sex-negative, and it also attributes sexual behavior and sexual diseases primarily to women. The Duke, who himself lives in an all-male fantasy world, seems to despise male–female sex, and Jacques in no way claims to enjoy sexual behavior. Shakespeare's usage of "libertine" in *Hamlet* is equally sex-negative. When Laertes warns Ophelia not to fornicate with Hamlet, she advises him to learn his own lesson (TLN 510–514; 1.3.47–51). Laertes himself never speaks of women or sexual desire. If Jacques's formerly libertine behavior has infected him with debilitating disease, and if Laertes might be in danger of following sexual desire to hell were he to become a "Libertine," Antony, according to his erstwhile ally Pompey, is currently a libertine. Pompey says, "Let Witchcraft ioyne [join] with Beauty, Lust with both,/ Tye vp the Libertine, in a field of Feasts/ Keepe his Braine fuming" (TLN 642–644; 2.1.22–25). We might accept Pompey's vision of Antony as the only practicing Shakespearean "Libertine," but his behavior in *Antony and Cleopatra* does not resemble Restoration libertine behavior; and, significantly, Restoration dramatists, despite their propensity to recreate Shakespearean characters as libertines, did not portray Antony as a libertine. Antony may be devoted to pleasure, but he is also devoted to his military honor; and he fails the Restoration's test for truly libertine sexual behavior because he shows no interest in multiple sexual conquests. We can see his culture's distance from heterosexuality in the fact that Shakespeare uses the word "libertine" in relation to these characters who do not satisfy the criteria for Restoration libertines.

Restoration characters rewritten as libertines include four who in their Shakespearean incarnations show no personal interest in sex with women: Sulpitius, Otway's version of *Romeo and Juliet*'s Mercutio; Aufidius in Tate's *Coriolanus*; and Quintus and Martius in Ravenscroft's version of *Titus Andronicus*. These characters were all rewritten as men devoted to sex with women, and in each case the rewrites show us how libertinism worked to define all men, even non-libertine men, as on a continuum of sexual desire for women. Unlike Shakespeare's Mercutio, who "does not address his own desire" for women (Bly "Bawdy" 108), Otway's Sulpitius despises women and love for women but espouses the libertine creed—the sexual pursuit of women for his own pleasure. He tells the Nurse that he is a sexual champion:

> A woman's man, my Sibyll, wouldst thou try
> My strength in Feats of amorous engagement.
> Lead me amongst the Beauteous, where they run
> Wild in their Youth, and wanton to their Wildness,
> Where I may chuse the foremost of the Herd,
> And bear her trembling to some Bank,
> . . .
> Throw my inspir'd Arms about her,
> And press her till she thought her self more blest
> Then *Io* painting with the Joys of *Jove*. (27)

In Otway's play, Sulpitius and other male characters insist that a man who would love a woman rather than sexually conquer her would be weakened by his devotion. In this insistence, they demonstrate the continuity between libertine sexual codes and one code of the homo-social imaginary. Sulpitius does not respect women, and he does not respect male–female love. But unlike Mercutio, he measures his masculinity in terms of his sexual prowess with women as well as in terms of his valor.

Although Shakespeareans have reviled Otway's Restoration revision, calling it "grotesque" and "a literary crime," in many ways Otway's play is a very accurate Restoration translation of Shakespeare's play.[11] Otway recognized *Romeo and Juliet* as criticizing male excess. As a Restoration dramatist, he interpreted that excess as necessarily sexual. All of his men understand their world in sexual terms. His feud is a political contest, fought between men who despise women but naturally desire them. Like Shakespeare's play, Otway's is suffused with violence, but Otway depicts a world of violent libertine and potentially libertine men pursuing their political ambitions to the death, and unlike Shakespeare, Otway removes his central love affair from the fray. Caius Marius junior is his play's heroic Romeo, tragically devoted both to his out-of-control father and to the beautiful, faithful Lavinia, who will follow him anywhere. Junior is not a libertine, yet he speaks the sexual language of the libertine, exulting in the "mighty Pleasures" and "th'highest expectation of Delight" that will be his when he attains sexual union with his beloved (30). And unlike Shakespeare's Romeo, whose love for Juliet makes him "effeminate" (3.1.109), Marius junior becomes a man in his love for Lavinia. Even his mad father is won by their true love, which the play purifies in contrast to the libertine sexual desire of the men who surround them.

In contrast to Shakespeare's *Romeo and Juliet*, Otway's revision, I would argue, depicts modern "true love." To depict that love, Otway had to correct Shakespeare's play, excising the Friar's speeches in favor of moderation and sequestering Marius junior and Lavinia's love affair from the violence in which it seems only accidentally embedded. In other words, whereas Shakespeare's play sees Romeo's and Juliet's desire as violent and fatal in itself, Otway's play isolates that desire, contrasting it to libertine excess and seeing it as a good in itself. In addition, Otway felt compelled to excise Romeo's previous attachment to Rosaline (an excision that would hold sway for the next 200 years).[12] Marius junior and Lavinia have always loved each other over their fathers' objections. Marius junior reveals his love to his father, and that love strengthens him, confirming his manhood. As in modern sexual ideology, this Romeo's true love exists in the context of libertine desire, partaking of its vocabulary that exalts male sexual pleasure with women, but rejecting its premise of inconstancy. Marius junior is a sexually desirous man, but unlike Sulpitius and the rest of the desiring men surrounding him, he has true love, love that absolutely includes sexual desire but that admits no prior attachments, love that helps to make a man a man.

In 1682, Tate rewrote Shakespeare's *The Tragedy of Coriolanus* as *The Ingratitude of a Common-Wealth: Or, the Fall of Caius Martius Coriolanus*. As did Otway, Tate created a villain out of an ambiguous male character, *Coriolanus*'s Aufidius, a villain primarily motivated by his own sexual pleasure. Tate does not shy away from Aufidius's love for Coriolanus as depicted by Shakespeare, but Tate recasts that desire as a feature of Aufidius's libertinism, his villainy compounded by an unquenchable desire for Coriolanus's wife. Tate and Shakespeare both represent Aufidius as intensely involved with Coriolanus and as measuring himself in terms of his rival. However, Shakespeare's Aufidius has no personal interest in Coriolanus's wife, Virgilia, whereas Tate's Aufidius is interested in nothing as intensely as he is in her.

Although Tate retains many of Shakespeare's lines, his libertine Aufidius lives in a different world, a world in which men are judged and judge themselves in terms of their success in sexual relationships with women. In Tate's play, Aufidius wants to kill Coriolanus in order to sexually possess Virgilia, and he condemns himself for failing to do so:

> I am a lazy Trifler, and unworthy
> To be possest o'th'Beauty that I Love,
> Or to be reveng'd upon the Man I hate:
> Why forc't I not my passage to his Heart?
> Then pamper'd in the Banquet of his Blood,
> Flown hot, as flame born *Pluto*, to the Rape;
> And quench't the Fervour in *Virgilia's* Arms. (55)

Like the libertine Sulpitius, the libertine Aufidius would like to see himself as a sexually aroused Roman god. He calls himself unworthy because he has failed to pursue indefatigably his own sexual pleasure. Coriolanus bars the way to Aufidius's sexual satisfaction with "th'Beauty that [he] Love[s]," as much as he does to Aufidius's political advancement, or to the hearts of his friends, the primary concerns of Shakespeare's Aufidius. In Tate's play, Coriolanus and Aufidius both unashamedly love women, and they conduct their relationship with one another over women's bodies and, crucially, in terms of its effects on the women involved. When all lie dying on the stage, Tate's Aufidius cries out to Coriolanus, "I charge thee Dye not yet, 'till thou hast seen/Our Scene of Pleasures: to thy Face I'll Force her;/Glut my last Minuits with a double Ryot;/And in Revenges Sweets and Loves, Expire" (60). Aufidius's plan for revenge defines him as a libertine, and it also differentiates him completely from Shakespeare's Aufidius, a man who plans and carries out his revenge in the court of men and male public opinion without reference to any personal desire for a woman. Shakespeare's Aufidius cares nothing for "Loves" "Sweets," whereas Tate's Aufidius would like to die tasting them. Tate's Aufidius even dies without exacting his revenge because he cannot stand the sight of Virgilia wounded and bleeding. Where Shakespeare's Coriolanus is humiliated and defeated because he listens to women, all men in Tate's *Coriolanus*, even the most villainous among them, attend to women and see that attention as natural.

Of course, as Sedgwick has shown us, a plan such as Aufidius's is homosocial at its core; but if Aufidius's revenge on Coriolanus in Shakespeare's play is entirely homosocial, a continuation of their exclusively male–male relationship, Aufidius's revenge in Tate's play is not only homosocial, it is also (hetero)sexually oriented. Tate's Aufidius revenges himself because of his "love" for Virgilia, because he feels that Coriolanus has beaten him in a sexual contest. He plans to glut his pleasure in sexual congress with Virgilia. In Tate's play, both of these men are oriented toward women, even though they still fight battles in terms of one another. Aufidius's rape plan makes him a villain, but the play sees his orientation toward women and sexual pleasure as natural. He wants to rape because he is a villain, but he desires women because he is a man. As Marius junior's discourse suggests, the libertine villain was on a continuum with the new sexually desirous elite men. Where Shakespeare's Aufidius could enact a homosocial revenge within the homosocial continuum that made Coriolanus (when he succumbs to the women in his life) a boy, Tate's Aufidius desires a sexual revenge upon a (hetero)sexually desirous hero.

The libertine redefinition of white masculinity is equally evident in Edward Ravenscroft's 1687 rewriting of Shakespeare's early play, *Titus Andronicus*. In Shakespeare's play, the evil Tamora's lover, Aaron, entraps Titus's sons, Quintus and Martius, for a murder they did not commit. Aaron brings them to the murder scene, telling them that he has seen a panther sleeping there. In Ravenscroft's adaptation, in contrast, Aaron entraps Quintus and Martius by means of a letter promising a sexual romp. The letter reads, "Your Expectations shall be rewarded with the Company of two Ladies, Young, and in our own opinions not unhandsome, whose sight shall not displease you; Love

giues the Invitation, and we believe you both Gallant Enough to
know how to use it, and to conceal our favours" (23). When Quintus
shows the letter to Martius, he assumes, correctly, that Martius will
savor the prospect of a sexual liaison:

> Quin. Now *Martius* do you blame the haste I made?
> My Earnest pressing of you hither. —
> Mart. No Lucky *Quintus*, — I am all on fire
> To see these Nymps, these kind and Loving ones.
> Quin. O Love! How I do long to taste thy Banquet!
> And revel with the fair Inviters.
> Martius. Be Quick-sighted as the Hungry Hawk,
> That's watching for a Morning-Prey. —
> Let nothing like a Goddess scape thine Eye. (23)

Quintus and Martius are not libertine villains; in fact, they are duped
good characters. But Ravenscroft attributes to them sexual tastes
that resemble the tastes of the libertine villains in other Restoration
Shakespeare adaptations. Like Otway's Sulpitius and Tate's Aufidius,
Ravenscroft's Quintus and Martius style themselves as sexual gods,
"on fire" to "revel" with "young," "kind," beautiful ladies. They are
distinguished from villains in that they will party only with willing
ladies; but their discourse is otherwise identical to libertine sexual
discourse. They are also naturally sexual men.

As well as rewriting sexually uninterested Shakespearean characters
as libertines or as on the libertine continuum, the Restoration rewrote
men who demonstrated sexual interest as libertines. These rewritings
might seem more plausible, but they are equally revealing of the new
sexual dispensation for men. Alcibiades, who appears briefly in *Timon
of Athens*, is a case in point. In Shakespeare's play, Alcibiades returns
from banishment to take his revenge on Athens. Perhaps because
Alcibiades reenters the play with whores (in whom he shows little
interest), Shadwell reinterpreted him as a libertine. Shadwell's
Alcibiades has a raging sexual appetite. He is already banished before
Shadwell's play starts, and the senate banishes him again during the
play. Toward the beginning of the play, Shadwell's Timon successfully
begs the senate to rescind their punishment of Alcibiades. Apemantus
warns Timon that recalling Alcibiades will bring chaos to Athens:

> Thinkst thou thy self thy Countries friend now *Timon*?
> His foul Riot and his inordinate Lust,
> His wavering Passions, and his headlong Will,

> His selfish Principles, his contempt of others,
> His Mockery, his various Sports, his Wantonness,
> The Rage and Madness of his Luxury
> Will make the *Athenians* hearts ake, as thy own
> Will soon make thine. (28)

As in Shakespeare's play, Shadwell's Alcibiades is an ambiguous character, neither wholly evil, as Apemantus makes him out to be, nor entirely altruistic. However, Apemantus accurately describes Alcibiades's sexual appetites. In the interview with the senate in Shadwell's play, a senator pays him a sarcastic compliment: "It was well done to get your friend King *Agis*/His Wife with Child in his absence"; and Alcibiades replies, "He was a Blockhead, and I mended his breed for him" (58). When Timon asks him why he brings whores with him to battle, Alcibiades answers, "after all the toils and hazards of the day/With men, I refresh my self at night with Women" (76). Alcibiades is a raging, sexually passionate libertine; he debauches his friends' wives and needs sexual release even after he fights. Before the action of Shadwell's play begins he was engaged to Melissa. Alcibiades sneaks back to Athens to see her, and when she welcomes him, he asks her directly to have sex with him before the "senseless formalities" of their marriage. Of course in this play (as it could never be in Shakespeare), Melissa's refusal is another sign of her perfidy. Alcibiades's request, however, is another piece of evidence that indicates his "inordinate lust." Shadwell recreates Alcibiades as a libertine without qualms, but Alcibiades in the end is not very different from Shadwell's Timon, at least in their dealings with women. Both desire the beautiful Melissa, and both have sex with other women. Alcibiades is perhaps more ragingly inconstant, but both characters, like the other Shakespeare characters transformed to libertines, confirm men's lust for women. Shadwell's play shows once again the continuity between libertine sexual desire and the sexual desire attributed to men with consciences.

Like *Timon of Athens*, Shakespeare's *Cymbeline* depicted two men who seem to have been equally at odds with Restoration sexual ideology. In *Cymbeline*, Cloten, the evil Queen's son, is a clown and also a rapist, and Iachimo, the Italian who instigates the wager on Imogen's virtue, is humiliated by his ignoble sexual posturing.[13] It appears that neither Cloten nor Iachimo was a credible villain for the Restoration; their sexual positioning (to Restoration eyes) made them need repair. Cloten looked like a fop in that he was self-involved and not a potent fighter;[14] however, he plans to rape Imogen, which would make him a libertine, a man without a conscience. Shakespeare's Iachimo resembled a libertine in his disregard for women's virtue, but he was not sexually interested enough, and he repents and is forgiven, which seems to have been unacceptable in the Restoration. Because both Cloten and Iachimo seem interested in women but also scornful of them, D'Urfey, who rewrote the play in 1682 as *The Injured Princess, or the Fatal Wager*, read them in ways that Shakespeare could not have foreseen, creating an alliance of a fop with libertine tendencies (Cloten) and a libertine (Jachimo). The libertine Jachimo becomes Cloten's co-conspirator, and both men teem with immoral excess and energy. In addition, D'Urfey invented a French libertine villain called Shattilion to make the wager with Ursaces (his Posthumus) over (his Imogen) Eugenia's chastity.[15]

D'Urfey rewrote Shakespeare's Cloten and Iachimo as drunk and sexually insatiable. It no longer made sense that Cloten's lust and immorality would mean, as they do in Shakespeare's play, that his mother controls him. In D'Urfey's play, Cloten conspires with his mother to enhance her power. He declares to her, "For thee I'le cut through all Opposers, / King, Husband, Daughter, Friend, I'le stop at none, / But on their bloudy Ruines build thy Throne" (7). D'Urfey's Cloten is still clownish, but he is also powerful in his own right; and his libertine sexual behavior is a feature of that power. This Cloten is "A dull Fop Suitor" styling himself a libertine (14). He tells his companion, Silvio, "you shall / Charm [Eugenia] with your Fingers, and you with your Tongue, / Whilst I, God *Mars*, brandish my Weapon; and if tonguing, fingerings and fighting, don't please her, / The Devil's in her" (21). These lines are D'Urfey's translation of Shakespeare's Cloten's speech to his musicians: "Come on, tune: If you can penetrate her with your fingering, so: wee'l try with tongue too: if none will do, let her remaine: but Ile neuer giue o're" (TLN 975–977; 2.3.12–14). As the note in the *Norton Shakespeare* wittily suggests, "it is unclear if [Shakespeare's] Cloten understands the bawdy import of his own words" (2986n.3). D'Urfey's Cloten, who sees himself as a god of war and sex, certainly understands his own sexual language. If Shakespeare's Cloten is a coward whose speech inadvertently reveals his clownish sexual obsession, D'Urfey's Cloten is just another man with libertine desire, styling himself a sexual god.

D'Urfey makes Posthumus's servant Pisanio into a courtier with a daughter, Clarina, who becomes an object of Cloten and Jachimo's libertine desires. Jachimo attempts to rape and kill Clarina with

Cloten's help. When Clarina begs for her life, Cloten and Jachimo exchange these lines:

> *Cloten* . . . Prithee art thou such a
> Fool to think we fear the Devil? *Jachimo*, show
> Her the contrary, rowze her, towze her, Boy, I'le
> Do thee an honourable kindness, and pimp for thee,
> For fear of disturbance.
> *Jachimo* A very friendly part, faith, my Lord: Come, Madam,
> You and I must be more familiar; nay, nay, no
> Strugling, my heart's a flame, and you must quench the fire. (38)

Jachimo and Cloten's friendship is based on their understanding that women are placed on earth for men's sexual satisfaction. This is part of the libertine creed, and, again, it is certainly a homosocial understanding of the world. It encourages male bonding over women's bodies. But it also makes a world vastly more (hetero)sexually oriented than *Cymbeline*'s world. D'Urfey's play understands men as men based on their sexual interest in women. The men in Shakespeare's play see Cloten as a weak woman, whereas the men in D'Urfey's play see him as a wild man. D'Urfey's villains' logic is libertine, but it is also the logic of a play that depicts libertine sexual desire as the extreme edge of normal male sexual desire.

As Shakespeare wrote him, Iachimo seems to have troubled the Restoration, although he makes perfect sense in *Cymbeline*. Iachimo's sexual desire, although relatively meager in Restoration terms, is predicted by his foreignness—in the authoritative vision of the Leonati that precedes *Cymbeline*'s denouement, Posthumus's dead father calls Iachimo, "slight thing of Italy" (TLN 3104; 5.5.158). Iachimo's bet with Posthumus revives a quarrel that Posthumus had previously had with a Frenchman over the chastity of women in their respective countries.[16] An Italian adventurer, Iachimo seems to enjoy both the quarrel and his own assertion of prowess with ladies, his stance as a "(that way) accomplish'd Courtier" (TLN 406–407; 1.4.80–81). But he does not address his own sexual desire anywhere else in the play, and he regrets his pretense that he has known Imogen intimately. At the end of the play, he is forced to his knees by his "heavy conscience," and Posthumus forgives him. Iachimo's meager desire would ultimately disqualify him as a Restoration libertine, and his conscience would be an additional barrier to such a reading, since libertines, by definition, lack a conscience.

This lack of personal interest in sex appears to have been inconsistent with an adventurous man, since D'Urfey felt compelled to have his Iachimo, Shattilion, reveal his own plan to debauch English women. D'Urfey created Shattilion as unrepentant, villainous, and sexually interested. He claims an identity as a thief "in Love," which he terms "the pleasant way of Larceny" (9). Unlike Shakespeare's Iachimo, Shattilion already has designs before the quarrel to try his hand sexually with the "Ladies" of Britain (8). Iachimo offers to kiss Imogen in the temptation scene; in contrast, Shattilion proposes a full-body encounter with Eugenia: "Let me seal my Passion/Upon thy snowy hands transported, then rove higher,/And ransack this white Magazine of Beauty" (17). In her bedchamber, he muses, "Sure none but I cou'd see thee thus, and leave thee/Thus in this lovely posture. But no more;/I've other business" (20). Shattilion, like a good libertine, never repents his attempt on Eugenia's virtue. He is a man after his own sexual pleasure. This lack of repentance made him a consistent male character for Restoration audiences. Shakespeare's Iachimo denigrates women as a libertine would (and as do so many other men in Shakespeare's plays); but he does not think about his own sexual pleasure as a libertine should. In contrast, Shattilion is a properly sexual Restoration wild man, helping to define Ursaces, D'Urfey's Posthumus, as a properly sexual Restoration man.

In Shakespeare's *Cymbeline*, Pisanio describes Cloten's pursuit of Imogen: "Away he postes/With vnchaste purpose" (TLN 3580–3581; 5.6.283–284). By the time D'Urfey wrote his play, men in plays were no longer imagined to have chaste purposes, since chastity outside of marriage was not a male goal. D'Urfey's *Injured Princess* has a prologue that introduces the play to the men in the audience:

> Old Plays like Mistresses, long since enjoy'd,
> Long after please, whom they before had cloy'd;
> For Fancy chews the Cudd on past delight,
> And cheats it self to a new Appetite.
> . . .
> Hence 'tis, that at new Plays you come so soon,
> Like Bride-grooms, hot to go to Bed ere noon!
> . . .
> As Husband after absence, wait all day,
> And decently for Spouse, till Bed-time stay!

Men can dwell on their former sexual exploits until old mistresses become sexually exciting once more. This reveling in former pleasures is equivalent to the sexual excitement of a newly married man who cannot wait until night falls for his sexual satisfaction, and it resembles a husband's heat for his wife "after absence." The libertine Jachimo is only the magnified version of the essential man, focused on his sexual pleasure. The bridegroom and the husband take that pleasure given willingly within or without marriage: they are not rapists, although they may be adulterers. Any man might have or desire a mistress, and all men see women as the source of sexual pleasure. The libertine as the naturally and primarily sexual man without the brakes of a conscience is a new development in English sexual ideology. He helped to remove the moral stigma that attached to the (hetero)sexually desirous man in Shakespeare. Though the Restoration libertine villain had extreme lustful masculinity, his lust was just that, the extreme version of what was newly taken for granted: the sexual desire for women that naturally belonged to men.

Edmund: The Libertine Star

Tate's Edmund, in his *King Lear*, another libertine, resembles all of these other Restoration Shakespearean libertines in his lauding of his own sexual desire and power. When Edmund sees Regan and Goneril, he exclaims, "Triumphant Queens!/With what Assurance do they tread the Crowd./O for a Tast of such Majestick Beauty,/Which none but my hot Veins are fit t'engage" (25). As do many of these other libertine characters, Edmund sees sex as a militaristic engagement that proves his male fitness. As in Shakespeare's *Lear*, Tate's Regan and Goneril are eager to have sex with Edmund, but Tate's Edmund also plans to rape Cordelia, who does not share their eagerness:

> . . . then to th'Field
> Where like the vig'rous *Jove* I will enjoy
> This Semele in a Storm, 'twill deaf her Cries
> Like Drums in Battle, lest her Groans shou'd pierce
> My pittying Ear, and make the amorous Fight less fierce. (28)

Like Sulpitius, D'Urfey's Jachimo, and Tate's Aufidius, this Edmund sees sex as a conquest. He is a consummate ladies' man in a modern sense, attracted to every beautiful woman he sees, playing one woman against the other in order to maximize his own sexual pleasure and, like a good libertine, seeing that pleasure as paramount. Tate adds a scene in which Edmund lounges in sexual congress with

Regan, swearing his constancy while he simultaneously plans his sexual escapades with Goneril.

Shakespeare does not stage Edmund's sexual encounters; nor does he present Edmund as primarily concerned with his sexual pleasure. Shakespeare's Edmund soliloquizes on his position between the two ravenously desirous sisters:

> To both these Sisters have I sworne my loue:
> . . .
> Which of them shall I take?
> Both? One? Or neither? Neither can be enjoy'd
> If both remaine aliue: To take the Widdow,
> Exasperates, makes mad her Sister *Gonerill*,
> And hardly shall I carry out my side,
> Her husband being aliue. Now then, wee'l vse
> His countenance for the Battaile, which being done,
> Let her who would be rid of him, deuise
> His speedy taking off. (TLN 2902–2912; 5.1.55–65)

Shakespeare's Edmund wonders which of the sisters he should "enjoy," but he is arguably more concerned with his political position, with maximizing his power in relationship to Goneril's husband Albany. He "sees the choice of sisters as merely a strategic problem" (Strier *Resistant* 221). Goneril's jealous fury might compromise his political position; but he also would be compromised politically by Albany's resistance to his plan to kill Lear and Cordelia.

Tate's Edmund would never contemplate enjoying neither sister. Tate revises this speech to make Edmund's sexual motivation paramount:

> neither can be held
> If both remain Alive; where shall I fix?
> *Cornwall* is Dead, and *Regan*'s empty Bed
> Seems cast by Fortune for me, but already
> I have enjoy'd her, and bright *Gonerill*
> With equall Charms brings dear variety,
> And yet untasted Beauty: I will use
> Her Husband's Countenance for the Battail, then
> Usurp at once his Bed and Throne. (54)

Tate's Edmund sounds like Shadwell's Timon: both subscribe to the libertine creed that celebrates male inconstancy and male sexual pleasure. This Edmund wants Goneril because she will bring him sexual "variety," and, unlike Shakespeare's Edmund, he is as interested in Albany's bed as he is in Albany's throne. Also unlike Shakespeare's Edmund, who finally succumbs to his conscience despite his nature, Tate's Edmund speaks the libertine creed: "But, Conscience, what have I to do with Thee?/Awe Thou thy dull Legitimate Slaves, but I/Was born a Libertine, and so keep me" (59). Tate's Edmund's god is his pleasure. He asks Regan to "Lull [him] in endless Sleep/That [he] may dream of pleasures too transporting/For Life to bear" (40). And he designs his plot against his family to maximize that personal pleasure. In soliloquy he promises, "And to my hand thy vast Revenues fall/To glut my Pleasure that till now has starv'd" (27). Shakespeare's Edmund deeply resents his exclusion from patriarchal inheritance. He desires all of the power within the political system that his bastardy disqualifies him from achieving. He is also naturally a "bastard," an embodied disruption of patriarchy and primogeniture. Tate replaces these motivations with the libertine quest for personal sexual pleasure.

(White) Men United

Together, the newly defined woman-loving friend and the libertine point to a consolidation of male identity as (hetero)sexually desirous, a consolidated identity new to English texts. In representations from Shakespeare's time, sexual desire for women divides men into categories that (ideally) correspond to their "natural" differences. Renaissance males are depicted as naturally divided by age, religious difference, rank (the primary identity category), nationality, and race (a category being constructed at the same time).[17] Only some adult white English men represent elite masculinity; and they can represent that masculinity only so long as they do not sink into the degraded feminized world of lust (or other uncontrolled states such as drunkenness).[18] In early-seventeenth-century England, sexual desire for women participates in a system that divides men, even white English men and boys against or, more properly, in relation to one another.

By rewriting all men as possessing natural sexual desire for women, Restoration Shakespeare adaptations dissolve differences between white men. These plays still depict a hierarchical world, but the natural differences between men based on sexual desire for women are beginning to disappear. In Shakespeare's *Taming of the Shrew*, Tranio, Lucentio's servant, takes Lucentio's identity, his social rank, so that Lucentio (Vincentio's son) can gain access to Bianca by pretending to be a Latin teacher. Tranio's elevation is the work of his master, and it will certainly be undone. In addition, Vincentio's rage in the first scene of act 5 indicates the potential gravity of such a masquerade, even in comedy. Vincentio sees the masquerade as treasonous: he cries, "oh he hath murdred his Master" (TLN 2465; 5.1.73).[19] When John Lacey rewrote *Taming* as *Sauny the Scott: or, the Taming of the Shrew* (1698), he opened the play with a dialogue between Winlove (his Lucentio) and Tranio. That dialogue resembles the dialogue between Lucentio and Tranio in the first scene of Shakespeare's play, but Lacey transforms Tranio into Winlove's peer. Winlove says to him, "Thou, *Tranio*, hast been my Companion . . . and tho' our Bloods give me Precedency (that I count Chance) My Love has made us Equal, and I have found a frank return in thee" (1). The "Precedency" afforded by blood is not "Chance" in Shakespearean texts. Rather, it is the truth of social life, the truth that renders such characters as *The Winter's Tale*'s Perdita and *Cymbeline*'s Arviragus and Guiderius naturally noble, brave, chaste, and respectful of hierarchy despite their temporary losses of identity and their rude upbringings (Perdita is raised by shepherds, Arviragus and Guiderius in a cave, and they are all ignorant of their royal births). It is also the truth that makes Viola and Sebastian in *Twelfth Night* suitable marital partners for Orsino and Olivia. "Be not amaz'd, right noble is his blood," Orsino assures Olivia after she finds she has married Sebastian (TLN 2430; 5.1.257). *Twelfth Night* shames Olivia's steward, Malvolio, utterly for his attempt to claim equality with Olivia's kin. In contrast to the world signaled in Winlove's speech to his servant, love between a male master and a male servant in the earlier world confirms their natural difference.[20] Rather than dissolving status differences, such love is appropriate because of the difference in rank.

By the eighteenth century, sexual desire for women was one of the features of life that brought men together. New categories of men were created on stage, categories such as the libertine, the fop, and the rake. But all of these categories of men shared sexual interest in women. Eighteenth-century fops, who were effeminate in manners and attentive to appearance, might be less sexually interested than other men, but they were still at least marginally desirous. If we look at Renaissance characters who resemble Restoration fops, characters such as Sir Amorous La Foole and Jack Daw in Ben Jonson's *Epicoene*, Oswald in *King Lear*, and the prissy Lord described by Hotspur in *1Henry IV*, they share a presiding interest in women. They are also like women. Hotspur scornfully describes the Lord as "Fresh as a

Bride-groome," as "like a Waiting-Gentlewoman," and as using "many Holiday and Lady tearm" (TLN 356, 377, 368; 1.3.33, 54, 45). In the Restoration, men in general are conceived as "Like Bride-grooms, hot to go to Bed ere noon!" (D'Urfey, epilogue to *The Injured Princess*). In Shakespeare's text, these desirous fops disqualify themselves as men; because they desire women, they are like women. In the Restoration, fops have less, not more, desire because they are like women. But they are united to other white men in that they all desire women.

The dissolution of status differences between men is very apparent in D'Avenant's *The Law against Lovers*. In that play, *Measure for Measure*'s Lucio is good friends with *Much Ado about Nothing*'s Benedick. If one takes the sexual codes of Shakespeare's world seriously, one can hardly imagine a more discordant pairing of Shakespearean characters, but the new sexual world emerging in the Restoration brought these men together naturally. Shakespeare's Lucio is a degenerate gentleman, riddled with venereal disease.[21] He is wedded to what he calls the "foppery of freedom" (TLN 224; 1.2.113). Lucio is so without self-control that when lechery becomes a capital crime under Angelo's rule, he is afraid to eat because "One fruitful Meale would set [him] too't" (TLN 2247–2248; 4.3.144–145).[22] Inevitably, given his proclivity for sex with women, Lucio lies, slanders, and behaves cravenly. The Duke, whom Lucio has unknowingly maligned to his (disguised) face, sentences him to marry one of the whores with whom he has disported himself. According to the Duke, Lucio limns his own character when he accuses the Duke of being, "a foole, a Coward,/One all of Luxurie, an asse, a mad man" (TLN 2899–2900; 5.1.494–495). Unlike Lucio, Benedick in *Much Ado about Nothing* is a brave soldier who fears being cuckolded. There is little evidence that this fear is connected to any previous dissipation. He feels safer with men than he does with women.[23] This makes him an honorable man and a brave soldier, just as Lucio's appetites make him an "asse" and a "Coward."

In D'Avenant's rewriting, however, Lucio and Benedick are the best of friends, brought together by their sexual desire for women, sexual desire that means that they are normal men with libertine tendencies, not that they are depraved. Benedick greets Lucio:

> *Lucio*, I am much pleas'd to see you well;
> It gives me hope that I shall have but few
> Sad Evenings here in *Turin*, if the
> Beauties which I left be not quite wither'd,
> Their Voices cract, and their Lutes hung on Willows. (276)

How could this be a Benedick? And how could even this Benedick be friends with the whoring Lucio? The answers to those questions lie in the construction of libertine character in the Restoration and in the sexual assumptions about men that support that construction of character. In Shakespeare's plays, both Benedick and Lucio scorn marriage. The logic that dissolved differences between these rewritten characters runs as follows: Since all men desire sex with women, this desire does not make a man an "ass" and a "coward"; therefore Lucio and Benedick are natural friends, and neither man is an "ass" or a "coward." The natural distinctions between men that disqualify Lucio for true gentlemanly status and that require that at the end of Shakespeare's *Measure for Measure* his status will diminish past reckoning have disappeared in this Restoration adaptation.

By the 1770s in America it was possible to claim that "all men are created equal." That late-eighteenth-century claim looks specious to my eyes, since in 1776 it meant white, property-owning, Christian men. However, even in its minimal form, such a claim does not belong to the same world as Renaissance texts.[24] In those texts, some men are created with the tenuous ability to control their bodily desires, and some men are not. Some men are men, boys are like women, and some men are like women. The stories of philosophical and political shifts and the story of emerging heterosexuality are related stories, stories that inform one another. The Restoration's temporary validation of adultery, its construction of the "chaste mistress," its revaluation of friendship, and its creation of the libertine as the wild version of the natural man, participated in creating the modern world as we know it, especially, but not only, in sexual terms. In sexual terms, the eighteenth century veered toward what is called "morality," but that new moral world was a world in which some of the basic tenets of heterosexuality had taken hold, in which white men could be defined as equal in terms of their sexual desire.

CHAPTER 4

"DOMESTIC TRAGEDY" AND EMERGING HETEROSEXUALITY

The rewriting of Renaissance drama continued through the long eighteenth century, and that rewriting was not confined to Shakespeare's works. Eighteenth-century authors also rewrote more minor works, including two of the central plays in the genre we now call "domestic tragedy." In 1943, Henry Hitch Adams defined and codified that genre to account for a group of plays written in the late sixteenth and early seventeenth centuries that in his eyes portrayed "common people . . . dealing with personal and family relationships" (1–2).[1] *Arden of Faversham* (1587–1592?), an anonymous play that was once part of the Shakespeare apocrypha, and *A Woman Killed with Kindness* (1603?), by Thomas Heywood, were seen by Adams as representative domestic tragedies. In the history of criticism of these plays, we can see a later genealogy of heterosexuality. In addition, twentieth-century reception of these plays shows us what is visible and invisible through heterosexuality's fully ground lens: this reception has ignored the plays' homosocial structures and has seen heterosexuality before it was born. But the eighteenth century was well aware that these plays did not display more modern sexual relations—this awareness prompted eighteenth-century dramatists to rewrite those plays to make them conform to the new understandings of sex, marriage, and masculinity that were to cohere into emerging heterosexuality. In this chapter, we will look at both ends of this process: the twentieth-century disregard of the homosocial imaginary and the eighteenth century's revision of it.

Only recently have critics become aware that the households *A Woman Killed* and *Arden* present are not modern.[2] As Garrett Sullivan notes, "Adams quietly guestures toward timeless conceptions of family, domesticity and realism, conceptions that in the case of *Arden* [*of Faversham*] prove to be quite misleading" (250n.48).

My readings of these two plays are indebted to this critical rereading of "domesticity," including work by critics such as Sullivan, Frances Dolan, Natasha Korda, Lena Cowen Orlin, and Wendy Wall; this work productively challenges previous assumptions about family and marital relations in the Renaissance. As this recent work suggests, Renaissance drama does not focus on nuclear families or on marriages in isolation from the kinship structures that were all-important in the late sixteenth century. *A Woman Killed with Kindness* and *Arden of Faversham* depict a world that centers on relations between men, and in this world, those relations should be the focus of male protagonists. These plays praise men who value male–male alliances above relations with women. In these plays, marriages are made in the service of inheritance, homosocial bonds, and financial gain. Although *A Woman Killed with Kindness* and *Arden of Faversham* gesture toward what historians have called "companionate marriage" as an ideal, like so many other texts of the homosocial imaginary they portray women's sexual desire and conduct as so dangerous and destructive that they may easily destroy marriage.[3]

As we shall see, *Arden of Faversham* and *A Woman Killed with Kindness* are as much tragedies of relations between husband and guests as they are marital tragedies, and as Dolan suggests, these plays are also tragedies of master–servant relationships (*Dangerous*). They share an understanding that adultery is a community problem. Gouge in *Of Domesticall Dvties* (1622) declares,

> [adultery is committed] Against ones *neighbour*, as the partie with whom the sinne is committed (for this sinne cannot be committed singly by one alone) the *husband* and *wife* of each partie (who cannot rest contented with any satisfaction) the *children* borne in adulterie (whom they brand with an indelible character of infamie, and depriue of many priuiledges that otherwise they might enjoy) the *alliance* and *friends* of each partie (to whom the griefe and disgrace of this foule sinne reacheth) the *whole family* appertaining to either of them (for this is a fire in an house) the *towne, citie*, and *nation* where such vncleane birds roost (for all the very *church of God* (the holy seed whereof is by this sinne hindred). (219)

Gouge, unlike Adams and other twentieth-century critics, does not imagine a private world of either marital or extramarital relations—instead, male–female sexual congress is a public act that makes and unmakes the Renaissance household. Though *A Woman Killed with Kindness* and *Arden of Faversham* are distinctly not Protestant conduct manuals, they share this common sense about adultery and sexual behavior, a common sense that we have seen in *King Lear* and the Renaissance Antony and Cleopatra plays and poems. *Arden* and *A Woman Killed* represent male–female sexual desire so negatively that they challenge the conduct manuals' attempts to establish marital sexual satisfaction as a goal for men. However, the language of love in these plays as well as the modern dominance of the heterosexual imaginary have misled critics, leading many of them to see these plays as promoting male–female sexual love. In this chapter, by showing that in Renaissance texts the language of love signifies very differently than it does in modern texts, I hope to defamiliarize that language, to make its workings in these plays as foreign to us as they were to the eighteenth-century authors who felt compelled to rewrite them.

When George Lillo and John Hoadly rewrote *Arden of Faversham* in 1759 and Benjamin Victor rewrote *A Woman Killed* as *The Fatal Error* in 1776, they made the plays into sentimental dramas.[4] Lillo, Hoadly, and Victor attempted to fix the flawed understandings of male–female relations that they saw in the earlier plays. Eighteenth-century authors did not yet believe that dramatic characters constructed in earlier centuries were fully psychologically developed human beings, whose foibles, including punning language and seemingly incongruous behavior, only more completely embroider their unique personalities.[5] This modern belief accounts partially, perhaps, for the failure of most twentieth-century critics to see that these plays, as well as Shakespeare's, violate basic premises of heterosexuality. The eighteenth century had neither this belief about dramatic character nor was the heterosexual imaginary so dominant as to enable playwrights and audiences to read Renaissance drama as if it espoused that imaginary's tenets. In rewritings such as Victor's and Lillo and Hoadly's, the difference of the homosocial imaginary was recognized as it was discarded and overwritten.[6] Although traces of that imaginary linger in the eighteenth-century rewrites, these plays challenge its basic tenets as they laud a new economic, political, social, and sexual order.

In his advertisement before *The Fatal Error: A Tragedy*, Victor declares that having read "a tragedy with a strange title, call'd, *A Woman kill'd with kindness*," he found the play unsatisfactory (81). Victor interpreted the play as a story of "matrimonial distress" (81). But, he says, he found that story defective on two grounds: that Anne consented to her own seduction and that, given her consent, Frankford could be "approved for his excessive tenderness, and forgiveness to such a criminal" (81). Anne and Frankford violated Victor's eighteenth-century concepts of femininity and masculinity. For Victor, a willfully fallen woman is irredeemably criminal, and a man who forgives such a woman is ridiculous (even, apparently, when she has starved herself to death in repentance for her sin). In response, Victor tells his readers, he wrote what he says is a new play, *The Fatal Error*. Although *The Fatal Error* owes more to *A Woman Killed with Kindness* than its advertisement claims, the play that Victor wrote regularizes both femininity and masculinity within the frame of emergent heterosexuality. Unlike *A Woman Killed with Kindness*, *The Fatal Error* embraces (as it helps to construct) the middle-class domestic family, a family that twentieth-century critics have been eager to see in the late-sixteenth-century play but that is wholly absent from that play's world.

The authors of the eighteenth-century *Arden of Feversham* were as interested as Victor was in correcting the faults of the earlier world. Faced with a female protagonist steeped in sin, they made her into a woman who has slipped but who aches for an unfallen life. Lillo and Hoadly were more forgiving of Alice (whom they called Alicia) than Victor was of Anne, but in Alicia they created an eighteenth-century woman whose repentance justifies her husband's love and desire. Although Lillo and Hoadly responded less harshly to Alice's adultery than Victor did to Anne's, all of these authors' responses come from a revisioned sexual world, a world in which adultery, and thus male–female sexual desire, figured anew. If adultery had to be temporarily valorized in the Restoration in order for male–female sexual desire to get a good name in the eighteenth century, it came back in eighteenth-century drama with a reviled vengeance but in a distinctly more personalized form. Rather than signifying the destruction of community relations between men as it had in the Renaissance, adultery in the eighteenth century signified the loss of personal male honor and the utter degradation of the woman in question.[7] In the Renaissance dramas of adultery that I have discussed in this book, adultery confirmed a story about women as old as the story of the faithless Eve. This is the story that Anne's reluctant fall and Alice's eager fall verify. In addition, many of these dramas of adultery, such as *King Lear*, *Antony and Cleopatra*, and the various relations of Antony's history in the late sixteenth century (chapters 1 and 2), are as much interested in the stories of their adulterers as they are in those of their adulteresses. In the earlier world, men's extramarital affairs were as central to representation as women's. Both men's and women's adulteries invoked the destruction of the social world, and stories of men's violations of patriarchal family and homosocial bonds were as significant as stories of women's violations of those same bonds. In the new eighteenth-century sexual world, in which men were supported for locating their identities in their wives, and in which all women were not expected to fall because of their sexualized natures, his wife's adultery was a personal nightmare for a man, a sign of his failure as a man rather than a sign of the inevitable perfidy of women. The rewrites of *Arden* and *A Woman Killed* show us the further emergence of the heterosexual imaginary and the family relations that helped to constitute it.

The Domestic Scene in *A Woman Killed with Kindness*

Adams devoted an entire chapter of his book *English Domestic or Homiletic Tragedy* to *A Woman Killed with Kindness*, which he calls "the best-known Jacobean domestic tragedy" (144). Where Adams saw domestic tragedy as "set in the domestic scene, dealing with personal and family relationships rather than with large affairs of state," as the twentieth century progressed, that domestic scene increasingly shrank to the space of the heterosexual bedroom. In 1951, Peter Ure further refined Adams's terms—Ure's criterion is "that the play concern itself with the relationship between husband and wife" (201). Subsequent work took this criterion as its premise. Rick Bowers in 1984 extols "the newlyweds' cocoon-like mutual adornment" (296). R.W. Van Fossen, in his introduction to *A Woman Killed*, asserts that the "play begins and ends with, and devotes most of its attention to, the relationship between husband and wife" (xxxiii).[8] Although this criticism has produced valuable insights about the play, it has also obscured the play's main concern: the Renaissance homosocial network. These critics write as if they are reading the eighteenth-century rewrite of the play, which does focus on the marriage in relative isolation.

This strain of criticism does not see the household and neighbor relations that are so significant in *A Woman Killed*. Frankford's household includes his wife, Anne; Frankford's friend, Wendoll; Cranwell, another male guest; Frankford's servant, Nick; his butler, Spiggot; at least two lower servants, Sisley and Jenkin; and the women caring for two unnamed and mostly unmentioned children who reside offstage. Where children may be central in representations of modern heterosexual households, the children in the Frankford household are nameless props, who Frankford orders brought out by maids to castigate Anne for her potential corruption of blood lines:[9]

> Frankford: Go bring my infants hither.
>
> . . .
>
> Away with them; lest as her spotted body
> Hath stain'd their names with stripe of bastardy,
> So her adulterous breath may blast their spirits
> With her infectious thoughts. Away with them. (G3v; 13.112–117)[10]

Modern domestic dramas of adultery focus on the confines of the bedroom or living room, invisible to the larger community. In Heywood's play, the entire Frankford household turns out to cry at Anne, "O Mistres, Mistres, what haue you done Mistres," and Anne exclaims that she is "Asham'd to looke [her] seruants in the face" (G3v, G4; 13.146, 152). The objects of Anne's shame, the servants rather than her consanguineous family, indicate the distance of this representation from a modern conception of the household, where the servants, if there were any, could not be conceived of as essential witnesses. Anne's adultery is, as Gouge puts it, a disgrace to "the *whole family* appertaining to either of them[,] . . . a fire in an house" (219). In *A Woman Killed with Kindness*, Anne's relationship with Frankford is a matter for the hall as well as the bedroom, and their bedroom can only exist in relation to the hall. Where late-twentieth-century American households grant married couples a privacy that may mask intra-familial domestic violence, in the late-sixteenth and early-seventeenth centuries, "marital relations were conducted within the broader context of the neighborhood" (Wrightson 99). The play shows us the neighborhood rather than the isolated marriage that some critics envision.

That neighborhood encompasses Frankford's household and also a group of aristocratic men whose exploits, including the exploits of Frankford's brother-in-law Acton, provide material for the play's subplot. The apparent dissonance between the two plots of *A Woman Killed with Kindness* has been a perennial critical problem, a problem that in its parameters shows how devoted critics have been to seeing the Frankford household as an avatar of middle-class heterosexual "domesticity." Van Fossen notes that the subplot involving Acton, Susan, and Mountford "has provoked condemnation and even ridicule on practically all counts, most notably for its lack of connexion with the main plot," involving Frankford, Anne, and Wendoll (xxxiii).[11] Many critics assert that the romantic elements of the subplot and its references to the pursuits of the nobility differentiate Frankford's "realistic" "middle-class" life from Acton's and Mountford's aristocratic fantasy.[12] However the play does not accidentally link the plots via an insignificant family connection; rather, it insists on the significance of the family connection—not heterosexual satisfaction—as the reason for and the ultimate justification of the marital tie. Kinship is the most powerful link between the two plots, and the success of that kinship even in the face of broken marital relations is the play's desideratum.[13]

A Woman Killed with Kindness shows Frankford and Anne as neither middle class nor living under the regime of heterosexuality;[14] instead, from the beginning of the play, they are imbricated in aristocratic master–servant, guest, and friendship bonds. Mountford congratulates Frankford on his marriage as follows:

> Master Frankford,
> Y'are a happy man Sir; and much ioy
> Succeede your marriage mirth: you haue a wife
> So qualified, and with such ornaments
> Both of the minde and body. First, her birth
> Is Noble, and her education such
> As might become the daughter of a Prince. (A3; 1.12–18)

Anne is worthy to marry Frankford in his friend Cranwell's assessment because they are both "Schollers, both yong" and "both [are] descended Nobly" (A4; 1.68).[15] Neither party derives from the middle class, and neither would qualify for admittance. In marrying Anne, Acton's sister, Frankford fulfills his marital function within his world: finding a partner who will connect him properly within the homosocial network.

The play's two plots are inextricably linked by the brother–sister and brother–brother relationships. Thus the subplot is not extraneous, as it might seem to be through the lens of heterosexuality. Wendoll, the guest who will sully Frankford's marriage, enters Frankford's home bearing news of Acton's fight with Mountford, a fight that takes place at a hawking match arranged at Frankford's wedding. Acton is Anne's brother and, as importantly, he becomes Frankford's brother in the originary marriage. Later in the play, Acton becomes Mountford's brother when he marries Mountford's sister,

Susan. The play resolves two contests between men—Wendoll's assault on Frankford's marriage and Acton's determination to ruin Mountford—with settlements over women's bodies, and the key term of both of these settlements is kinship: Susan's sacrificial marriage resolves the feud between Mountford and Acton; and Anne's literal sacrifice preserves the kinship between Acton, Frankford, and Frankford's heirs. Indeed, the play recognizes the exact analogy between Susan's capitulation to Acton and Anne's death. Frankford kills Anne with his "kindness" in exiling her, and, by paying her brother's debts, Acton "will fasten such a kindnesse on [Susan]/As shall orecome her hate and conquer it" (E4v; 9.66–67).[16] Both of these acts of "kindness" make kinship between men.

A Woman Killed points repeatedly to the fact that Frankford and Anne's wedding links not only the two of them but, as importantly, Frankford and Acton. In the wedding scene, Acton names Frankford "Brother," "brother," and "good brother, Frankford" (A3, A3v, A4; 1.12, 42, 73). And the final deathbed scene demonstrates that the supreme achievement of that wedding is the alliance between men. Critics have interpreted Anne's deathbed scene as an intimate reconciliation and remarriage. For example, Leonora Leet Brodwin argues that, in this scene, Frankford and Anne's "love reaches that full commitment that can 'unite [their] souls' and so create a true marriage" (117). However, in the play, like the original marriage, this deathbed remarriage is witnessed by the neighborhood, and it becomes an occasion to reiterate Frankford and Acton's alliance. As Frankford pardons Anne and she devotes her shrived soul to God, Acton declares,

O master Frankford, all the neere alliance
I loose by her, shall be supply'd in thee;
You are my Brother by the neerest way,
Her kindred hath fallen off, but yours doth stay. (I3v; 17.101–104)

Anne dies in this scene, but Frankford and Acton remarry one another.

Leanore Lieblein argues that the adultery in the play "is a violation— of the spouse's body, of the marriage bond, and of the moral order" (192). I am suggesting that the adultery between Wendoll and Anne violates especially the play's ideal of a brotherhood of aristocratic men. In Gouge's terms, Wendoll's and Anne's affair is an act directed against "the *alliance* and *friends* of each partie (to whom the griefe and disgrace of this foule sinne reacheth) [and against] the *whole family* appertaining to either of them" (219). Wendoll has the potential to destroy the blood tie between Frankford's children and Acton as well as the marital tie between Frankford and Acton. Frankford's display of the children demonstrates the strength of that threat. Thus, Wendoll endangers the bond between men that Anne has cemented in her marriage to Frankford. Acton's speech reconstitutes that bond over her dead body, and her dead body indicates that the characters clearly value that alliance more than her life. Indeed, if we view the play through the lens of kinship rather than the lens of heterosexuality, Wendoll is immediately visible as potentially dangerous, because, as he himself notes of Frankford's intimacy with him, "this kindnesse growes of no alliance 'twixt" them (C3v; 6.33). In addition, Wendoll's crime violates the ideal of male friendship that should assist in preserving this world. Had Wendoll behaved as a proper friend, as Cranwell does throughout the play, the link between Acton and Frankford would have remained inviolate.

Thus Wendoll traduces two vital bonds between men: the marriage of Acton and Frankford, and his own friendship with Frankford. When Wendoll speaks to the audience after he and Anne have been banished, he speaks first of Frankford: "When I but thinke of master Frankfords loue,/And lay it to my treason..." (H4v; 16.38–39). Before Wendoll illicitly approaches Anne, he castigates himself for an act that will "scratch [his] name from out the holy booke/Of [Frankford's] remembrance, ... rend [Frankford's] hart/To Whom [his] hart was ioynd and knit together" (C3; 6.47–50). Framing the adultery this way seems acutely counterintuitive in the context of late-twentieth-century domesticity. After all, as Lieblein's argument indicates, adultery seems to be an innately heterosexual crime — at least in a world that allows marriage only between a man and a woman and authorizes sex only between men and women. As we have seen, however, adultery was not yet reconfigured in those terms in the English Renaissance. Wendoll's priorities are exactly in line with the priority given to male friendship in Renaissance texts (see chapter 3). Anne's part in the adultery is clearly a problem, since she must die in payment for it; however, the marriage between Anne and Frankford is just as clearly not the play's goal, since the play can reconstitute primary bonds over her dead body. The play focuses not on saving the marriage for the children's sake, but, instead, on killing Anne for the blood line's sake, in order to save the male–male kinship bond.

Breaking and Making Homosocial Bonds

Seen as a whole rather than as two barely related plots, *A Woman Killed with Kindness* depicts a world where homosocial alliances disintegrate as men fight and sexually betray each other. In this disintegrated world, Acton resolves to revenge himself by shaming Mountford's kin: "They say he hath a pretty wench / To his Sister: Shal I in my mercy sake / To him and to his Kindred, bribe the foole / To shame her selfe by lewd dishonest lust" (D3; 7.79–82). Just as the play makes bonds between men in marriage, here Acton imagines his revenge accomplished on Mountford and his kin by means of his sexual conquest of Susan. In Acton's initial impulse, his assault on Susan's chastity will solidify his hate relationship with Mountford. A focus on homosocial bonds makes resonant the seemingly extraneous scene of Susan's appeal to her family and Mountford's "Allies" to extract her brother from jail. (Mountford has gone to debtor's prison rather than succumb to the aptly named Shafton's plot to bilk him of his ancestral property.) Mountford instructs his sister to "Go to . . . [his] Kinsmen and Allies" to ransom him (D3; 7.67–68). But Susan encounters a cold world, which disregards kinship bonds as well as male friendship. Their uncle denies her, saying, "He was my Brothers sonne—why Neece, what then? . . . He lost my kindred when he fell to neede" (E3v, E4; 9.4, 17). Tydy, their cousin, declares: "Call me not cozen. Each man for himselfe; / Some men are borne to mirth, and some to sorrow, / I am no cosen vnto them that borrow" (E4; 9.34–36). Sandy and Roder, supposedly allied to Mountford, also reject her appeals, Roder despite Mountford's having placed him "Rent-free . . . in that wealthy farme / Of which [he is] possest" (E4; 9.27–28). The play clearly condemns Acton's sexual revenge fantasy, and it condemns Mountford's uncle's, cousin's, friend's, and tenant's measurements of the bonds between men in terms of an economic system that disregards friendship, status, and kinship ties. All of these broken bonds between men indicate the significance of kinship, tenant, and friendship ties. Without them, the world is lost to lust and greed.

If those bonds are reknit by Susan and Acton's marriage, their union is not a modern wedding. Acton accepts Susan as a marriage partner, saying to *Mountford*, "I seale you my deere Brother, her my wife" (H3; 14.146); and Mountford replies to *Acton*, not to Susan: "Rich in your loue I neuer can be pore" (H3; 14.152; my emphases). Acton resolves the subplot in a final speech spoken to his new brother Mountford:

> Al's mine is yours, we are alike in state,
> Let's knit in loue what was opposd in hate.
> Come, for our Nuptials we will straight prouide,
> Blest onely in our Brother and faire Bride. (H3; 14.153–156)

These men speak a language recognizable to us as the language of heterosexual love, but they speak it to one another. The priority ascribed by both Acton and Mountford to each other is so alien to modern sensibility that it has been almost inaudible to critics. But if we cannot hear their language, it is unexceptional in the play. And that language—"I seale you my deere Brother" and "Blest onely in our Brother"—and that priority—"Brother" before "wife," "Brother" before "Bride"—is not just a feature of an aristocratic, fantastic subplot that we can separate from a "bourgeois domestic scene." Their words are *the* language of this "domestic" tragedy, just as their homosocial priorities are the priorities of Renaissance representation generally. Wendoll's lament as an adulterer reads the same way, as does Frankford's language about the sexual crime. When Nick tells him of Anne's and Wendoll's affair, Frankford exclaims, "Man, woman, what thing mortall may we trust, / When friends and bosome wiues proue so vniust?" (E; 13.82–83). In the world Frankford laments, friends are the priority.

With the bond sealed between Mountford and Acton, all that is left to renew the aristocratic brotherhood disrupted by adultery and the feud is Anne's death. Anne, the woman whose adultery threatened the kinship network, will die; Susan, the woman who offered to die to defend her chastity, will live so that her husband and brother can remain rich in their love for one another. Acton has the penultimate speech in the play, and he addresses a stage audience of "Brothers and Gentlemen." And it is to his brother Acton that Frankford responds to finish the play. Anne lies dead on her bed on stage, but standing next to her is the brotherhood of men formed in the play: Frankford, Acton, Mountford, and Frankford's faithful friend and house guest, Cranwell. Strikingly, however, the lens of heterosexuality in the twentieth century led many critics to ignore that reconstituted brotherhood in favor of the marital couple. However, though Anne and Frankford speak of their love for one another, the play does not focus on that love but rather on the bonds between men that their love makes and her neglect of it unmakes.

Frankford is originally happy in his marriage: he praises her wifely virtues and expresses care for her health, and Anne also seems to treasure Frankford. But their relationship is clearly subordinated to the homosocial bonds that it enables and perpetuates.

The Fatal Error and (Hetero) Sexually Desirous Men

When Victor rewrote *A Woman Killed*, he rejected its homosocial kinship focus; he, not Heywood, made relations between the husband and the wife the focus of the play. In that revision we can see the family and marriage refigured in the terms of emerging heterosexuality. *The Fatal Error* is a three-act play with a smaller cast than *A Woman Killed*. Victor retains the surname of the central couple, Frankford, but calls the husband "Sir Charles" and the wife "Lady Frankford." The marital scene Victor created is not yet as constricted as it will become in later centuries: although the play constructs a more private scenario for the couple, they live in a household full of extramarital characters. Lady Frankford has a brother, Lord Bellgrove, who has recently returned from the Continent, and the Frankfords are entertaining Mr. Cranmore and his sister, Emeline, as house guests. Two servants also have parts: Humphry and Juletta. Crucially, Victor rewrites Anne's adultery as a rape: with Juletta's help, Mr. Cranmore (the play's Wendoll) has raped Lady Frankford the night before the action of the play starts. The play opens with Cranmore alone on the stage repenting his abuse of Lady Frankford and his treachery toward his friend, but most of the play depicts his desperate ploys to hide the matter from Frankford. In the first act, Cranmore enlists the complicit Juletta in a plot to explain Lady Frankford's distress by attributing it to her concern about Bellgrove (Cranmore claims that Bellgrove has attempted to seduce Emeline).

In the next scene, we see the thoroughly disordered Lady Frankford, who accuses Juletta and rages at Cranmore. Cranmore persuades her to keep the story of her rape from her husband for his own good. Then Sir Charles returns as promised and finds his house in an uproar. His wife is miserable and ill, and Cranmore attributes her misery to Bellgrove's attempted seduction of Emeline. Sir Charles accuses Bellgrove, who acquits himself, leaving Sir Charles bewildered. Bellgrove expresses interest in Juletta to Cranmore who, worried that she will expose him, threatens Juletta into silence. In act three, Juletta runs to Bellgrove for protection from Cranmore.

Bellgrove then hides where he can hear Lady Frankford accusing Cranmore and rushes out to kill him. Finding Cranmore dying, Sir Charles assumes Bellgrove killed him over the Emeline business, but Cranmore confesses to the rape. Meanwhile, Lady Frankford has taken poison and reveals on her death bed that Juletta let Cranmore into her bed chamber and that her own "fatal error" was "being prevail'd on to conceal [her] injury" (140). Sir Charles forgives her, and the play ends with Sir Charles and Emeline weeping over her corpse and Bellgrove delivering a sentimental speech about the effects of guilty love.

Unlike *A Woman Killed*, which condemns Anne's and Wendoll's lust and subordinates Frankford's desire for his wife to the homosocial network, *The Fatal Error*, like Restoration Shakespeare, portrays lust for women as the natural state for all men. Cranmore and Bellgrove both have inordinate desire for women, and their illicit desires mark them as corrupt, although to varying degrees. But this Frankford also demonstrates his desire for his wife from the beginning of the play, and his is clearly approved. In *A Woman Killed*, two significant men, Mountford and Frankford's friend, Cranwell, display no interest in women. In contrast, each of *The Fatal Error*'s significant men sees women or a woman as the center of his life. Male sexual desire for women is thus naturalized: it may have illicit aims, but it is the condition of masculinity. Certainly Cranmore has enjoyed his sexual feat. When Juletta laments that she helped him to rape her mistress, he boasts, "Oh, 'twas glorious mischief! By which I equall'd JOVE when he enjoy'd ALCMENA!" (87). Although this is sentimental drama, Cranmore sounds just like Otway's Sulpitius and Tate's Edmund (chapter 3). Cranmore says, "the King's Exchequer cou'd not draw me through half the dangers, the irresistible charms of this woman have made me leap into" (126). Unlike Wendoll, Cranmore finds women more appealing than money or status, and, though he opens the play lamenting his treacherous act, through most of the play he understands and glories in his fall as the condition of his virility. Bellgrove, who is much less vicious, is also fixated on women's charms. When her brother blocks his "harmless gallantries" aimed at Emeline, he craves a substitute, and he explains his desire to Cranmore, who has represented himself to Bellgrove as a sexually experienced man. With Cranmore's apparent consent, Bellgrove vows to transfer his attentions to Juletta: "you must admit that my situation here, at my time of life, must be a little unpleasant, if I must be deprived of every female to pass a lively hour with" (123). His assumption that young men need women with whom to pass their time is the assumption of a rake, and in a play that lauds the bourgeoisie, his rakish behavior condemns him. Significantly, however, this sentimental drama of the eighteenth century draws its character types and its assumptions about male sexual desire from the model of Restoration drama.

In the Renaissance, Cranmore's desire for Lady Frankford could also have been a sign of his iniquity; and Bellgrove's callous aristocratic desire for women is obviously a feature of the *The Fatal Error*'s Whiggish discourse. However, *The Fatal Error* declares its allegiance to a nascent heterosexual imaginary in its depiction of approved sexual desire in its godly, staid protagonist, Sir Charles Frankford, and in its elimination of the homosocial love language that surrounded *A Woman Killed with Kindness*'s Frankford. In Victor's play, heterodesire becomes the condition of masculinity, not one of its many possible fallen states. Frankford announces his return to the household in a letter to his wife:

> "Dearest, Best Belov'd,
> "This envious post will out-run me—I
> "follow with a lover's haste, to the arms
> "Of my adorable wife   C. F." (106)

This ardent missive sends Lady Frankford into paroxysms of shame, and it also defines Frankford as a lover, happily anticipating sexual congress. Rather than dishonoring Frankford, his anticipation is one aspect of his approved masculinity. Unlike the heroes of the earlier plays, who (should) find their centers in their homosocial networks, Frankford locates his identity in his wife, who, unmolested by Cranmore, would have guarded it jealously. Thus, *The Fatal Error* rejects two central assumptions of Renaissance household dramas such as *A Woman Killed*: that men can trust at least some of their male friends more than they can trust their wives, and that wives do not need to be raped in order to fall.

Whereas *A Woman Killed*'s Frankford speaks lovingly of Anne after he has discovered her sin, at the beginning of the play, his relationship with his friend Wendoll is clearly as central to his identity as is his marriage.[17] When Wendoll enters the household, Frankford tells him,

> You are ful of quality and faire desert,
> Chuse of my men which shal attend on you,
> And he is yours, I will allow you sir,

Your man, your gelding, and your table,
Al at my owne charge, be my companion. (C; 4.68–72)

In the scene in which Wendoll declares his love to Anne, she has returned from seeing her husband off, and she tells Wendoll that her husband spent his time before leaving searching for Wendoll in order to leave him master of the house:

Nay more, he wils you as you prize his loue,
Or hold in estimation his kind friendship,
To make bold in his absence and command
Euen as himselfe were present in the house. (C3v; 6.73–76)

Anne explains, "Sir you are much beholding to my husbande, / You are a man most deere in his regard" (C3v; 6.87–88). Just as Frankford is as wounded by Wendoll's trespass as by Anne's, Anne cannot believe that Wendoll would betray the man who loves him so much; She counters Wendoll's declaration of love to her with her comment about her husband's love for Wendoll: "he esteemes you / Euen as his braine, his eye-bal, or his hart" (C4; 6.113–114). Some modern critics criticize Frankford's devotion to Wendoll, arguing that Frankford even invites his own cuckolding. However, it may be that the play is instead condemning Wendoll's failure to respond in kind.[18] In texts of the homosocial imaginary, the ideal of male friendship may be unreachable, but it is still the ideal. In comparison, *The Fatal Error* almost ignores male–male love and the centrality of male relations. Its Frankford should be wholly devoted to his female "Best Beloved."

The Family versus the Sexualized Aristocracy

The Fatal Error's emphasis on women as the center of men's existence is coupled with a critique of aristocratic behavior, which the play associates with loose sexual desire for women. Aristocratic lineage, the lineage that is saved in *A Woman Killed with Kindness* by Anne's death and Susan's marriage to Acton, is devalued in the eighteenth-century play as is the aristocrat, Lord Bellgrove. Bellgrove pursues Emeline for his own enjoyment, with no marital intentions, and he easily transfers his erotic pursuit from Emeline to Juletta. In Renaissance drama, illicit and transferable lust such as Bellgrove's is the mark of clowns, servants, and debased foreigners, not of aristocrats *per se*.[19] After the opening wedding scene in *A Woman Killed with Kindness*, the play shows the Frankford household servants and farm servants dancing with "countrie Wenches." Their talk teems with bawdy suggestion. Jack Slime, a farm servant, assures the household servants that "thogh we be but country fellows, it may be in the way of dancing, we can do the Horse-tricke [whore's trick] as well as seruingmen" (B2; 2.13–15). Thus, the play asserts that the servant world is a world of whoredom and fornication. Among the tunes the servants and wenches contemplate dancing to is "John Come Kiss Me Now" and "The Cushion Dance," a dance where all the men and women kiss (2.33–35; see Chappell 288). In the earlier play, unbridled lust is associated with debased servants and the self-hating Wendoll who, tellingly, sets off for the Continent at the end of the play.

In *The Fatal Error*, in contrast, such lust separates the newly exalted gentleman, Sir Charles Frankford, from the hereditarily titled aristocrat, Lord Bellgrove; and the play signals the contrast between the two in the language they use for love. Sir Charles confines his love and sexual desire to his wife and speaks an unornamented language of love. In contrast, Lord Bellgrove, falsely courting Emeline, speaks as if he were a Petrarchan lover, in a discourse already under assault as tired in the late sixteenth century but still admissible then as a language of romantic love:[20] Bellgrove says, "Is it my Emeline? Or some angel that has assum'd her form to claim more adoration—'tis she herself! And come abroad thus early to add fresh fragrance to the flowers!" and "No rose, nor lily—no hyacinth—are of the sweetness, whiteness, softness, as my Emeline" (92). His outdated, elaborate metaphors sound stilted in comparison to Frankford's love language, and they are distinctly not to the dominant taste of the eighteenth century, a taste formed by the decorous standards espoused by essay writers for journals like the *Spectator*. Emeline's replies to Bellgrove's speeches might have appeared in any of Addison's essays on social behavior. She tells Bellgrove, "if you will descend into the vale of common sense, I shall have no exception to converse with you" (93). When Bellgrove calls her reaction "barbarous *English* severity," and compares it to the reaction of "the ladies [he has] left in *Italy* and *France*" who would have welcomed his addresses, Emeline replies, "My Lord, our mode of education (as you know) differs greatly from theirs—The freedoms of good breeding, (as you term it) and gallantry with them, wou'd be esteem'd downright rudeness with us" (94). Bellgrove, in his own terms, is not a wicked "debauchee" and is enough of a good Englishman to be unable to help "approving her conduct" (94). In *The Fatal Error*, Petrarchan lovemaking has become a mark of debased Continental style.[21]

The Fatal Error's substitution of a (hetero)sexual nationalist imaginary for an aristocratic homosocial settlement is obvious in Sir Charles's interview with Cranmore about Bellgrove's supposed attempted seduction of Emeline. Sir Charles declares that "This young Lord [Bellgrove] shall not only regulate his behaviour, but repent what he has done, or depart directly—No ties of blood shall influence me when virtue and honour are concern'd" (113). Sir Charles holds maidenly virtue, and his own honor as that virtue's knight, higher than his ties of blood. In an almost embarrassingly obvious celebration of English Whiggish morality, Sir Charles soliloquizes,

> What insolent liberties these young men of quality indulge themselves in! As if title and fortune gave them privilege to insult all they think beneath them—but as such noble profligates are generally born fools, they are, of course, strangers to the happy laws of their country, by which the subjects of England are protected in their persons and property! What a glorious constitution! (113)

Significantly, however, Sir Charles is as (hetero)sexually desirous a man as Lord Bellgrove; what differentiates them is Bellgrove's disrespect for female virtue, not, as might distinguish men in earlier plays, their relative abilities to disregard feminine wiles and sinful desire.

Uneven Emergence, Again

Though I have been emphasizing *The Fatal Error*'s distance from its predecessor's homosocial imaginary, the play is not a product of the full-blown heterosexual imaginary, which might see its seducer as completely unrepentant and even sexy (think of late-twentieth-century soap opera), driven by natural, if twisted, desire. Traces of the homosocial bonding between Wendoll and Frankford remain in *The Fatal Error*, although they are literally traces, having no real effect on the play's action. The play opens with Cranmore sounding like the self-castigating Wendoll: "I have abused the virtuous wife of my best friend! my benefactor! . . . Thou god of thunder, withhold thy speedy vengeance on a villain! A villain, and a traitor to his fond, believing friend!" (85). And when Lady Frankford upbraids him in their first scene together, Cranmore says, "I have injured my friend! The best of men—a worthy gentleman" (101). Also, as Cranmore dies, he declares, "Oh, Lady Frankford! I have ruined the best of women—and wrong'd the best of friends!" (135). In his phrasing in these speeches, Cranmore could indeed be the repentant and self-hating Wendoll. In fact, Victor takes Cranmore's opening speech almost word for word from one of Wendoll's soliloquies, in which he calls himself "A villain, and a Traitor to his friend" (C3; 6.21–25). However, unlike Wendoll, Cranmore has no more repentant speeches until his death speech.

Likewise, *The Fatal Error* shows us a household with servants that recalls but translates *A Woman Killed*'s household relations. Throughout *A Woman Killed*, servants interact constantly with their masters and mistress. In contrast, in *The Fatal Error* the family and the servants become two worlds within a house rather than one world under the master as patriarch. Frankford's manservant, Nick, is an intimate member of his master's household. He holds his master's interests closest to his heart, and he is the one who enables Frankford to detect and expose his wife's and friend's adultery. Nick and, finally, Frankford understand that their homosocial bond is more durable and longer-lasting than Frankford's marriage, and Nick will sacrifice himself in order to prevent his master from living as a cuckold. In contrast, Sir Charles's servant, Humphry, understands his individual interest as more important than his duty to his master. He says, "To give my suspicions of the horrid secret in this family, would be neither prudent nore safe—I fear there will be a fatal discovery at the arrival of my poor master" (96).[22] Humphry even lies to his master. When Sir Charles asks him what has caused Lady Frankford's illness, he replies, "My Lady's fears for you—and your long absence, Sir—but your happy return will, I hope, soon restore health and peace again" (120). Significantly, the play does not condemn him for the lie or for guarding his own interest. In this lack of condemnation we can see the homosocial imaginary's peeling plaster. Whereas earlier household tragedies, such as *A Woman Killled*, see the bonds between superior and subordinate men as sacrosanct and, ideally, as more durable than the marital bond, and while they punish subordinate men who disregard their homosocial bonds, *The Fatal Error* approves Humphry's self-interest and even makes him something of a moral center.[23] Humphry's new self-centered status shows that though traces of the homosocial imaginary persist in *The Fatal Error*, the play is well on the way to embracing a new sexual world, a world in which every man should love and live for himself.

Arden of Faversham and the
Homosocial Imaginary

If *A Woman Killed with Kindness* shows us a Renaissance kinship network restored, the anonymously authored *Arden of Faversham* displays that world destroyed by lust. Adams considered *Arden*, a play based on the actual murder of a husband by his wife, her lover, and her servant, the "finest" of the "domestic" tragedies (108). Perhaps because *Arden* is more brutal than *A Woman Killed*, and because the play alludes continually to Arden's economic activities, this play has inspired less idealizing, domesticating criticism.[24] Even those late-twentieth-century critics of the play who focus on Arden's and Alice's marriage have tended see the marriage and adultery plot in the context of, or at least in relation to, Arden's economic ambitions.[25] Catherine Belsey reads Alice Arden as challenging the institution of marriage and the regulation of sexuality, but Belsey links those challenges to what she characterizes as a "world of economic individualism" (*Subject* 132). Like Belsey, Frank Whigham argues that Alice and Mosby "mark the onset of a new erotics, drenched in anger but (or perhaps—and so) dreaming of a new notion of marriage" (78). But Whigham also sees these adulterous partners as embedded within myriad other social struggles activated by the dissolution of the monasteries.

Despite Belsey's attention to economic matters, Sullivan and David Attwell criticize her for failing to attend to the larger economic world. In Attwell's analysis, Belsey errs in seeing Alice's dissent as divorced from the rise of what he calls the "middle-class bloc" (332). Sullivan criticizes Belsey for relying "on a public/private binary more appropriate to the late eighteenth and nineteenth centuries than to early modern England" (242–243).[26] In contrast to Belsey's Arden, divided between acting as a rapacious landlord and acting as a loving husband, Sullivan posits an Arden who identifies primarily as an "estate manager" and an Alice who challenges the transmission of property. These readings of the play elaborate and extend earlier-twentieth-century readings, all of which see *Arden of Faversham* as exploring social and economic change.[27] Notwithstanding the conflicts between these suggestive readings, what links them all is a vision of the play as either nostalgic for a pre-capitalist and pre-enclosure social order or as documenting the rise of a new economic man and sexually free woman. These critics frame *Arden* as the middling sort's *King Lear*—they make precisely the same moves that *King Lear*'s critics have made toward positioning the play as a harbinger of the economic world to come.

However, if we read *Arden*'s sexual ideology without the blinkers of the heterosexual imaginary, *Arden of Faversham*'s social relations look neither nostalgic nor emergently modern. Rather, in a move characteristic of "domestic" tragedy of the homosocial imaginary, *Arden of Faversham* laments an idealized Renaissance world foreign to modern heterosexuality. In sexual and in economic terms, *Arden of Faversham* is securely a text of the homosocial imaginary. Alice's inordinate sexual desire is not a quest for some essential freedom that will be attained with late modernity; instead it resembles the outrageous sexual desire that Medieval moralists assigned to women.[28] The play defines women as a group as obsessed with lust, and both women's and men's lusts are catastrophically destructive. Arden's sexual love for Alice negates the homosocial bonds that should constitute the social world, and his sexual love determines his tragedy as much as does his grasping quest for higher rank.

As critics suggest, the play links Alice's lust to Arden's greed, but this link does not indicate emerging modern economic and sexual relations. Rather, as we have seen, it is a staple of premodern understandings of sex.[29] Lust and greed are related sins of a fallen world. Instead of reading the "repeated" contemporary "interpretations of the events" of the murder "as so many attempts to elicit a definitive meaning for Alice Arden's crime" (Belsey *Subject* 135), we can read them as so many versions of a sermon against lust and greed, alternatively stressing the one sin over the other, and also pointing to the essential links between sins. If *Arden of Faversham* hints at the emergence of what is called "bourgeois" ideology, in terms of sexuality, those hints are not contained in either Alice's lust or Arden's greed. Rather, they may appear in Arden's servant Michael's doomed obsession with Alice's servant, Susan. In this play, as in many of Shakespeare's comedies, the character who resembles the heterosexual imaginary's virile (in the modern sense) romantic man is a denigrated servant. But that proto-modern man does not look strong and handsome. Michael's sexual desire is linked to cowardice, for his lust, like Arden's, debases him.

Fear of Hetero-Desire

The title page of *Arden of Faversham* claims that within the play the reader will see that Arden was "most wickedlye murdered, by the means of his disloyall and wanton wyfe." That page promises that the play will show "the great malice and discimulation of a wicked woman," and *Arden* certainly fulfills that promise. Though Arden sometimes sees Alice as a loyal, adoring spouse, in front of the audience, Alice is a hypocritical, lustful, homicidal, primal force, the embodiment of the misogynist fantasy that so obsessed men of the homosocial imaginary. *Arden of Faversham*'s title page seems to point to Alice as one particular wicked woman, implying that other women might be good in comparison. However, the play reveals a common sense in which all women are potential Alices, the (embattled) common sense of the homosocial imaginary. *Arden of Faversham*'s title page also indicates disgust with male and female sexual desire, a disgust it shares with *A Woman Killed with Kindness*. *Arden*'s title page explains that the play will show "the vnsatiable desire of filthie lust," and once again the play fulfils its title page's promotional promise. In the play, all sexual desire between men and women is destructive and insatiable. As Dolan suggests, "the play so closely associates desire, affection, and violence that the murder plot becomes the consummation of Alice's and Mosby's affair" (*Dangerous* 55).[30] Alice lusts after Mosby insatiably and at the cost of her marriage and any Christian principles. Michael and the Painter will murder to obtain Susan. Less obviously to a modern audience, Arden's sexual desire for Alice blinds him and dooms him to die at her hands. In the play, male–female sexual desire has the potential to destroy everything and affords satisfaction to no one.

This potential destruction does not (only) predict the modern world as Belsey argues it does; it is also the threat that consolidates the homosocial imaginary. Like the sermons, stories, and plays in Medieval and Renaissance England that inveighed against lust and greed, *Arden of Faversham* invokes the apocalyptic results when those sins are let loose upon the world. Because we now live in a world that has canonized greed (albeit ambivalently) and valorized lust, at least in approved heterosexual unions, Alice's unrestrained desire can look appealing and even as if it predicts modernity—this I think helps to explain its allure to critics as astute as Whigham and Belsey. But neither the ambivalent canonization of greed nor the selective valorization of lust was inevitable. The theatrical appeal of greedy and lustful characters also does not argue for either their modernity or their heroism.[31] After all, throughout his incarnation in literary texts, the devil has been attractive. No one was therefore required within or by those texts to model themselves after him. If we look closely at the play's language, Alice's desire is nothing but apocalyptic in Christian and therefore Renaissance English terms.

The play carefully paints Alice's desire as so heinous that to identify with her would be to reject Christ. Alice declares, "Loue is a God and mariage is but words" (TLN 102; 1.101), and "oathes are wordes, and words is winde" (TLN 451; 1.436).[32] Alice elevates what she calls love, or in Renaissance terms, the sin of lust, to the godhead. Later in the play after a short spate of repentance, Alice declares to Mosby, "I will do pennance for offending thee, / And burne this prayer booke, where I here vse, / The holy word that had conuerted me" (TLN 1381–1383; 8.115). Once again, Alice replaces Christ with her lust; she will offer her penance to Mosby and as a function of that penance destroy what she herself calls "holy" scripture. The "words" that found the Christian order and the "oaths" that tie the homosocial world together become dematerialized in her anarchic dedication to sexual pleasure.[33]

Alice's dedication to lust above "oaths" allies her to the murderer, Black Will, certainly a devil in the play's theological landscape.[34] Greene tries to hold Black Will to the bargain they have struck with a caution to Black Will to "thinke vpon thyne oath." But Black Will replies, "Tush, I haue broken fiue hundred oathes! . . . Tell me of gould my resolutions fee" (TLN 881–884; 3.81–84). As they do for Alice, "oathes" mean nothing to Will, who has dedicated his life to greed. In addition, Will's name connects him to the lust inspired by and embodied by Alice.[35] Black "Will" is the will of the devil, the will that Alice has invoked.[36] Although Alice pretends to dismiss "words" when they impede her sinful progress, she never hesitates to use them to advance her cause, and her monetary temptations move Black Will's greed to murderous heights: He swears, "Such wordes would make one kill 1000. men" (TLN 2147; 14.132). Like Alice, Will is eager to extend his murderous plans to the larger community. Alice prompts Greene to conspire with Will and his companion, Shakebag, to murder Arden. In response to Greene's importunities, Black Will asserts, "giue my fellow / George shakbag and me, twenty Angels, / And if thoult haue thy owne father slaine, / That thou mayst inherit his land, weele kill him." And Shakebag adds, "I [Aye] thy Mother, thy sister, thy brother, or all thy kin" (TLN 757–761; 2.87–90). Will and Shakebag's greedy, murderous proclivities are more than indiscriminate, although they are that as well. The murderers will commit the most heinous crimes in a patriarchy, the destruction of the father and the kinship network that should sustain each man's and woman's world.

Arden of Faversham depicts Alice's and Mosby's lust as infectious as well as world-threatening. Promised Susan by Alice, Arden's servant, Michael, declares, "Why then I say that I will kill my master/Or any thing that you will haue me doo" (TLN 167–168; 1.162–163). Michael's lust for Susan eradicates his loyalty to his master and replaces it with a will to murder. If, in the relationship between Frankford and Nick, *A Woman Killed with Kindness* celebrates loyalty and service, in *Arden of Faversham*, lust has perverted that essential homosocial bond. Ten lines after his vow to Alice, Michael is planning fratricide: "For I will rid myne elder brother away:/And then the farme of Bolton is mine owne./Who would not venture vpon house and land:/When he may haue it for a right downe blowe" (TLN 177–180; 1.172–175). Alice's homicidal lust has let murderous desire loose in *Arden of Faversham*'s world. Greene is surely right to suggest to Michael that he loves Alice (and her promotion of anarchic murderous desire) better than he does his master (TLN 932; 3.131). Even more terrifyingly within the homosocial imaginary, Michael will kill his master for his own desire; desire for Susan has turned Michael into the nightmare servant, serving his own lust at the expense of his master's life.

True Love for Alice and Mosby?

Only if we read Alice's love as private and heterosexual can we see her declarations to Mosby as heroic paeans in which marriage "is identified as an impediment to true love" (Belsey *Subject* 133).[37] This formulation requires a definition of "true love" that would not appear as common sense for at least another hundred years. We saw that definition's growing pains in Restoration Shakespeare and we will see them as well when the eighteenth century rewrites *Arden*; but that definition does not apply to the adulterous relationship in the sixteenth-century *Arden of Faversham*. Not only are Mosby's and Alice's actions demonized, but both parties in the affair repent. The playwright strategically places their repentance scenes at the center of the play and at its end, and both scenes should prevent us from reading Alice and Mosby as true heterosexual lovers. Because he is wholly motivated by greed, Mosby is never a lover committed to either his sexual satisfaction in Alice or to his personal communion with her. Alice is only that lover when she has fallen grievously. The play depicts that grievous fall, and it never glorifies what it conceives as sin and the devil's work. Critics who discount a Christian moral frame in favor of a modern reading of character may distrust

Alice's final meditation upon her "sauiour Christ,/Whose bloode must saue [her] from the bloode [she] shed" (TLN 2525–2526; 18.10–11). But that meditation makes sense both in terms of her momentary earlier reliance on a prayerbook and in terms of the play's dissection of the sin of lechery. To discount that frame in favor of some kind of transhistorical "true love" is to believe that the play might be committed to atheism.[38] However, in both of Alice's repentance scenes she reconstructs the force and significance of (what the play clearly sees as) the supra-material substance of God's word. In the first repentance scene, Alice asks Mosby to "conceale the rest [of their affair], for tis too bad,/Least that [her] words be carried with the wind./And publisht in the world to both [their] shames" (TLN 1329–1331; 8.63–65). In addition to showing the significance of Alice's words in the play's actions—as people kill at her bidding—the playwright demonstrates that, under God's influence, Alice herself can see the force of both "words" and "wind." The play equates Alice's love with atheism and heresy, and her own eventual disgust with that love reconstitutes the social world that in the play is aligned with Christian doctrine. Alice's lust is, therefore, heretical and socially anarchic, and only her denial of it will save her.

Martin White suggests that if Alice is inspired by "her irresistible sexual passion for Mosby," Mosby "is motivated by the more mundane, though no less compelling, desire for wealth and social status that his relationship with Alice promises to provide" (*Arden* 1982, xxiv). The influence of the heterosexual imaginary is evident in White's assessment of Mosby's desires as more "mundane" than Alice's. Under the fully developed heterosexual imaginary, sexual passion can be elevating and even transcendent; it can and should exist in a separate realm than material desire—that is, greed. In the late sixteenth century, in contrast, even, and possibly especially, when marital sexual communion mimicked heaven, it was only and ever firmly mundane. In a 1607 wedding sermon, Robert Wilkinson reminds his audience that sexual communion in marriage is both temporal and temporary:

Lastly, lest any Man doat too much upon this Heavenly Ship of Earthly Joys, we must remember, That as a Ship is not a place of continual Habitation, but only for Passage; so is the Society of the Wife, though comfortable and joyful for the time, yet lasting only for a time; a Help to hold him up and comfort him, during this transitory, short, and troublesome Pilgrimage; but then there is another, a happier, a more lasting Marriage with the Lamb. (7)[39]

Wilkinson admits that marriage and presumably marital sex can feel "heavenly," but he characterizes the joy as finally "earthly." Life is only a "transitory, short, and troublesome Pilgrimage," and marriage on earth only a fleeting shadow of the "happier . . . more lasting Marriage" with Christ. Though marriage is an "earthly" phenomenon, adultery, Alice and Mosby's sin, is far below "mundane." All conduct manuals and wedding sermons agree on this point, and these "domestic" tragedies seem designed to reinforce this point. Adultery is a nest of "vncleane birds" (Gouge 219) and "the sauage rudenesse of the bruit creatures" (Whately B2). So Frankford, in *A Woman Killed* characterizes his "polluted bed-chamber" as "Once [his] terrestrial heauen, now [his] earths hel" (F3; 8.14–15). The sin of greed is hardly more "mundane" than adulterous lust in these texts; both sins are beastly and debasing.

Alice is no heroine of heterosexuality, an ideology that unrepentantly champions "true love" and sexual transcendence and an ideology that neither links sexual desire with death nor envisions women as suffering from unrestrained desire. Furthermore, as White suggests, Mosby, the object of Alice's lust, is not at all motivated by hetero desire. Mosby has been read by critics as a failed lover, a lover not worth Alice's investment. However, Mosby is essentially Alice's counterpart in sin. If Alice may be redeemed by the blood of the Lamb, Mosby cannot reach redemption because he ends the play blaming Alice. He calls her "strumpet" and cries out "Fy vpon women" (TLN 2528, 2550; 18.13, 34). Rather than resembling the modern husband or adulterous lover committed to sex, Mosby sounds remarkably like Milton's fallen Adam, who at first quite traditionally blames his partner in sin rather than repenting his own. Mosby also sounds like the Adam of the fourteenth-century York Mystery Plays who cries "Ah! Eve, thou art to blame,/That thus enticed thou me" (*Wakefield* 70).[40] Though Mosby employs the language of romantic love to placate Alice, he aspires to Arden's rank and his gold rather than to his place as Alice's lover, and he condemns Alice for entrapping him.

The language of romantic love in this play and in *A Woman Killed* makes it difficult to recognize essential ideological differences between representation today and Renaissance representations. We may believe we recognize that language as the coin of heterosexuality because, spoken by women to men and men to women, it sounds much the same today as it did in Heywood's and the *Arden* playwright's England. In *A Woman Killed with Kindness*, Wendoll declares his love for Anne in terms that could be used by modern male, romantic, heterosexual lovers: "And when I meditate (O God forgiue me)/It is on her diuine perfections" (C3; 6.10–11); "For you Ile hazard all, why what care I:/For you Ile loue, and in your loue Ile dye" (D; 6.137–138). But the romantic language that Wendoll speaks to and about Anne exists in the context of, and as defined by, the love language of homosocial bonding: "I loue your husband too,/And for his loue I will ingage my life" (D; 6.141–142). Wendoll's romantic language also indicates his failed Christianity since Anne can not have "diuine perfection." In *Arden of Faversham*, Alice proclaims, "mosbies armes/ Shal compasse me, and were I made a starre,/I would haue none other spheres but those./There is no nector, but in Mosbies lypes" (TLN 2160–2166; 14.145–148). Earlier in the play she cries, "for what is lyfe but loue:/And loue shall last as long as lyfe remaines,/And lyfe shall end, before my loue depart" (TLN 1698–1700; 10.87–89). These speeches might play well in modern movies and Broadway musicals. In dominant twentieth-century representations, this language was limited to and, therefore, constitutive of heterosexuality.[41] However, in *A Woman Killed with Kindness* and in *Arden of Faversham*, men also use these terms to speak to and of one another. Moreover, in each of these same speeches Alice plans the murder of her husband. By linking murder plans and the language of romantic love in these speeches, the playwright indicates their consonance in this context. Only the heterosexual imaginary's lens can separate Alice's love language from her murder plans and see that language as the language of "true love."

Over the centuries, the language of romantic love has participated in quite different epistemologies of social relations. Within those different understandings, this language may not imply sexual desire, or it may imply sexual desire between men, between women and men, or between women. Twentieth-century dominant American culture limited that language to heterosexuality. Renaissance England clearly did not; even Restoration England, as we have seen, accepted that language easily when spoken between men. This language of romantic love, which today continually reinvents the heterosexual imaginary, once functioned to sustain the homosocial imaginary of Renaissance England. Such language does not define a discourse; rather it is a vocabulary employed and deployed in the service of various ideologies. A modern Alice could speak of her "true love" today, and we could subscribe to it without endangering our souls. However, Alice's culture very actively discouraged that response. As Orgel suggests, love "is a language that implies everything and nothing" (42). This explains how Renaissance English poetry written by a man to flatter a male patron finds its way to Hallmark Valentine's Day cards.[42] And it explains how we could have misread Alice as a lover rather than a sinner.

Franklin versus Alice: Arden's Lustful Emasculation

If Alice is no true lover, Arden's love for Alice damns him as surely as does his ambition. His sexual desire for her blinds him and leads him to sacrifice homosocial bonds for deadly marital bonds. In scene 13 of the sixteenth-century play, we see Dick Reede, a man whose family Arden has defrauded, importuning Arden for his money. Arden denies him and Reede curses Arden. In the play's epilogue, Franklin suggests that Arden's neglect of Reede has contributed to his murder. Arden's economic machinations certainly contribute to his horrible death, but, during the play, Arden's governing problem—the problem that debases him and removes him from the safe world of men—is his overwhelming and emasculating sexual love of his wife: "Sweet love," he tells her, "thou knowst that we two Ouid like/Haue often chid the morning, when it gan to peepe" (TLN 60–61; 1.60–61). Alice refers to this sexual involvement later as she masks her designs on his life: "The time hath bene . . . That honors tytle nor a Lords command,/Could once haue drawne you from these armes of mine" (TLN 1612–1614; 10.14–16). And Arden reassures her that he "hould[s] [her] dearer then [his] life" (TLN 1630; 10.31). To the modern eye, this involvement might make Arden a sympathetic if misguided fellow; indeed the eighteenth-century Arden, as we will see, is depicted in exactly these terms, although he is not as misguided as the earlier Arden since his wife, Alicia, is not evil. If we read Arden's sexual involvement with Alice in Renaissance terms, however, Arden can sound as blasphemous as Alice when he speaks of his desire: "deare I holde hir loue, as deare as heauen" (TLN 39; 1.39). This is exactly the mistake that Wilkinson's sermon warns against. The play will display Arden's commitment to Alice as both a theological and a social error. Mosby's plan to kill Arden with a poisoned portrait of Alice condenses the play's attitude toward Arden's desire for his wife: the lust that would lead him to gaze on her forever is poisonous. Arden values Alice and her sexual pleasures above heaven and at the risk of his life. The play rewards that commitment with death at her hands.

A more modern play might offer its central male character a true woman in exchange for the woman who has failed him. This is the move that Shadwell makes in his *Timon*, as we saw in chapter 2. In contrast, *Arden of Faversham*, like *A Woman Killed with Kindness*, values homosocial bonds above any male bond with a woman. Rather than creating a female character to console Arden, the playwright invented Franklin, Arden's devoted friend from the beginning of the play; no comparable character appears in the play's chronicle source. If Alice and Mosby are not true lovers, Arden and Franklin are true friends, bound by the codes of gentle male friendship and also by their joint alliance with the Lord Protector.[43] In the opening scene, Arden says, "Francklin thy loue prolongs my weary lyfe, / And but for thee, how odious were this lyfe" (TLN 9–10; 1.9–10). And Franklin's love does prolong Arden's life throughout the play. From the start, where Mosby and Alice plot to murder Arden, Franklin acts as his savior, supplying mithridate to counteract Alice's poison, with the anthem, "My lyfe for yours" (TLN 399; 1.385). Unlike the poisoned facsimile of love shared by Arden and Alice, Franklin and Arden share reciprocal and solicitous love.

In the chronicle source for the play, Arden condones Alice's ongoing affair with Mosby in order to secure his own place among her noble friends. The chronicle says, "he was contented to winke at hir filthie disorder, and both permitted, and also inuited Mosbie verie often to lie in his house" (Holinshed 1062–1063). The chronicle's version of the events in Kent is a tragic story of the homosocial imaginary in which the protagonist values his links with other men at the expense of countenancing adultery, a sin that threatens essential familial links by potentially producing illegitimate progeny. The play, for the most part, replaces that story with another story of the homosocial imaginary in which Arden's desire for Alice binds him to Mosby, the man who is betraying him, at the expense of Franklin, the man who truly loves him. The play stages a contest between Franklin and Alice in the aftermath of a brawl between Franklin and Mosby. Although the play depicts a household with intimate relationships between servants, guests, and the marital couple, Alice invokes a privileged marital bond to counter Franklin, when she says of him "men of such ill spirite as your selfe. / Worke crosses and debates twixt man and wife" (TLN 1987–1988; 13.146–147). At the end of the scene, Franklin offers this choral interpretation:

> He whome the deuil driues must go perforce,
> Poore [Arden] how lone he is bewitcht,
> And yet because his wife is the instrument,
> His frends must not be lauish in their speach.
> (TLN 1993–1996; 8.152–155)

Despite Franklin's discretion, Arden chooses Alice, the "instrument" of the devil, and her lover Mosby, over his friend. Michael informs his mistress that "When Mosbie bled, [Arden] euen wept for sorrow:/And raild on Francklin that was cause of all" (TLN 2040–2041; 14.32–33). Because Arden trusts Mosby and Alice, he misguidedly blames Franklin; that trust leads him to his subsequent and consequent death at their hands. And if *Arden* stages Alice's betrayal of her husband, it is equally concerned with Arden's betrayal of his friend. Both betrayals combine to destroy Arden, and both have their roots in Arden's excessive sexual desire for Alice. Protestant conduct manuals were attempting to endorse a special relationship between man and wife, albeit within the frame of the social and sexual codes of the homosocial imaginary. This play and *A Woman Killed with Kindness* warn their audiences of the consequences of privileging that special relationship when women are so much less trustworthy than loving friends. By making Alice the hypocritical spokesperson for that special relationship, the play subverts it emphatically.

The Base Origins of Heterosexuality

"True love" as we may understand it today, love maintained in the face of death, exists in this play only between male friends and in the basest of men. In the heterosexual imaginary's terms, one "true lover" in the play might be Michael, who says, "Faith I care not" about dying "seeing I die with Susan" (TLN 2553; 18.37). Rather than rendering him heroic in the play, however, his love for Susan contributes to his characterization as feminine. Michael is a coward, both spineless and inept, and he also explicitly compares himself to a female bird in a love letter to Susan in which he claims that "as the Turtle true, when she hath lost her mate, sitteth alone" he has lost track of his master's overshoes in his distraction over Susan's absence (TLN 792–793; 3.5–6). In this letter and in many of Michael's other scenes, his lines are so funny and full of malapropisms that it seems likely that Michael's was a clown's part. And his love for Susan resembles the love of Shakespearean clowns for women. He signs his letter to Susan "Yours Michaell, or els not Michaell" (TLN 801; 3.15). In *Arden of Faversham* as in many other Renaissance English representations, the man founding his identity in a woman is an effeminate clown.

Michael's sentiments are seconded in the play by the base Painter [Clarke]. The Painter approves of Alice's murderous plan in terms that Michael will repeat in his final words. Clarke tells Alice, "you shew a noble minde, / That rather than youle liue with him you hate, / Youle venture lyfe, and die with him you loue, / The like will I do for my Susans sake" (TLN 276–279; 1.269–272). Both the Painter and Michael may sound romantic within a modern frame. But within the homosocial imaginary, both men sound like debased sinners obsessed with lust. The more developed character, Michael, shows the male face associated in the Renaissance with the attitude toward a woman that we might call "true love" today; he looks nothing like the heroes of modern romance precisely because his love for Susan cannot be heroic in Renaissance terms. The keyword in the Painter's speech is "noble." The Painter is neither noble in rank nor in his behavior, and his judgment of nobility must, therefore, be suspect. Again, the language of romantic love is wickedly deceptive in Michael and the Painter's discourse. It can seem to predict modernity's devotion to love affairs that transcend death, while, in context, it signals the eternal death that in Renaissance England was the canker of illicit, and sometimes licit, male–female love.

Another way to read Michael and the Painter and their evocations of "true love" is to see them as actual kernels of male heterosexual identity. In sexual terms, Michael identifies himself in a way that should seem familiar from the libertine characters created in Restoration Shakespeare and the Restoration generally. Challenged by Shakebag, who says to him, "we heare / You haue a pretty loue in Fevershame," Michael replies, "Why haue I two or three, whats that to thee" (TLN 934–936; 3.133–135). Michael's saucy reply proleptically resembles the cocky boast of the libertine. Just as likely to have multiple women in his plumed (e)masculinity, Michael will die for love. His willingness to die for love, however, differentiates him from the Restoration libertine. He is a more modern male ideal character in terms of his relations to women, acknowledging the potential to love many women sexually, but loving one to the death. If Michael's character can be read as such a kernel today, however, in his Renaissance play he is nothing but a buffoon, a low-born, silly man.

Outcast from the homosocial network that in the play should constitute proper masculinity and the social world, Michael and the Painter look like the dregs of the Arden household. This is how Arden identifies them to Franklin: "Susan my maid, the Painter, and my man [Michael], / A crue of harlots all in loue forsooth" (TLN 811–812; 3.24–25). "Harlot," today, is an archaic word for a sexually loose woman, the only definition that survives from earlier usage (*OED* "harlot" 5c.). The *OED* records three obsolete usages of the word that might suit Arden's usage. In relation to men, "harlot" could signify a "rogue" or a "fornicator" (*OED* "harlot" 1) or, less pejoratively, "a male servant" (*OED* "harlot" 3). It could also be "[a]pplied to unchaste persons of both sexes" (*OED* "harlot" 6). The *OED* finds this usage only in a late-sixteenth-century Scottish text, but it is a possibility here.⁴⁴ What Arden's usage of "harlot" in relation to Michael signals is Michael's debased status in the play—he is both a menial servant and a fornicator. The history of "harlot" points to the general lack of differentiation between low status and propensity for fornication; in addition the history of "harlot" points to the lack of differentiation between genders in the period. Michael's love for Susan makes him like Susan, and it confirms his lowly status.

Michael's defiance of the homosocial imaginary's approved masculinity is not only located in his debased clown's identity; this defiance is also vexed from within. So, just as Mosby and Wendoll do, Michael understands, even as he transgresses, his place within the network of men and the propriety of that place. As Arden's man, Michael speaks the words of a loyal servant but with the kick that signals his own debasement: "And he whose kindly loue and liberall hand,/Doth challenge naught but good deserts of me,/I wil delyuer ouer to your hands" (TLN 970–972; 3.169–171). If the oath that Michael has sworn to Alice "for Susan's sake" is "nearer then a masters loue" as he says it is (TLN 1077–1078; 4.65–66), Michael may be a very early version of a modern man, trading alliance with his master for alliance with a woman. In a distinctly Renaissance formulation, however, Michael's devotion to Susan is either a feature of, or very deeply linked to, his cowardice, even in the scenes of his internal conflict. For Michael does not lock the doors to Black Will and Shakebag because he has momentarily chosen his master over Susan. Rather he locks the doors because he fears for his own skin.

When emerging heterosexuality looks for heroes, it will look well above Michael, both on the level of rank and of seriousness. It will look to characters like the noble Antony, like Benedick, like Frankford, hardly the menial servants in their respective plays. However, when *Arden of Feversham* and *A Woman Killed with Kindness* were rewritten in the eighteenth century, authors had to reconstruct their more elevated characters radically in order to make them into heroes of emerging heterosexuality and in order to align heterosexuality with bravery. The eighteenth century and the centuries that followed were either unwilling or unable to see the proleptic heterosexuality of the clown.

They relocated it to their more prominent men, making what was a mark of debasement into a mark of respectability.

Arden in the Eighteenth Century

George Lillo's *Arden of Feversham* (completed by John Hoadly) is self-consciously a historical drama,[45] yet Lillo almost completely ignores what modern critics might see as the stuff of history: Arden's economic ambitions. Instead, the Lillo–Hoadly *Arden* focuses on the marriage; and like the marriage at the center of *The Fatal Error*, the marriage this *Arden* creates testifies to the growing strength of the heterosexual imaginary. As in *The Fatal Error*, we can see in this *Arden* some gasps of the dying homosocial imaginary. For example, as the play opens, Arden says he must "find in friendship what [he's] lost in love" (182). But the eighteenth-century Franklin befriends Alicia and the ideal of eighteenth-century marriage as much as he befriends Arden. This play, unlike the earlier *Arden* and unlike *A Woman Killed*, celebrates companionate marriage rather than companionate friendship. Likewise, we see a few gasps of the passionate, uncontrollable woman in the new *Arden*'s Alicia, but that woman very quickly disappears from this play. This Alicia does not stab her husband at the play's end; instead, she tries to abort the murder plot, only to be overpowered by Mosby, newly crafted in this play as an almost-reluctant libertine.

In the eighteenth-century *Arden*'s murder scene, Arden tries to read his own story through the lens of early-seventeenth-century Protestant doctrine. He cries out,

> How have I doated to idolatry!
> Vain, foolish wretch, and thoughtless of hereafter.
> Nor hop'd, nor wish'd a Heav'n beyond her love.
> Now, unprepar'd, I perish by her hate. (227)

Were this the Arden of the anonymous play, he would be right. His love of his wife would have been idolatry, and it would have led directly to his murder. But in this play, he judges Alicia unfairly, for he believes that Alicia has conspired against him to the end. However Alicia, quite unlike the earlier Alice, spends very little of the play's time conspiring against Arden. In act 2, she attempts to stab her sleeping husband, but her conscience stops her. Arden wakes, and she repents bitterly in the face of his dismay at her sin. In the third act, she denies Mosby her love, which she calls her "loose desire," but, under duress, promises to love Mosby again should it ever be "lawful" (207). Even then, she deeply regrets her promise (208). In act 4, she reconciles with Arden, and, though she regrets her promise to her former lover, Mosby, she never regrets that reconciliation. Arden is quite mistaken when he believes that he has "perish[ed] by her hate." He dies listening to her assuring him that she loves him unconditionally: "I who despis'd the duty of a wife,/Will be thy slave" (227).[46] This sentimental play tugs heartstrings over Arden's mistaken belief that his wife has betrayed him again. Rather than arguing, as the anonymous *Arden* does, that a man should find his identity in God and his faithful male friends, this eighteenth-century *Arden* argues that marital happiness is a reliable center for a man.

Unlike the Arden of the earlier play, this Arden is a rising-middle-class hero, heroic in his integrity in two related eighteenth-century realms: the domestic world (in the process of becoming more narrowly defined), and the world of business. This Arden is never fooled by Alicia; indeed, he fools himself about her when at the play's end he distrusts her though he should not. Alicia, even when she betrays him (briefly), calls him a "slumb'ring lion" (188); and he is the play's lion, never the greedy, sniveling pig that his predecessor sometimes resembles. This play offers audiences a God-fearing hero who is both a loving husband and a respectable businessman. This Arden, like his predecessor, has been granted "rich abbey-lands" by an aristocratic patron (189), but he has stolen from no man. Thus, the sixteenth-century story of Arden's greedy rise to wealth and power, a story that most late-twentieth-century critics might argue is the guts of Arden's chronicle history, lives on in this play only in a very attenuated fashion.

One illustration of the earlier Arden's greed appears in a scene in which a sailor tries to dissuade Reede from approaching Arden. The sailor says, "His [Arden's] conscience is too liberall, and he too nigardly" (TLN 1835; 13.2). In *Keywords*, Raymond Williams traces the history of the word "liberal," attending to its political senses and usages over time, but the word is equally instructive for a history of sexuality. *Arden*'s sailor is using "liberall" to mean "Free from restraint; free in speech and action." The *OED* observes about this type of usage, "[i]n 16–17th c. often in a bad sense: Unrestrained by prudence or decorum, licentious." Shakespeare, in particular, attaches this meaning of "liberal" to sexual license.[47] The dictionary cites this usage's last appearance in a *Tatler* piece by Richard Steele in 1709 (*OED* "liberal" 3a.). Over the course of the eighteenth century, "liberal" 's pejorative usage, signifying without "restraint," that is, relation to God's law, disappears. According to the *OED*, by the end of the eighteenth century "liberal" is used to mean "Free from narrow prejudice" and especially "Free from . . . unreasonable prejudice in favour of traditional opinions or established institutions" (*OED* "liberal" 4.a. and 4.b.). *Arden*'s sailor is, rightfully as it turns out, accusing Arden of a conscience "too liberall" to care for other men in his social network. In the history of the world "liberal" we can see the gradual (and always uneven) secularization of the English world, a transition in which what was viewed as a negatively valued violation of tradition becomes a freedom from "unreasonable prejudice." In "liberal" 's mutation from a word that could signify condemned sexual licentiousness to a word that could signify freedom from "unreasonable prejudice" the consequences of that uneven secularization in the sexual world become visible. Arden's devotion to the faithless Alice and his neglect of Reede signify Arden's ungodly liberality. The eighteenth-century *Arden* shows us a different world. Reede neither appears nor is mentioned in the play. This Arden is the sentimental family man who loves and desires his wife legitimately, and he is also a legitimate businessman.

Adultery and Eighteenth-Century Male Identity

In *The Fatal Error*, Victor refigures Anne's adulterous affair as Lady Frankford's rape so that he can rationalize Frankford's forgiveness. The eighteenth-century *Arden* takes another path to the same destination. Alicia is an adulteress, a fact that brands her but does not compromise her husband's heroism. Rather, the play documents his heroic struggle with his personal honor. Arden says, "Adul'tress! dost thou kneel/And weep, and pray" (183). This newly branded Alicia, according to Arden, has cost him too much:

> my just right to false Alicia's heart,
> (So dearly purchas'd with a husband's name,
> And sacred honour of a gentleman)
> I shall assert myself, and thus secure
> From further violation. (190)

If women were purchased in marriage in the earlier patriarchal world, the deal was made between men, often between the father and the son-in-law, and that deal was then imagined as cementing the link between the men in question. The eighteenth-century Arden, born in a world that still depends on marriage settlements, and thus on the purchase of women, imagines that deal differently: Alicia has been purchased at the cost of her "husband's name" and "the sacred honour of a gentleman."[48] Should Arden lose what, therefore, is his "just right," he has lost aspects of his male self, not any connection to the larger social world. The language of rights that Arden uses to figure his relationship with Alicia emerges from a political landscape in which (white) men are understood as having potentially equal relations. Women in this system are purchased by individual men at the cost of an honor invested in women's fidelity.

The personal investment in question should look quite familiar to us today. It is an investment system that can still structure marital and other heterosexual relations; it determines the personal shame that a man may feel when he is sexually rejected in favor of another man. Because this system seems so familiar, myriad modern readings of Renaissance plays project this investment system back onto male characters struggling with their beliefs in their wives' infidelity. Despite what might feel like the emotional truth of these readings to a twentieth-century audience, they are a result of the blinders of the heterosexual imaginary, not a result of attention to the details of the drama in question. The contrast between how the anonymous *Arden* and the Lillo–Hoadly play stage Arden's encounter with his wife and her lover should help to remove these blinders so that we can see more clearly the difference in what adultery might have meant to the audiences in question.

The Lillo–Hoadly scene in which Arden asserts his "just right" to Alicia's heart is a radical rewrite of a scene from the earlier play. The scenes have similar structures: in both scenes, Arden and Franklin come onstage and find Alice/Alicia with Mosby, and Mosby asks Arden about the Abbey lands. Arden's reply to that question in the later *Arden* sparks his speech about his "just right" to Alicia's heart. Also in both scenes, Arden and Mosby quarrel about Alice/Alicia; and, in both, Mosby's use of his sword is in question. But here the similarities end. The original Arden dismisses Greene's claim to the lands by asserting his "letters patents" from the king. To this assertion of ownership, he attaches his claim to his wife:

> But I must haue a Mandat for my wyfe,
> They say you seeke to robbe me of her loue,
> Uillaine what makes thou in her company,
> Shees no companion for so base a groome. (TLN 312–315; 1.302–305)

In this speech and in the rest of the scene, Arden stresses the disparity between his and Mosby's statuses—he is a gentleman, and Mosby is a "groome."⁴⁹ Arden feels disgust that such a "base minded peasant" might presume to court his wife (TLN 334; 1.323). Mosby's fury at Arden's status insult prompts him to threaten Arden, and Mosby's threat provides an occasion for Arden to further insult Mosby on status grounds. Arden pulls Mosby's sword and disputes Mosby's right to wear a sword at all because he was once a man who worked with a needle—Arden calls him a "goodman botcher" (a tailor who mends clothes) (TLN 326; 1.315). The argument between the two men occupies about twenty-five lines, and it revolves around Mosby's status in the world and Arden's scorn even for Mosby's new worldly position, attained through patronage, which Arden characterizes as the position of a "Ueluet drudge" (TLN 333; 1.322).

Arden calls Mosby "Uillaine," [villain] a word whose transition in meaning shows us the move from the status-dependant world of Renaissance England to an eighteenth-century world that imagines men as relatively equal. Originally signifying "a low-born base-minded rustic; a man of ignoble ideas or instincts [,] in later use," "villain" came to mean "an unprincipled or depraved scoundrel; a man naturally disposed to base or criminal actions, or deeply involved in the commission of disgraceful crimes" (*OED* "villain" 1.). Mosby is a sexual criminal, and Arden is using the word "as a term of opprobrious address" (*OED* "villain" 1.), both to signify Mosby's depravity and to signify Mosby's low birth, as Arden's assertion that Alice is "no companion for so base a groome" shows. *A Woman Killed* uses "villain" in a similar manner. Wendoll calls himself "a villan" and a "Slaue" for wronging "the most perfectest man / That euer England bred a Gentleman" (C2v, C3; 6.1, 3, 19–20). Born to the same rank as Frankford, nevertheless, he behaves like a "base man" (C3; 6.36, 44). When Wendoll approaches Anne to seduce her, he asks to have printed on his face "The most stigmaticke title of a villaine" (C3v; 6.86), and, in his next speech, as he fights with himself over his desires, he asks, "shal I purchase to my fathers crest / The Motto of a villaine" (C4; 6.95–96). He says as well, later in that scene, that his attempted seduction will brand him in the world's eye: he will "incurre / The general name of villain through the world" (C4v; 6.134–135). Wendoll understands the status stakes of his betrayal of friendship; he knows that, should he betray a generous gentleman patron, he will sully his own family name. Between these Renaissance plays and their eighteenth-century rewrites, "villain" ceased to function so doubly. Rather than signifying the relative social status of these pairs of men—Frankford and Wendoll and Mosby and Arden—"villain" came to figure only the moral difference between relatively equal men. What were, in the earlier plays, arguments about rank, become arguments about male personal honor reconceived as separable from social status.

Arden asserts his right to Alice with the line "I must haue a Mandat for my wyfe" (TLN 312; 1.302). Alice should be Arden's not because of any contract between them but in the same manner that the Abbeylands are his, by command. Mosby threatens to interrupt a status system in which Arden is the recipient of his superior's gifts. To be more exact, Mosby is not attempting to shortcircuit that system or to transform it. He wants Arden's place in that system, his status as a gentleman, and Arden is determined to keep Mosby in his place as a manual worker. Mosby wants to "sit in Ardens seat" (TLN 1297; 8.31), and that desire motivates his pursuit of Alice.[50] The contest between men in the play's first scene is a contest over mastery. These men want to master one another, and Arden wants back his mastery over his wife, but the status fight between the men has clear priority: after Arden claims a mandate for Alice, neither man mentions her until Mosby begins to lie about his affair (TLN 337; 1.326).

The scene in the revised play may have structural similarities, but Lillo and Hoadly completely transform the subject matter of the quarrel between Mosby and Arden. The eighteenth-century playwrights, I imagine, were disapproving of the idea that a dispute over a fallen wife might move seamlessly into a dispute over worldly status between men. Their Arden wants badly to fight Mosby over the challenge to his "just right" to Alicia. Mosby won't defend himself, and Arden is further personally humiliated by Mosby's cowardice. He calls Mosby a "shame to manhood" and expresses his fury that Mosby's "shameful cowardice" might "protect a villain" (130). In Lillo and Hoadly's usage of "villain" we can already see the transformed world to which this play belongs, for that usage contains no trace of the status/rank insult contained in the earlier Arden's usage of the word. This "villain" in the word's modern sense has committed the "disgraceful crime" of having sex with another man's wife; in addition he is shaming "manhood" generally by being too cowardly to fight Arden over Alicia.

This scene, then, constructs, as it refers to, a general category of "manhood" that does not exist in the original play. If in the anonymous *Arden* Mosby has insulted Arden's gentlemanly rank by presuming to approach his wife when Mosby is only a "botcher," in the eighteenth-century play, Mosby has insulted "manhood" in general by refusing to fight for a woman. In many Renaissance plays, men insult their own manhood precisely because they *will* fight over women.[51] In *A Woman Killed* Frankford's first impulse after catching Anne and Wendoll in bed together is to kill them both, but when a servant stops him, he thanks her for saving him "like the angel's hand." His concern is the condition of his soul, not his sense of personal honor or manhood. In the eighteenth-century *Arden*, Mosby's refusal to fight over Arden's adulterous wife shames "manhood" generally. This general shame presupposes a world in which individual men are not categorically defined by their ranks. In the scene in the late-sixteenth-century play, Franklin is as concerned about Mosby's status as is Arden. When Mosby proclaims (falsely) "to God and . . . to the world" that Arden has insulted and wronged him, Franklin says, "Why canst thou deny, thou wert a botcher once" (TLN 331; 1.319–320).[52] As Arden and Franklin's comments about Mosby's lowly status indicate, there was no general category of manhood in the Renaissance founded on sexual or marital relations between men and women. Men were divided along status lines, not united by their desires for women and their concerns about women's honor (a shaky category at best). The eighteenth-century Arden takes for granted a newly categorical "manhood" based in relations to women—a category familiar to this day. In this categorically defined "manhood," all who would be men would defend their own sexual honor against assault, would fight over a woman. In this eighteenth-century play, Mosby is a "villain" for refusing to fight over a woman, a refusal that might make him a hero in, for example, a Shakespearean history play.

In the eighteenth-century scene, Arden's heroism is defined by his distinction from Mosby's villainy. He, unlike Mosby, will willingly fight over Alicia, and he, unlike Mosby, is personally devastated by her fall. Whereas this scene in the original play fades into the scene in which Alice tries to poison Arden with his breakfast broth, in the eighteenth-century play, the scene ends with a long speech from the conflicted Arden who is vowing to "hate" and "forget" Alicia "if [he] can." He describes the difficulty of keeping this vow:

> No easy task for one who doats like me.
> From what a height I'm fallen! Once smiling love
> Of all its horrors robb'd the blackest night,
> And gilt with gladness ev'ry ray of light,
> Now tyrant-like his conquest he maintains,
> And o'er his groaning slave with rods of irons reigns. (131)

This speech encapsulates the play's portrait of a heroic ardor; it simultaneously can demonstrate to us the continuities between the discourse of the homosocial imaginary and the emerging heterosexual imaginary. The word "dote" is a keyword in the earlier world's imagery of sexual enslavement. Kent, as we saw in chapter 1, tells Lear that he is "not . . . so old" that he will "dote" on a woman for the sake of her (and his) "thing" (TLN 568–569; 1.4.34–35). Shakespeare's Antony laments the "doting" that caused him to follow Cleopatra to his military doom (TLN 2039; 3.11.15). And, in the eighteenth-century Arden's speech, "doat" evokes the imagery of male enslavement these earlier texts customarily associated with the word when it implied a sexual relationship between a man and a woman. Using Niklas Luhmann's vocabulary, the "referent" in this eighteenth-century usage of "doat" seems identical to its "referent" in these Shakespearean texts and in so many other texts of the homosocial imaginary (8; see introduction). Arden, like Shakespeare's Antony, is bemoaning his enslavement, the power his sexual desire for a woman has to conquer him. However, this speech takes what Luhmann would call a "new perspective" on the sexual relationship Arden has previously enjoyed with Alicia. Rather than envisioning that relationship as inherently debasing, this speech envisions it as a "height." When Alicia loved him faithfully, Cupid was his savior, not his "tyrant." In the speech, Arden does not regret his life of doting; rather he (and the world around him) approves of that life when its object contentedly dotes by his side. The relationship saved him from the dark, enlightened even the light, and only when Alicia strayed, did Cupid become "tyrant-like." The earlier world uses the word "dote" to signify Venus's and Cupid's tyrannical natures, their investments in conquest, and the slavery of their victims. This Arden uses the vocabulary that, in the earlier world, functioned to denote Cupid's tyranny to signify, instead, Cupid's essential goodness, if only women would stay faithful (as they naturally should). Arden is a hero, then, for doting, a formulation that is unlikely in the earlier world.[53]

"Even Friendship here Would seem Impertinance"

The heroic doting Arden of the eighteenth century finds an ally in an utterly transformed Franklin. Rather than playing Arden's lover, more devoted than his wife, the eighteenth-century Franklin plays a friend to the marriage, a marriage that should be all in all for Arden.

This Franklin seems utterly uninterested in a fantasized male–male world—he is now the cheerleader for male–female sexualized marriage. In addition, the play physically excludes him from the marital couple's conversations. The sixteenth-century Franklin witnesses the internal workings of the marriage as a matter of course, but the eighteenth-century Franklin politely excuses himself from what he (and the play) sees as none of his business. In the position of the eighteenth-century Franklin in Arden's household, we can see a further shrinking of male–male love, from the center of male life to the periphery; we can also see an increasingly marked boundary between public and private that accompanied the development of the heterosexual imaginary.[54]

Lillo and Hoadly remove Franklin from Arden's side even when Alicia is nowhere to be seen; they, seemingly, are leery of the bond between these men that the earlier play takes for granted. In the original play, Franklin accompanies Arden on his trip home from Rochester, and when the two men meet Lord Cheiny, who invites them both to supper at his house, Arden excuses himself from dining that night because Bradshaw is waiting at his house. Lord Cheiny makes Arden promise to dine with him the next day and to bring Franklin (TLN 1539–1557; 9.98–115). Lillo and Hoadly rewrite this scene so that Arden is traveling alone. When Lord Cheyny (spelled differently in this play), invites him to supper, he excuses himself: "Franklin, my lord, who is my guest at present,/Expects me at my house" (203). Franklin is now a "guest at present," someone who does not belong by right to Arden's household. In the opening scene of the anonymous play, Franklin offers Arden a better option than living at home, angry and jealous. He says, "ly with me at London all this tearme," and Arden agrees (TLN 53, 51; 1.1.53, 51). When Arden broods about Alice's behavior back in Kent, Franklin counsels him: "Then stay with me in London, go not home" (TLN 1034; 4.28). Michael leaves the doors of the London house unlocked to let the murderers in and then panics and alerts his master and Franklin, who enter together, from the same room, and perhaps from the same bed.[55] The stage direction reads "Here enters Fran. & Arden" (TLN 1099). Lillo and Hoadly omit the London relationship between the men, but they keep Michael's dilemma over the unlocked doors. As in the original play, in the rewrite, Arden and Franklin talk together and then go to bed; however, when Michael sounds the alarm, Lillo and Hoadly's stage direction reads *"Enter* ARDEN *and* FRANKLIN, *undress'd, at several doors."* Since the men are in Kent, and Arden is sleeping with

Alicia, the stage direction seems excessive. Why is it necessary to specify that Arden and Franklin come in "*at several doors*"? The revised stage direction may be a sign of emergent "homosexual panic" on the part of these eighteenth-century authors.[56] Whereas twentieth-century criticism neglects Arden and Franklin's love relationship, as if it were not Arden's primary bond and the play's vision of a safe love-haven, the eighteenth-century rewrite may display, in this altered stage direction and in its reinvention of the relationship, its anxiety about the shape of Renaissance male–male friendship.

However, the eighteenth-century play does not completely abandon love between men. Alicia says to Maria that "Franklin's company" is as welcome to Arden as the grant of abbey-lands (186). In addition, a trace of the language of love between men persists in this *Arden*. In his rage at Franklin holding him back from killing Mosby, Arden offers to "tear" Franklin's "officious hand"; then, coming to his senses, he says to Franklin, "Pardon me, sweet friend" (191). Significantly, however, this love-language is the only trace of the developed love vocabulary employed between the two friends in the earlier play, and, equally significantly, this eighteenth-century Franklin does not use the language of love to talk about his friend Arden. Instead, he is completely focused on the health of his friend's marriage, on his friend's love for his wife. In the original play, Franklin counsels Arden to stop obsessing about Alice's sexual crime: "Gentle Arden leave this sad lament,/She will amend, and so your greefes will cease/Or els shele die, and so your sorrows end" (TLN 1027–1029; 4.21–23). If Alice neither amends nor dies, Franklin says, others have borne double Arden's woes patiently. Franklin's concern is his friend's mental well-being. He offers Arden two options that would ensure that well-being, and those options seem equally satisfactory: either Alice will stop fooling around with Mosby, or she will die and Arden will be rid of the problem of a faithless spouse. The eighteenth-century Franklin would never offer these options.

In that play, Arden's well-being is absolutely predicated on the well-being of the marriage, and the play and Franklin approve that predication entirely. In conversation with Maria, Franklin hopes that Arden will relent and restore his life with Alicia: "Their mutual peace, Maria!/For his can ne'er be found but in Alicia" (213). As a whole, the eighteenth-century *Arden* parenthetically adds "this is as it should be" to Franklin's claim. The play even implies that, despite Alicia's fall, their mutual peace might have been restored. The play's tragedy is that Arden could not avoid Mosby's villainy (in the modern sense of the word). The earlier play makes exactly the opposite point in its portrayal of Arden and Franklin's relationship: Arden should have founded his identity on his friendship with Franklin rather than on the well-being of his marriage. Where the sixteenth-century *Arden* sees marriage as quicksand, the eighteenth-century *Arden* believes in sexually fulfilling (for the man) marriage as a rock, and Franklin's part in the play is to assure Arden of that rock's firmness. Of course, Alicia is a crumbling rock, but the play and Franklin do not really believe in her lack of solidity. When Mosby, insincerely, claims that Arden's doubts about Alicia are figments of his imagination, Franklin goes further and calls them "[i]mpossible to thought" (190). He finds Alicia's sexual slip unthinkable, and, in some odd way (odd, since she *has* fallen), so does the play. When Arden says that he will need to learn to live without Alicia, Franklin replies, "Pray heaven forbid!" (191). Far from offering his own bed as the alternative to Arden's restless life with his wife, as Franklin's progenitor does, this Franklin assumes that Arden will find his peace in bed with Alicia.

Lillo and Hoadly turn the door-locking incident to their own ends, ends that erode loving male friendship and shore up loving marriage. They also rewrite to similar ends the incident in *Arden of Faversham* in which Mosby is wounded. The scene of that wounding in the original play is almost incomprehensible if Arden is to be read as a hero; in the anonymous *Arden*, he is cuckolded in front of his face, and he rejects his friend who would be his savior in favor of the fiends who will destroy him. Franklin and Arden encounter Mosby and Alice arm in arm, exchanging "sugared" kisses and taunting Arden about his horns. Franklin takes out his sword. Then Black Will and Shakebag enter and try to kill Arden, and in the ensuing brawl, Franklin stabs Mosby and saves Arden. Apparently unwilling to believe his own eyes, Arden accepts Alice's shamelessly inaccurate interpretation of the incident and rejects Franklin's correct interpretation. This is the crucial moment in the play when Arden spurns Franklin for Alice and, thereby, seals his doom. Lillo and Hoadly wanted no part of this story, which can not fail to depict Arden, at the very least, as an idiot. However, if they were to reach the play's tragic end, they needed to have Arden trust Mosby enough to let him back into his house. This incident served that purpose in the original play, and it serves the same purpose in their revision. They rewrite it as Mosby's design:

> *Mosby* I've thought a way—
> That may be easy under friendship's mask,
> Which to a foe suspected may be hard.

Green Friendship! impossible—
Mosby—You know him not. (213)

Arden is characterized in this conversation, and in the ensuing action, as slightly credulous. Michael says that he has an "easy heart" that will be won by a "seeming benefit" (213). Will and Shakebag then feign an attempt on Arden's life, and Mosby saves him. Once again, in the eighteenth-century play, Arden walks alone, without Franklin. When Franklin enters the scene, Arden tells him of his new-found friendship with Mosby, and when Franklin still distrusts Mosby, Arden interprets that distrust as jealousy. Franklin says, "I like [Mosby] worse than ever," and Arden replies, "Because I like him better. What a churl" (220). This Arden is a dupe, but he has not mis-interpreted what he saw with his own eyes. The quarrel between the two friends is no longer a quarrel that pits Franklin against Alice. Arden's mistake in this play is his susceptibility to friendship.

As in the distinctions between premodern and modern misogyny (chapter 1) and between attacks on different sexual standards (chapter 2), the distinctions between the lessons these two *Arden*s teach about friendship are fine, but they are, once again, vital to rec-ognize. Both plays show a man mistaken when he chooses between male friends; both *Arden*s show the dangers of male friendship;[57] but the plays ultimately take quite different paths. The original *Arden* chooses friendship over marriage, whereas this eighteenth-century *Arden* chooses marriage over friendship. After the fight, this Franklin walks off in a fit of pique. Thus, he is not at Arden's house to save him when his false friend attacks. Friendship, after all, is not worth as much as male–female love, and this is what this Franklin himself says again and again.

In comparison to earlier representations, the sanctified realm of male friendship is desecrated in this play, and the desecration of that realm seems to have been a necessary step in the construction of the heterosexual imaginary. Hand in hand with that desecration went, as the eighteenth-century *Arden* shows directly, the construction of a realm of marital privacy, a realm only barely emergent in the English Renaissance, but relatively firmly constructed in the mid-eighteenth century. Although Orlin argues for "developing ambitions for personal privacy" in the English Renaissance, her survey of English houses indicates "that privacy was not an object of the architecture of the period" (*Private* 8, 185). As Orlin suggests, domestic tragedies of the sixteenth century show us marriage in public.[58] Not only do they offer the audience a window into marital disarray, they also show us that marital disarray displayed before the servants, the neighbors, and friends. In the sixteenth-century *Arden*, the neighbors have been talking about Alice and Mosby from the beginning. This neighborhood gossip provokes Arden's distress about the affair. Arden's servant, Michael, is also privy to Mosby and Alice's affair and quietly present during intimate conversation between man and wife. As significantly, Arden and Alice conduct their marital business in front of Franklin at all times. No one remarks upon his presence in their most intimate conversational moments. The eighteenth-century *Arden*, in contrast, shows us a relatively modern realm of marital privacy. Contemplating confessing her sin to Arden, Alicia says, "Nay, could I live with public loss of honour,/Arden would die to see Alicia scorn'd" (215). Arden's male "honour" depends on Alicia's public reputation, a reputation that this play guards from even the couple's close friends. Where English Renaissance drama continually stages the most public male sexual suspicion, this play invokes a private world between husband and wife—privacy for sex and intimate conversation about sex, privacy that might guard male as well as female reputation. In order that Arden and Alicia may have their intimate conversation, Franklin and Maria leave the room, and Franklin tells Maria, "we'll withdraw—even friendship here/Would seem impertinence" (215). Though Franklin's comment affords friendship a privileged place, it has become a secondary relationship at best. The male friend belongs, with his female counterpart, outside the bedroom walls.

Sentimental Drama and the Heterosexual Imaginary

When eighteenth-century playwrights rewrote Renaissance plays as sentimental dramas, they may well have been reacting "against what was viewed as the excess, impropriety, and debauchery of Restoration Age drama" (Murfin and Ray 440). In the context of a genealogy of heterosexuality, however, they show instead their indebtedness to the sexual world inaugurated in the Restoration. Eighteenth-century playwrights share Restoration Age drama's newly born belief in all men as lovers; they share its character types, and at least in terms of male friendship, they share its priorities. The eighteenth-century Mosby is a species of libertine. After Michael assures Mosby that Alicia will remain true to her husband, Mosby exclaims, "Have I then slighted her whole sighing sex,/Bid opportunity and fortune wait;/ And all to be forsaken for an husband!" (212). This Mosby is, from time to time, nervous about his abandonment of moral values, but he never regrets his sexual desire. Mosby's greed and Alice's lust have been decoupled in this play, and Mosby has been granted the lust above all. If Alice is the ultimate world-overturning anti-heroine of *Arden of Faversham*, Mosby is the libertine anti-hero of the later play. His plotting speech opens the Lillo and Hoadly play, giving him the inaugural place in this play that the Restoration Edmund has in Tate's *Lear* (chapter 3). In contrast, a discussion between Franklin and Arden opens the earlier play, just as a discussion between Kent and Gloucester opens *King Lear*. The same shift occurs in Victor's rewritten *Woman Killed*. Heywood opens his play with a conversation between men, and Victor opens his with Cranmore's account of his own desire. In this switch from beginnings in male friendship to beginnings in individual male libertine desire, we can see how indebted sentimental drama is to the sexual codes of the Restoration. These eighteenth-century sentimental dramas rewrite the sexual worlds of their prototypes; they belong wholly to the new sexual world inaugurated in the Restoration.

CHAPTER 5

OTHELLO IN THE SEVENTEENTH AND EIGHTEENTH CENTURIES AND THE COLONIAL ORIGINS OF HETEROSEXUALITY

Unlike most of Shakespeare's other plays and unlike *Arden* and *A Woman Killed with Kindness*, *Othello* held the stage largely without adaptation throughout the Restoration and eighteenth century. Actors and managers cut the play for production, but its basic plot and especially the relationship between Othello and Desdemona remained intact, although those cuts and critical interpretation established a Desdemona who conformed to emerging gender ideals for women.[1] In this chapter I contend that, as well as picking up, adapting, and newly valuing the sexual mores from representations of debased English servants, the emerging ideology of heterosexuality newly valued the sexual interests of Othello, who in his original incarnation was written as overly sexually interested. In early-seventeenth-century England, the male racial or ethnic other who was deeply invested in women was read as uncontrolled, weak, and unproductive. However, by the middle of the eighteenth century, as we have seen, a man's sexual desire for, and investment in, a woman could be seen as proper and even heroic.

This argument has a double bearing on *Othello* and the history of its editing and production. First, I claim that, in 1604, Shakespeare portrayed Othello as debased precisely because of his passionate involvement with his wife. This involvement meant that his masculinity was suspect, as the play explicitly shows when "Housewiues make a Skillet of [his] Helme," as he fears (TLN 622; 1.3.273). When Othello demonstrates his overwhelming love for his wife he is automatically degraded. In the play, his love signals his lack of control, a lack of control that the play proceeds to demonstrate.

Othello resembles numerous other stereotypical seventeenth-century Moors, Indians, and other foreign and alien men, men represented as connected to, and obsessed with, voracious female sexuality. The folio text of the play makes a problem of this stereotype by cleverly placing it in Roderigo's mouth, when he calls Othello "a Lasciuious Moore" (TLN 139; 1.1.124). Nevertheless, both the folio and the quarto eventually confirm the image, which is used finally to skewer Othello. His worst fears about his involvement with his wife become his reality. Second, I contend that since Othello's passionate involvement with Desdemona turned out, historically, to conform to emerging understandings of ideal, dominant, masculine sexual engagement with women, the eighteenth century misrecognized him as a proper man just as it misrecognized his wife as a passionless woman. These linked misrecognitions are yet another window into the uneven emergence of the heterosexual imaginary.

In the early seventeenth century, the complex, and perhaps even contradictory, character Desdemona conformed to dominant understandings of women. Although she is chaste, she is also sexual, and she talks very freely. Whether we see her with Peter Stallybrass as an inconsistent character who touches all the bases of represented womanhood in the early seventeenth century, or read her as a complex character who can be chaste, open-mouthed, and sexually interested at the same time, she is hardly exceptional either as a Shakespearean woman or as a represented early-seventeenth-century woman.[2] Othello, in contrast, is othered by his blackness from the beginning of the play and throughout its action. His blackness matters, and, as Arthur Little, Michael Neill, Karen Newman, Virginia Vaughan, and others have shown, his blackness matters in sexual terms. During the long eighteenth century, however, to conform to emerging gender ideals that cohered in the infant heterosexual imaginary, Desdemona's character had to be edited and misread to excise any hint of sexual interest, whereas Othello's character, especially his passionate love of his wife, was left intact because it approximated a new normality for dominant men. Unlike the stories of so many other Shakespearean men and women, Othello and Desdemona's love story was not altered because it, unlike those other stories, was becoming the story of life.[3]

The critics and editors discussed in this chapter may disagree with one another strenuously about the text of *Othello* and about its cruxes, but they share an ideological playing field. Early-seventeenth-century England did not share that field; indeed, to that culture, that field's boundaries and markers might have looked deformed and utterly strange. In the critical and editorial disputes over (and ultimate agreement about) *Othello*'s lines, we can see both the emergence of that new playing field and its bumps and fissures. In this chapter, I also attend to nineteenth- and especially twentieth-century commentary on some of the same textual cruxes and stubborn lines that preoccupied eighteenth-century critics. That later history can help us to better understand the contours of the imaginary being formed in the eighteenth century. And a look at aspects of the fully formed twentieth-century heterosexual imaginary can show us how, while the eighteenth century approaches that imaginary, it did not fully embrace it.

The Sexualized Colonial Imagination and the Emerging Heterosexual Imaginary

As well as having racial insults thrown at him by other characters, as the play progresses, Othello associates himself with reviled blackness and also, ambivalently, with the "Turbond Turke," "the base Indian" (in the quarto), and "the base Iudean" (in the folio). In Renaissance travel narratives and other texts, men in each of these categories were stereotyped as passionately involved with women. In her indispensable book on *Othello* in its Jacobean context, Vaughan uses Richard Knolles's *Generall Historie of the Turks* to illustrate her argument about the Jacobean understanding of male passion. Knolles's *Generall Historie* shows us a passionately jealous Turk who murders his wife because he is "more amorous of her person than secured in her vertues" (qtd. in Vaughan *Othello* 79). Vaughan suggests that while Othello's "behavior suits contemporary conceptions of male desire and susceptibility to passion, it is also imbricated in" racial discourse and images of foreign others (88). However, Vaughan must reach into these racial and xenophobic discourses precisely because *Othello* does not confirm Jacobean understandings of dominant male behavior and passions. Whereas Jacobean people saw passion as potentially unmanageable, they attributed the ability to control passion differentially according to a man's social group or age, and/or ethnic or racial category, as they also attributed that ability differentially to men and women. Thus, as we have seen, household servants/clowns and many women are represented as having little control over their passions, where dominant, fully sanctioned men are represented as relatively unsusceptible to passion and excess. In Shakespeare's time, and in his texts, racially and ethnically othered men were represented in the same sexualized terms as women and base men.[4]

As Vaughan notes, Shakespeare was surrounded by texts about exotic others that coupled foreign, and especially racially and ethnically othered men, with unbridled desire for women. Travel narratives from the period continually depict men who, though they may look to late-twentieth-century eyes as if they are living in a male heterosexual's paradise, are actually described this way as a sign of their disempowerment. For example, in his 1624 *Generall Historie of Virginia, New England and the Summer Isles*, Captain John Smith describes the man he calls the Emperor Powhatan, who, Smith says, "hath as many women as he will, whereof when he lieth on his bed, one sitteth at his head, and another at his feet, but when he sitteth, one sitteth on his right hand and another on his left. As he is weary of his women, he bestoweth them on those that best deserve them at his hands" (II 127). Smith's Powhatan desires multiple women, using them and then discarding them to others of his people, and these men presumably take Powhatan's women happily as a sign of their emperor's favor. In *The True Travels, Adventvres, and Observations of Captaine Iohn Smith, In Europe, Asia, Affrica, and America, from Anno Domini 1593–1629*, a 1618 narration of some of Smith's earlier adventures, the peripatetic Captain describes the Crym-Tartars who keep a "great number of captived women to breed upon." Smith relates the ways in which these men "maintaine themselves in this Pompe. Also their wives, of whom they have as many as they will" (III 195). Although Smith's description of the Crym-Tartar princes is cribbed from a thirteenth-century text, it resembles his pseudo-ethnographic report on the Indians in Virginia. Both texts depict the leaders of these foreign "nations" surrounded by women. To a well-interpellated gentle or noble man of the period, Powhatan's and the Crym-Tartar princes' love of numerous women renders them effeminate. Smith's descriptions make this point on more than one level. Smith writes that Powhatan, as well as being surrounded by women, is practically beardless, a physical fact that Smith draws attention to because in Renaissance England the ability to grow facial hair signified adult manliness.[5] Likewise, Smith describes the Crym-Tartars' attire—their rich furs, lined with plush, or taffeta, or robes of tissue—attire that for Smith is another sign of debased masculinity. In Smith's narratives generally, taffeta is a fabric associated with players and idle effeminate creatures.[6] Smith's narratives are examples of the stereotype that linked ethnic others to unbridled lust for women. His narratives indicate also how indiscriminate that linkage was. For Smith and his English audience, Crym-Tartars share sexual mores with Native Americans.

Black Africans fell into the same sexualized category in early-seventeenth-century representation. Travelers' tales associated Moors and other African men (themselves often lumped together arbitrarily) with sexual desire for women.[7] In volume two of his *Principal Navigations*, Richard Hakluyt includes a 1566 text called *A description of the yeerely voyage or pilgrimage of the* Mahumitans, Turkes *and* Moores *vnto* Mecca *in* Arabia. The author of that text describes a Cairo that houses "people of all Nations, as Christians, Armenians, Abexins, Turkes, Moores, Iewes, Indians, Medians, Persians, Arabians, and other sortes of people . . . The rest of the people in Cairo are for the most part marchants which goe and come, and the remnant are Moores and other base people" (II 200). In the same section of the text, the author states, "The women of this countrey are most beautifull . . . and are very libidinous, and the men likewise, but foule and hard favoured" (II 201). Unlike eighteenth-century critics, who stress Othello's royal descent, texts that Shakespeare could have read in Hakluyt often postulate an essentially undifferentiated black African population and depict that population as sexually excessive. A 1554 account of John Loke's second voyage to *Guinea* that, like Othello's own story of his travels, speaks of men "hauing their eyes and mouth in their breast" (Hakluyt II 332), contains this discourse on "the people of Africa":

> It is to be understood, that the people which now inhabite the regions of the coast of Guinea, and the midle parts of Africa, as Libya the inner, and Nubia, with divers other great & large regions about he same, were in old time called Æthiopes and Nigritæ, whom we now call Moores, Moorens, or Negroes, a people of beastly living without a God, lawe, religion, or commonwealth. (II 331)

Lok tells of a "people of Libya called Garamantes, whose women are common: for they contract no matrimonie, neither haue respect to chastitie" (II 331).[8] These texts associate African men and women with sex outside of marriage and with sex with multiple partners.

In his masterful study of the construction of racial and ethnic identities through the stories of Noah's sons, Benjamin Braude does not "find any medieval Christian source explicitly connecting [Noah's son] Ham, sex, and blackness" (132). However, by the early seventeenth century, a specific story involving male–female sex was told about Ham. In that story, retold by George Best in Hakluyt, Ham is cursed with blackness because he would not refrain from having sex with his wife during the flood. According to Best, God commanded that Noah and his sons "should vse continencie, and abstaine from carnall copulation with their wiues." Noah's son Cham believed that the first son born after the flood would inherit "all the dominions of the earth." Therefore, he disregarded his father's commandment and "vsed company with his wife." The son, Chus, born from that union was cursed to be born "blacke and lothsome" and "remaine a spectacle of disobedience to all the worlde" (Hakluyt III 52). Best's 1578 tale, by now well-known in *Othello* criticism, is both a story about the unbridled sexual activity associated with blackness in the period and also a Renaissance story of sex in the service of illegitimate inheritance.[9] Ham's sin resembles the sin of Shakespeare's Aaron in *Titus Andronicus* who glories in the fact that his adulterous affair with Tamora might make his son the emperor. Thus Best does not accuse Cham of being unable to control his sexual desire. He accuses him of carnal incontinence motivated by the lust for patriarchal rights over the whole world. Nevertheless, the story, like so many others in the period, linked blackness with male–female sex.

The stories told and collected in the early seventeenth century about Africans', Turks', Jews', and Indians' sexual proclivities do not match up neatly with one another. All of these groups were linked to sex, but not all to the same kinds of sexual behavior. To the modern eye, a Turk's or a Jew's excessive involvement with his wife does not look like either Ham's ambitious desires or Indian and African desires for multiple wives. However, the distinctions we might make between these stories are modern ones based on our understanding (cultivated under the heterosexual imaginary) that a man's passionate desire for his wife is a good thing. Under the homosocial imaginary, these distinctions were neither simple nor clear. Once a man became involved with a woman, he could succumb to the excesses of passion. These could be expressed in a passionate involvement with one woman—as in the cases of Othello and Elizabeth Cary's Herod (*The Tragedy of Mariam*). These excesses could also be expressed in the desire for many women. Sometimes texts link these two proclivities, but either form of desire might render a man effeminate. This is why Othello's desire for Desdemona links him to Hakluyt's "lascivious" Moors.

During the later seventeenth century and the eighteenth century, charges of sexual misbehavior in Africa became more focused on what people still generally see as outrageous sexual acts and desires. As Winthrop Jordan notes, Africans were accused of having enormous "members" [penises] and of sex acts with apes. Texts increasingly stigmatize African women as "hot and lascivious" (35). Thus, as dominant white women in England were purified of sexual desire for men, women in Africa were increasingly sexualized. And as codes for white masculinity in England began to include sexual desire for women, texts increasingly represent African male sexuality as unusual. In the early seventeenth century, Othello's passionate involvement with his wife helped to form a discourse on racial otherness that defined him as a normal Moor but an inadequate dominant man. As the eighteenth century defined Othello as a legitimate man, it also associated blackness with more exorbitant sexuality. The emergence of race as an identity category during the seventeenth and eighteenth centuries intersects with the story of emerging heterosexuality; and both stories are visible in *Othello*'s vicissitudes over the two centuries.

In the early seventeenth century, *Othello* both contributed and reacted to contemporary ideas of race, including the story of Ham. As Roderigo's disparaging comment shows, *Othello* invokes the stereotype of the "lascivious" black man that still lives with us today. But that stereotype's endurance should not blind us to the twists and turns it has taken along the way. For, as we have seen repeatedly, throughout history images and stereotypes are taken up and used in the interest of competing ideologies. Whereas, in 1950s America, black men's supposed sexual prowess and interest in (white) women might be used as sticks with which to beat black men and simultaneously might be objects of envy for white men, in 1604, Othello's sexual interest in his white wife indicates that Venice cannot trust him with command. Rather than rendering him hyper-masculine in a threatening manner, this sexual interest debases and feminizes him, enabling his officer Cassio to accept unquestioningly Iago's judgment that "our General's Wife, is now the General" (TLN 1438–1439; 2.3.309–310). Although this judgment is rendered by the play's devil, all the men in the play share the belief that a man's love for a woman weakens and softens that man. Shakespeare's characterization of Roderigo is evidence of this tenet of the homosocial imaginary, since his character is composed equally of weakness and sexual desire. Cassio knows that Othello, even when caught in the snare of his own involvement with Desdemona, would not like to see his officer "woman'd" (TLN 2359; 3.4.194), and so Cassio avoids being seen with

Bianca. The play associates Othello with the stereotypical "lascivious Moor," and that association degrades him in the eyes of the men in the play.

Just as Othello's racial identity partly determines his passion for Desdemona, race also figures into eighteenth-century criticism of the play. The history of *Othello* criticism in the long eighteenth century is both a history of the uneven development of racism in literary criticism and a history of emerging heterosexuality; and those histories interact in fascinating ways.[10] In the late seventeenth and early eighteenth centuries Thomas Rymer and Charles Gildon were scandalized by Othello's blackness. Rymer roared angrily in 1692 that "With us a Moor might marry some little drab, or Small-coal Wench" whereas Shakespeare has him marry the daughter of a senator (134). He was shocked that the Venetian senators would countenance the marriage: "Should the Poet have provided such a Husband for an only Daughter of any noble Peer in *England*," he contends, "the Black-amoor must have chang'd his Skin, to look our House of Lords in the Face" (139). Tellingly, Rymer also objects to Desdemona because of her open mouth, her "importuning and teizing" of her husband, a characteristic that was absolutely denied by later eighteenth-century critics. In 1710, Gildon agreed with Rymer that the match was impossible and that it reflected disparagingly on Desdemona's character. He claimed that "on common Womens admitting a *Negro* to a Commerce with her every one almost starts at the Choice. Much more in a Woman of Vertue . . . Custom having put such a Bar as so opposite a Colour, it takes away our Pity from [Desdemona], and only raises our Indignation against [Othello]" (410). These critics focused on racial difference rather than love and used that difference to denigrate Desdemona as well as Othello.

Although Gildon and Rymer agreed so completely about the inappropriate match and seem to have fully voiced a concept of miscegenation that was still being formed in legal and other discourses, theirs were the minority views among literary critics and editors as the eighteenth century continued.[11] Most eighteenth-century critics enjoyed the prospect of Othello and Desdemona's love more than they feared Othello's blackness. *Othello* was an exceptionally popular play throughout the period, provoking critical responses such as Charlotte Lennox's in 1753 that the play "has always been esteemed one of the best of *Shakespear's* Tragedies" (125) and Elizabeth Griffith's that "This Play, in my opinion, is very justly considered as the last and greatest effort of our Author's genius, and may, therefore, be looked upon as the *chef d'oeuvre* of dramatic composition" (1775 519). Throughout the century, editors placed *Othello* at the end of Shakespeare's complete works, seeing it as epitomizing Shakespeare's genius.[12] Thus, most commentators either refuted or disregarded Rymer's earlier vicious criticism of the play.[13] In 1733, Lewis Theobald furiously disagreed with Rymer, arguing that, while Giraldi Cinthio in the primary source text "design'd his Tale [as] a Document to young Ladies against disproportion'd Marriages," Shakespeare's moral in *Othello* is "that a Woman may fall in Love with the Virtues and shining Qualities of a Man; and therein overlook the Differences of Complexion and Colour" (*Works of Shakespeare* 371n.). More than forty years later, Lennox asserted of the Desdemona–Othello match that, "Such Affections are not very common indeed; but a very few Instances of them prove that they are not impossible; and even in *England* we see some very handsome Women married to Blacks, where their Colour is less familiar than at *Venice*; besides the *Italian* Ladies are remarkable for such Sallies of irregular Passions" (131). Lennox and Theobald believed with Rymer and Gildon that racial differences were significant, but such differences paled for Theobald and Lennox before the power of true love. While Lennox saw the marriage as "irregular," she saw it also as evidence that Desdemona and Othello possessed a "marriage of true minds."[14] Lennox writes, "There is less Improbability in supposing a noble Lady, educated in Sentiments superior to the Vulgar, should fall in love with a Man merely for the Qualities of his Mind, than that a mean Citizen should be possessed of such exalted Ideas, as to overlook the Disparity of Years and Complexion, and to be enamoured of Virtue in the Person of a Moor" (132). The exaltation of male–female love was so attractive and powerful for the vast majority of *Othello* critics and editors by 1733 that the color issue became either a sign of the extent and beauty of Othello and Desdemona's love—as it is for Theobald and Lennox—or insignificant in the face of that love.

Indeed, as the ideology of heterosexuality moved into dominance by the beginning of the nineteenth century, Othello's love and especially his passionate nature became so appealing that Samuel Taylor Coleridge and the critics and producers who followed him whitened Othello so as to reconcile their approval of his character with established racism. In his 1818 lectures on Shakespeare, Coleridge famously asserted that "as we are constituted, and most surely as an English audience was disposed in the beginning of the seventeenth century, it would be something monstrous to conceive this beautiful

Venetian girl falling in love with a veritable negro" (179).[15] Coleridge misreads Shakespeare's England as sharing his nineteenth-century values, values shaped by England's participation in slavery and the hardening of racial distinctions. Coleridge lauds Othello's passion and simultaneously produces an Othello who is not "Negro." In the eighteenth century, after Theobald, the power and approval of passionate love between a man and a woman trumped Othello's racial difference. Subsequently, as blackness became an unavoidable stigma in the nineteenth century and many aspects of the heterosexual imaginary became absolutely dominant, Othello had to be a whitened lover.[16]

Othello, the Perfect Lover

Shakespeare's Othello could be shamed by his love for Desdemona, love that leads him to risk his "occupation" for his obsession with a woman. Eighteenth-century readers, critics, and audiences, however, admired Othello as a lover. Othello's vow, "My life vpon her faith" could look weak and naive in the early seventeenth century (TLN 647; 1.3.295). By the middle of the eighteenth century, this vow looked like normality. Early acting versions of the play cut none of Othello's professions of love. In fact, Othello was perfected as a lover in one Restoration version where minor cuts made him a younger man, playing up his "nobility, dignity [and] poise."[17] Francis Gentleman's notes to the Bell acting edition of 1777 explain of the character that "his appearance should be amiably elegant, and above the middle stature; his expression full and sententious, for the declamatory part; flowing and harmonious, for the love-scenes; rapid and powerful, for each violent climax of jealous rage" (10). Othello was to be the picture of elegant manliness, and his "love-scenes" were his most "harmonious" moments, "flowing" naturally from his character. Gentleman approves Othello's interjection, "If she be false, Heauen mock'd it selfe:/Ile not beleeue't" (TLN 1910–1911; 3.3.282–283). According to Gentleman, "The sudden effect of *Desdemona*'s personal appearance, is pleasing and natural; for the heart which truly loves, unless grossly imposed on, always judges favourably" (50). In James Thomas Kirkman's memoirs of Charles Macklin's theatrical career, Kirkman compliments Spranger Barry's first performance of Othello (1746): "*Mr. Barry* was, beyond all doubt, one of the most pathetic lovers on the English Stage, and stood greatly indebted to the excellent instruction of Mr. Macklin" (I 299). For Kirkman, the part offered Barry the opportunity to play a lover who would excite his audiences' passions. Thanks to Mr. Macklin's coaching, Barry could do this successfully. Mr. Barry "happily exhibited the hero, the lover, and the distracted husband" (I 302). Commenting upon Sir Francis Delaval's Othello, played for a select audience in 1751, Kirkman exclaims, "But what he was peculiarly superior to every person in, was the natural expression of the lover and the gentleman" (I 339). Shakespeare's Othello fails as a general and a man because obsessive jealousy, caused by his investment in his wife, subsumes his martial identity. He cries out, "[f]arewell: *Othello's* Occupation's gone" (TLN 2000; 3.3.360). But the eighteenth-century's Othello was magnificently a lover—this was his occupation. His devotion to his true love makes (common) sense in the eighteenth century.

The aptly named Gentleman's detailed analysis of Othello refers to the redefinition of masculinity that accompanied the transition between the homosocial and the heterosexual imaginary. In that redefinition, as we have seen, men were expected to repress violent instincts, to enjoy a newly-defined domestic sphere in which to express their love for women, as well as to isolate that domestic sphere from the world of business. Colley Cibber declared in 1740, "in *Othello* we may see [the actor], in the Variety of Nature: There the Actor is carried through the different Accidents of domestick, Happiness, and Misery, occasionally torn and tortur'd by the most distracting Passion, that can rouse Terror, or Compassion, in the Spectator" (478). Cibber sees *Othello* as a play about a man's domestic life, defined as the life between a man and his wife; and, crucially, Cibber approves that life as the focus of drama. This new space of domesticity, sexual desire for women, and love, rather than threatening a man's masculine identity as it did under the homosocial imaginary, now confirms and establishes his virility, in that word's modern sense.

Gentleman admires what he sees as Othello's delicacy in explaining his conduct with Desdemona to the senators. In the first act, before he tells the senators how he won Desdemona, Othello excuses his lack of eloquence: "Rude am I, in my speech,/And little bless'd with the soft phrase of Peace" (TLN 420–421; 1.3.82; this is the folio reading; the quarto reads "set phrase of peace"). Gentleman's note says, "*Othello* here modestly charges himself with what his oratory, through the whole scene, contradicts; and there is infinite beauty in so doing; it was a nice task to relate his course of love, and he could not express himself with too much diffidence and delicacy, on such an occasion" (15). In his note, Gentleman uses the word "nice" in the complimentary sense defined by the *OED*: "delicate, needing tactful handling" or "punctilious, scrupulous, sensitive" (*OED* "nice" 11b. 7d.). According to the *OED*, both of these definitions postdate *Othello*. The dictionary finds the first usage as "delicate" in 1617 and as "sensitive" in 1647. In 1604, "nice" could have meant "wanton, loose-mannered; lascivious" (*OED* "nice" 2a.); Shakespeare uses the word in that sense in *Love's Labour's Lost* when the foolish lover Armado's boy tells him to dance and sing like a "Rabbet on a spit" because "these are humours, these betraie nice wenches that would be betraied without these" (TLN 788, 791–792; 3.1.15, 17–18). "Nice" could also denote "effeminate, unmanly" (4b.) or "not able to endure much" (4c.). The transition in definitions from the earlier period into the more modern parallels the transition that masculine identity underwent during the same time. By the time of Gentleman's criticism, sensitivity and delicacy have become virtues in men whose primary identity is not warlike. These are virtues that define the newly sanctioned private sphere for men. Gentleman can use "nice" to describe Othello's task because that task was becoming a "nice" one in the more modern sense; rather than rendering Othello effeminate, for Gentleman and his later eighteenth-century audience, Othello's delicate handling of his love affair in public is a sign of his masculinity.

In the second scene of the play, Othello metadramatically declines to fight in the streets with Brabantio's men: "Were it my Cue to fight [he says], I should haue knowne it / Without a Prompter" (TLN 302–303; 1.2.81). Gentleman comments, "This is a spirited resolve. A brave man will always decline violence, when he can do it with honour" (12). This eighteenth-century Othello should, when possible, be an honorable lover rather than a volatile warrior.[18] Shakespeare's culture was already involved in redefining masculinity away from warrior identity; but such redefinitions, visible in a play such as *Romeo and Juliet*, did not, as Gentleman's criticism does, oppose a negatively defined warrior masculinity to a positively defined hetero-lover masculinity. Indeed in texts from Shakespeare's time, the critique of warrior excess was often accompanied by a critique of excessive desire for women, as it is in *Romeo and Juliet*. In addition, in Shakespeare's plays and culture, desire for women could easily be seen as disrupting proper masculine attention to war, as it does in a play such as *Antony and Cleopatra*. Othello, of course, is employed by the Venetian state as a warrior, and Desdemona loves him as a warrior. The play worries the question of his warrior identity constantly, but it by no means sets up an idealized private sphere to which he should devote energy. Rather, Othello and other characters

in the play see his marriage as a public event and as potentially conta-
minating his warrior duty. Gentleman's reading of Othello's task as
"nice" in a dominant eighteenth-century sense is a strong misreading
indicating his and his culture's ideological concerns; in fact, *Othello*
presents Othello's misplaced obsession with his own love for
Desdemona as emasculating and, therefore, as congruent with the earlier seventeenth-century senses of "nice" that were fading from the
word by Gentleman's time.

In an associated strong misreading, Gentleman approves of
Othello's speech in response to Desdemona's request to accompany
him to Cyprus. That famous speech culminates,

> No, when light wing'd Toyes
> Of feather'd *Cupid*, seele with wanton dullnesse
> My speculatiue, and offic'd Instrument:
> That my Disports corrupt, and taint my businesse:
> Let House-wiues make a Skillet of my Helme,
> And all indigne, and base aduersities,
> Make head against my Estimation. (TLN 618–624; 1.3.269–275)

Gentleman (mis)reads this speech as "a delightful flight of fancy"
and calls it "natural for a man of sense, who, though he bows to the
shrine of love, stedfastly attends to the important concerns of life"
(20). But Othello's lines are far from fanciful. Othello does not see
love as a "shrine" at which he must worship when not attending to
"the important concerns of life." Instead, in this speech,
Othello attempts to ward off the threatening "lightwing'd Toyes/Of
feather'd *Cupid*" that might blind him, destroy his reason, and
"corrupt" his abilities as a soldier and commander. The "man of
sense" that Gentleman constructs in this comment is not the
Othello of the play who clearly sees love as potentially turning him
into the debased Verdant, loving the vile enchantress Acrasia and
languishing in Spenser's Bower of Bliss; rather Gentleman's "man of
sense" is a new eighteenth-century man, content, and even
delighted, to bow to the "shrine of love."

This new Othello who loved to love was not born fully formed,
nor was his formation uncontested. In 1761, Victor commented
that "*Othello's Love* is excessive, even to the Degree of Dotage"
(*History* II 10).[19] Victor's comment indicates that, throughout the
period in which the new dominant man as lover emerged, a man's
love for a woman could still render him impotent in some eyes.[20]

However, as a commentary on Othello's love, Victor's assessment swam against the tide that brought in the new man. This new man is the Othello William Warburton saw in 1747 when he edited Shakespeare's complete works. Choosing between the quarto's "set" and the folio's "soft" in Othello's apology for his "rude" speech, Warburton chose "set," the quarto reading. His note explains, "This apology, [containing the word soft] if addressed to his *mistress*, had been well expressed. But what he wanted, in speaking before a *Venetian* Senate, was not the soft blandishments of speech, but the art and method of masculine eloquence" (291).²¹ Like Gentleman's "man of sense," Warburton's Othello should have a space for love in which he speaks sweetly and gently, and a space for business, in which his speech should be characterized by hard "method." Warburton's choice of the quarto's "set" was by no means universally adopted. But Warburton's own eloquence on the point reveals his eighteenth-century investment in separate spheres and also in Othello as a lover.

In 1748, an edition of *Othello* appeared in Dublin with an "Index of the Characters, Sentiments, Similes, Speeches and Descriptions" (100). The short index has four subheadings under the heading "Othello":

Othello, his Service of importance to the State, own'd by *Iago*   7
—owns himself of Royal Descent, and Love the sole motive of his
     marrying *Desdemona*   9
—seized and insulted by her Father   11
—accus'd by him before the Duke, he relates the whole progress
     of his Amour   14

The subheadings echo Warburton's and Gentleman's elevation of the lover Othello. Whereas these subheadings dignify him as royalty and as vital to Venetian security, the index focuses on Othello's relationship with Desdemona. And, according to the index, the purport of that marital relationship is not his jealousy or his murder of his wife, neither of which rate entries. Rather, the index highlights Othello the lover. It both purifies his love for Desdemona and reads this sole motive completely positively, linking it within one subheading to Othello's "Royal Descent." The index also seems to sympathize with his plight as a lover by indicating that Brabantio has insulted him. Finally, the index asks readers to attend to the scene that attracted Gentleman's and Warburton's comments, the scene in which Othello narrates the course of his love affair. Othello's courtship stories matter more to this index's Othello than any of his subsequent actions in the play. The Dublin edition's index presents Othello to its readers as the heroic eighteenth-century lover.

Desdemona's Kisses

In the early seventeenth century, there were two significantly different *Othello*s, the quarto text published in 1622 and the 1623 folio version of the play.[22] The folio text has about 160 more lines, and it does not contain the quarto's oaths. The folio text seems, therefore, to be some sort of revised text of the play, the oaths excised to make the play conform to the 1606 Profanity Act.[23] Virtually all modern editions of *Othello* use the added folio lines, but one apparent revision from the quarto to the folio has disturbed editors since Alexander Pope. In the quarto, in the middle of Othello's long speech explaining how he won Desdemona, he says, "My story being done,/She gave me for my pains a world of sighs." In the folio, Othello says, "My Storie being done,/She gaue me for my paines a world of kisses" (TLN 503–504; 1.3.157–158). In his 1709 *Works*, Rowe printed "kisses."[24] Fourteen years later, Pope noted, "It was kisses in the later editions. But this [sighs] is evidently the true reading: the lady had been forward indeed to give him a world of *kisses* upon the bare recital of his story, nor does it agree with the following lines" (491). All of the eighteenth-century editors after Pope followed his suit, and a number, including Warburton and Samuel Johnson, copied Pope's note as well.[25] The second clause after Pope's colon makes interpretive sense. In the rest of this speech, Othello seems to say that after the incident in question he still had to woo Desdemona. But the sense of Pope's interpretation does not fully explain its nearly universal adoption over the centuries. Rather, the story of that adoption is a story of what might be called, adapting Sedgwick, sexual-woman panic: the panic that Desdemona could be a sexual woman, "forward" enough to kiss Othello repeatedly.

The eighteenth-century Desdemona could not be sexually active enough to have given Othello "a world of kisses" before their marriage. That would make her, in Pope's words, "forward indeed." However, "kisses," as the recent *Norton Shakespeare* notes, is as credible as "sighs"; it just constructs a sexual Desdemona who, over the centuries, has made editors squirm. The footnote in the Norton edition comments, "It is hard to explain 'kisses' as a textual error; its plausibility depends on how forward one imagines Desdemona to be" (2110n.5).

Consciously or not, the Norton editor repeats Pope's term, "forward," for the Desdemona that the Norton edition, it seems, is prepared to imagine even where Pope and so many editors since him were not.

The eighteenth-century's consensus over "sighs" instead of "kisses" is a sign of the power of the aspect of the emerging heterosexual imaginary that has been much discussed in histories of gender: the desexualizing of dominant women.[26] And the concern over those "forward" "kisses" through the twentieth century is a sign of that imaginary's power over the next two centuries. In his 1886 New Variorum *Othello*, Horace Howard Furness printed "She gaue me for my paines a world of kisses," but his note has the same effect as printing "sighs" for "kisses." In that note, Furness copies Pope's comment and then remarks on it in brackets, "And yet we must remember that kissing in Elizabeth's time was not as significant as it is now. See the openness with which, in II, I, Cassio kisses Æmilia" (59n.182). Furness was a very careful reader of Shakespeare, but his comment shows that he shares Pope's investment in a desexualized Desdemona. Although Furness prints "kisses," he removes Desdemona's "kisses" from sexual suggestion by postulating a different standard of kissing, and then by offering Desdemona's kisses as equivalent to Cassio's greeting kiss to Æmilia. However, in that scene, Cassio excuses his kiss as "bold" (TLN 868; 2.1.99). In addition, the conversation between Iago and Othello at the beginning of act four about the hypothesized "kiss in private" between Cassio and Desdemona shows that kisses could always be sexually suspect even in "Elizabeth's time." Othello exclaims, "An vnauthoriz'd kisse?" (TLN 2374; 4.1.2) in response to Iago's offhand "to kisse in priuate." Surely Desdemona's "world of kisses" would have been unauthorized except by her lover.

The trajectory of those kisses through the twentieth-century Arden editions of the play is equally informative. M.R. Ridley, in 1958, prints "sighs." He has an extended footnote:

> *kisses* is as difficult to account for as to accept, and the motion of F's [the folio's] Desdemona would surely have blushed at herself. The word can hardly have been a misreading of *sighs*, however ill-written, yet it is hard to imagine anyone making the alteration deliberately. Perhaps the compositor had recently been setting a passage in which "world of kisses" occurred, and it stuck in his mind. (30n.159)

The emerging eighteenth-century heterosexual imaginary constructed the Desdemona that Brabantio wished was his daughter. In his note,

Ridley adopts Brabantio's language—"so still, and quiet, that her Motion/Blush'd at her selfe"—to describe the Desdemona his criticism creates. Ridley's blushing Desdemona is a sign that the desexualized dominant woman still holds court in his text. As an editor, he is hard-pressed to "imagine" that the word could be a compositor's mistake, since "sighs" and "kisses" do not resemble one another. In order to account for the Desdemona his common sense demands, however, Ridley can easily conjure up a fictional compositor with "kisses" on his mind. By 1996, after the rise and fall of the twentieth-century sexual revolution, Honigmann prints "sighs" with absolutely no commentary. Either Honigmann felt that the choice was self-evident or felt that, by the 1990s, the explanation for the choice would be almost embarrassing. Either possibility demonstrates the sway that the heterosexual imaginary being developed in the eighteenth century still holds over our own lives and stories.

"wench" and "wretch" in the Eighteenth Century

As we have seen, Othello's total loving investment in Desdemona made him a flawed and racially othered man in the early seventeenth century and a perfect man for the eighteenth century. This investment is epitomized in his aside about his wife, "Excellent wretch: Perdition catch my Soule/But I do loue thee: and when I loue thee not,/Chaos is come againe" (TLN 1691–1693; 3.3.90–92). The history of the rejection of the word "wretch" in this speech sketches in miniature ideas about femininity that helped to constitute the emerging heterosexual imaginary. In 1733, Theobald decided that Othello's use of "wretch" was utterly inappropriate and therefore must not be Shakespearean. Theobald emended "wretch" to "wench" because, he says, "*Wretch* can scarse be admitted to be used, unless in Compassion or Contempt . . . It is to be observ'd, that in SHAKESPEARE's time, *Wench*, *Lass*, and *Girl* were not used in that low and vulgar Acceptation as they are at this time of day; but very frequently with Dignity" (431). For examples of dignified uses of "wench," Theobald turns to other instances in *Othello* and to *Antony and Cleopatra*. Theobald's emendation was almost universally acclaimed and adopted throughout the century. In 1744, Thomas Hanmer adopted "wench." Echoing Theobald, Hanmer notes "the word *Wench* heretofore carried in it a sense no ways scornful or disparaging, such as modern times have annex'd to it: It signified a young woman, often an amiable woman, so that some have thought it a corruption only from the word *Venus*" (*Works of Mr. William Shakespeare* 488). Hanmer likewise refers to *Antony and Cleopatra* and to *Othello* and, one-upping Theobald in knowledge of early texts, also cites John Fletcher's *The Bloody Brother*. Gentleman agrees in his notes that "we think *wench* much more eligible than *wretch*" (44). The *Othello* edition published in 1753 uses "wench," as does the 1761 *Othello*, and the *Othello* published in 1771. All of these editor/critics were devoted to a love relationship between Othello and Desdemona that would preclude his calling her anything that might be construed as derogatory (although the *Othello*s published separately may be reprints without editorial attention behind them); and all of them found "wretch" vastly more derogatory than "wench" and therefore nonsensical.[27]

Theobald finds it inconceivable that Othello could regard Desdemona with "Compassion or Contempt"; however, his search for a substitute for "wretch" reveals more than just his investment in Othello's unambivalent loving regard for his wife. The word "wench" is only one of the bevy of Renaissance words for women that encodes the fluid relationship under the homosocial imaginary between women and whores. Like "mistress," the usage of which I discussed in chapter two, "wench" in early-seventeenth-century English slides easily between categories that did not become delineated until the eighteenth century.[28] Thus Falstaff can say of Mistress Quickly, "and is not my Hostesse of the Tauerne a most sweet Wench," meaning a sexually active woman, and Prospero can respond to Miranda's question with "Well demanded, wench," meaning a young girl (*1Henry IV* TLN 153–154; *Tempest* TLN 244). Othello certainly means "young woman" when, after the revelations following Desdemona's death, he laments, "Oh, ill-Starr'd wench,/Pale as thy Smocke" (TLN 3572–3573; 5.2.270–271). But Iago's address to Æmilia, "A good wench, giue it me" (TLN 1952; 3.3.317), is much more ambiguous, since he regards all women including his wife as potential or realized whores. Wench could, indeed, signify in the purified way that Theobald desires, but it was always dangerously close to the meaning he wishes to deny — the "low and vulgar Acceptation as they are at this time of day." Theobald's own examples fly in the face of his purifying desires. Agrippa calls Cleopatra "Royall Wench" and continues "She made great *Cæsar* lay his Sword to bed,/He ploughed her and she cropt" (TLN 941–943; 2.2.232–234). Since this is a direct sexual reference, it hardly affords Theobald the dignity he desires in Othello's speech.[29] However, given Theobald's immersion in the emerging heterosexual imaginary, all these instances could be subsumed under the understanding that Othello must have meant to call his wife a beautiful, virtuous woman.

Hanmer's discussion of "wench" is equally ideologically informative. Like Theobald, he attributes the "scornful" and "disparaging" senses of "wench" to "modern times." Remarkably, in his defense of the word's former innocence, he observes that "some have thought it a corruption only from the word *Venus*." In his "only," Hanmer constructs a chaste goddess of love that Shakespeare would not have recognized. From the evidence of both Shakespeare's Venus in the narrative poem *Venus and Adonis* and his banishment of Venus from *The Tempest*'s chaste wedding masque, Shakespeare imagined a classically lascivious Venus, a Venus akin to Cleopatra, the "Royal Wench."[30] That Hanmer can posit a goddess of love without lust is a sign of his embrace of a world in which women are not automatically seductresses.[31]

In the world of Fletcher's *Bloody Brother*, Shakespeare's world, the lines are never drawn in this way: "wench" and Venus simultaneously denote womanhood and sensual abandon. Hanmer cites Fletcher's text to justify his choice of "wench," but that text shares with Shakespeare the homosocial imaginary's vision of women. In *The Bloody Brother*, the murderous Rollo and his brother Otto have a virtuous mother, Sophia. Aubrey, Rollo's kinsman, taking probity's part in the nasty fraternal dispute between Rollo and Otto, exclaims of Sophia, "May never womans tongue/Hereafter be accus'd, for this ones Goodnesse" (C3). Later in the play, Aubrey again lauds Sophia: "O womans goodnesse never to be equall'd,/May the most sinfull creatures of thy sex,/ But kneeling at thy monument, rise saints" (D4v). Gisbert and Aubrey, both approved characters in a Manichean play, point to Sophia's singularity. "Womans tongue" generally is flawed and can only be redeemed by the example of this "one"; Sophia's virtue is "never to be equall'd"; but singular as it is, it will redeem the mass of "sinfull creatures" who define the remainder of womankind. Hanmer's "wench" is a world apart from Fletcher's seventeenth-century notion of womanhood.

Probably aware that "wench" was a problematic substitute, when he reaches this line, Johnson abjures the emendation. He provides Theobald's note to "excellent wretch" and then comments,

the meaning of the word *wretch*, is not generally understood. It is now, in some parts of *England*, a term of the softest and fondest tenderness. It expresses the utmost degree of amiableness, joined with an idea, which perhaps all tenderness includes, of feebleness, softness, and want of protection. *Othello*, considering *Desdemona* as excelling in beauty and virtue, soft and timorous by her sex, and by her situation absolutely in his power, calls her *Excellent Wretch*. (391)

Johnson wants to keep Othello's language, and he also wants that language to confirm his interpretation of Desdemona. For Johnson, the word "wretch" can speak both to Othello's love and to Desdemona's delicacy. Resorting to regional language differences, Johnson asserts that although it seems harsh to many (less-informed critics), "wretch" is actually a term of endearment, even an exceptional term, expressing "the utmost degree of amiableness." And, for Johnson, the term fortuitously combines the most perfect love with the acknowledgment of "feebleness" and "softness." In the word "wretch," Johnson sees Othello, the heroic lover, and Desdemona, the mild, desexualized wife.

A Fair Wife or a Fair Face?: Cassio's Beauty

Neither Desdemona's "kisses" nor Othello's "wretch" can properly be called a textual crux. Each of these words was disputed in the eighteenth century, but neither presents problems of meaning in themselves. However, *Othello* contains some famous cruxes, including the point early in the first scene where Iago calls Cassio "A Fellow almost damn'd in a faire Wife" (TLN 23; 1.1.20). Since Cassio is so evidently unmarried, in the late twentieth century, commentators generally dismissed Iago's comment as probably a slip either by the author or a compositor,[32] but in the eighteenth century Iago's line created a firestorm. Before 1733, individual editions of *Othello* printed the line as it appears in the quarto and folio.[33] Once again, Theobald was the first editor to object to Iago's line, but, after Theobald's 1733 *Works*, the line was seen as immensely troubling. All of the emendations of the eighteenth century failed to produce an entirely satisfactory explanation for Iago's comment. A 1774 letter of David Garrick's reads, "I have receiv'd another letter from Mr. Swan with his remarks upon that difficult passage in Othello—*A fellow almost damn'd in a fair wife*" (923). Garrick's and Swan's dismayed exchange follows forty years of scrambling by editors to explain Cassio's "faire Wife" away. In a 1764 individual edition of *Othello*, Halhed Garland got rid of the problem by cutting "almost damn'd in a fair Wife" completely. However, most eighteenth-century editors after Theobald, intent on constructing an infallible author, chose instead to emend the line to say what they believed Shakespeare must have meant. Their emendations and the commentary surrounding them point to the uneven erasure under the emerging heterosexual imaginary of two commonplaces of the homosocial imaginary: the association between female fairness and damnation and the discourse of male beauty.

Even though, given the grammar of Iago's speech, the referent for "almost damn'd in a fair Wife" seems to be Cassio, a number of editors decided that the lines must somehow describe the married Iago. Theobald explains that Shakespeare followed Cinthio's novel

> in giving the villanous Ensign a fair Wife . . . And it is a very good Reason for rejecting *Iago*, because he was a married Man, and might be thought too much govern'd by his Wife to be capable of this Charge. And this was a natural Objection in an unmarried General, as *Othello* was when he chose his Officers. *Iago* therefore was the Fellow *almost damn'd in a fair Wife*: which is an Expression obscure enough to deserve a short Explantion. The Poet means, *Iago* had so beautiful a Wife, that she was his *Heaven on Earth*; that he *idoliz'd* her; and forgot to think of Happiness in an After-State, as placing all his Views of Bliss in the single Enjoyment of her. In this sense, *Beauty*, when it can so seduce and ingross a Man's Thoughts, may be said *almost to damn him.* (373)

Theobald's emendation satisfied him completely on one count. Iago is a married man, and since Othello was unmarried when he (in Theobald's construction of the speech) made the comment, Iago's marital status was a legitimate cause for suspicion. In Theobald's explanation, we can see two aspects of the homosocial imaginary that remained residually active through Theobald's time: Wilkinson's strictures about the joys of marriage not being preferable to the joys of heaven (chapter four), and the concern over mixing women and business. This latter concern remains residually active today, especially in the realms of the military and of sports.[34] But Theobald's explanation was still troublesome, as the accretion of his own and other commentaries on it reveal. For even given the unmarried Othello's suspicion of marriage (before he knew better?), how was Theobald to explain the "obscure" "expression" "almost damn'd in a fair wife"? To handle this problem, Theobald invokes Wilkinson's religious context. Iago's obsession with his fair wife, his tendency to worship at her shrine, made him forget his debt to worship only God.

Theobald must invoke this context in order to account for a phrase that could hardly have puzzled anyone in the early seventeenth century. As in medieval texts, innumerable texts from the late sixteenth and early seventeenth centuries allude to the damnation that can result from having a "fair wife." Donne could very easily posit the impossibility of finding a woman both "true and fair." Shakespeare also creates characters and situations based on this identification of fairness and infidelity. The identification of fairness and infidelity motivates Hamlet's and Lear's misogynist rages, as it does Posthumus's, Leontes's, and Claudio's suspicions. That association animates Rosalind's and Beatrice's humor, and it is confirmed in the actions of some of Shakespeare's women, notably Tamora, Cressida, Cleopatra, and Cymbeline's Queen.[35] All of Shakespeare's comic and tragic heroines must contend with this association, even if only to prove it false. Although, and even because, it is so often contested and found to be groundless, the association of female beauty and male hell is part of the common sense of Renaissance England. What is astonishing is not so much the ubiquity of that association in Renaissance England, but its invisibility under the emerging heterosexual imaginary.

Due to that invisibility, Theobald's invention was very widely taken as *Othello*'s truth. Warburton's note to "a Fellow almost damn'd in a fair Wife" reads: "These are the words of *Othello*, (which *Iago* in this relation repeats,) and signify, that a *Florentine* was an unfit person for command, as being always a slave to a fair wife; which was the case of *Iago*" (276). Although there is absolutely no evidence in *Othello* that Iago was ever a slave to Æmilia, and although the play even offers abundant evidence to the contrary, Warburton accepts Theobald's invention unconditionally. And Warburton was not alone in thinking that Theobald's explanation accounted for the puzzling line. In his *Revisal*, Benjamin Heath comments on the line, "I apprehend the meaning of Othello's reflection on Iago is, that, notwithstanding he had a fair wife, he had little chance of going to heaven, as by the watchfulness of his jealousy he made it extremely difficult for her to do her part towards sending him thither" (551–552). Heath slightly modifies Theobald's invention. Without questioning Theobald's allotment of the "fair wife" to Iago, Heath spins his own fantasy to explain what he, with Theobald, sees as Othello's words in Iago's mouth. Heath's explanation involves woman's place as the guardian of male spiritual virtue, a commonplace of the later eighteenth and nineteenth centuries. Other eighteenth-century editions of *Othello* accept Theobald without comment, using typographical signs to indicate that the "fair wife" belongs to Iago.[36]

In his 1744 edition of Shakespeare's works, Hanmer came up with another way to solve the problem of Cassio's "fair wife." He lets Iago's line refer to Cassio by substituting the word "phyz" [face] for "wife." In the note to this new word he says that "wife" must be a mistake since Cassio is clearly unmarried, "on the other hand his Beauty is often hinted at, which it is natural enough for other rough soldiers to treat with scorn and ridicule" (440). Theobald's invention made Hanmer uncomfortable, but he would not countenance an apparent Shakespearean error that could not be corrected. To make sense of Iago's epithet for Cassio, Hanmer invented another scenario that satisfied him and many of his eighteenth-century colleagues (and presumably their readers). He asserts that the cause of Cassio's troubles—his potential damnation—is his physical beauty, since, he says, "it is natural enough for other rough fellows" to "ridicule" and "scorn" a man for physical beauty. Like Theobald's, Hanmer's suggestion was frequently adopted, especially after the middle of the eighteenth century. A 1753 *Othello* says that Cassio was "almost damn'd in a fair phyz," as does an *Othello* whose publication date says 1755, and an *Othello* published in 1761. In his collected works, Edward Capell substitutes "fair face" for "fair wife."

Once again, in Hanmer's emendation, we can see a crucial shift in "common sense" between the early-seventeenth-century homosocial imaginary and the heterosexual imaginary emerging in the eighteenth century. Under the homosocial imaginary, and crucially in Shakespeare's plays and poetry, Cassio's "fair face" would not be an object of laughter, even for "rough fellows." Throughout Shakespeare's canon, and in the literary texts surrounding that canon, male beauty is admired, praised, and very often associated with roughness, if roughness is defined as military might or valor. The examples are so numerous that they indicate the common sense of Shakespeare's culture. For instance, Sebastian in *Twelfth Night* is clearly very pretty. Repeating Sebastian's (Viola's) assertion of gentility to herself, Olivia says of him, "I am a Gentleman. Ile be sworne thou art./Thy tongue, thy face, thy limbes, actions, and spirit,/Do giue thee fiue-fold blazon" (TLN 586–588; 1.5.261–263). Sebastian has a fair face (so fair that he cannot be distinguished from the fair Viola), but he is certainly rough, as he demonstrates in his treatment of Toby. No one in the play is laughing at his beauty, not even the rough seaman Antonio. When Antonio believes that Sebastian has deserted him he laments that Sebastian's beauty conceals a false heart: "Vertue is beauty, but the beauteous euill/Are empty trunkes ore-flourish'd by the deuill"

(TLN 1889–1890; 4.1.334–335). Sebastian is the "beauteous euill" who has stolen his heart. In *Romeo and Juliet*, Capulet's wife urges Juliet to "Read ore the volume of young *Paris* face, / And find delight, writ there with Beauties pen" (TLN 427–428; 1.3.84–85). Paris, like Sebastian, shows his bravery later in the play, as he draws his sword on Romeo, whom he believes is desecrating Juliet's tomb; and no one in the play laughs at Paris's pretty face. The presumably male narrator of *Venus and Adonis* praises "rose-cheeked" Adonis's beauty as lavishly as does Venus:

> At [Venus's words] Adonis smiles as in disdaine,
> That in ech cheeke appeares a prettie dimple;
> Loue made those hollowes, if him selfe were slaine,
> He might be buried in a tombe so simple. (241–244)

Cupid himself has crafted Adonis's gorgeous dimples as his final resting place, but the poem never indicates that the friends with whom Adonis plans to hunt the boar are guffawing at his fairness. Of course, Shakespeare's sonnets abound with praise of the young man's "louelinesse" (4.1). In Shakespeare's texts, men may suspect beautiful men and boys of seducing susceptible women, but they seldom associate male beauty with timidity, nor do they hesitate to praise it. Just as, as we have seen so frequently, the language of love between men is unexceptionable in the early seventeenth century, so male beauty is not divorced from roughness.

By 1744, however, the association between male beauty and weakness had become quite tenable. As the eighteenth century progressed, commonplaces of the heterosexual imaginary were entering dominant discourse, although they had not taken hold as firmly as the historical evidence on behavior suggests they might have. Despite the emergence of a subculture that we could today label homosexual and the vastly increased prosecutions for sodomy in early-eighteenth-century London, literary texts from the period do not manifest the suspicious fear of both love language between men and male beauty that today makes men (including even very young boys) laugh uncomfortably. The fearful homophobia that features so prominently in today's heterosexual imaginary was only emergent.[37] Hanmer's "fair phyz" suggestion is a sign of this emergence, but it is not an indication of dominance. In Johnson's and Steevens's edition's variorum-like collection of commentary on "almost damned in a fair wife," they cite

Thomas Tyrwhitt's *Observations and Conjectures, &c. printed at Oxford,* 1766, which includes the commentary, "The great difficulty is to understand in what sense any man can be said to be *almost damn'd in a fair wife; or fair phyz,* as Sir T. Hanmer proposes to read. I cannot find any ground for supposing that either the one or the other have been reputed to be damnable sins in any religion" (358–359). Tyrwhitt cannot make sense of Shakespeare's text, but neither can he make sense of Hanmer's emendation. For him, neither a "fair wife" nor a "fair face" would damn a man. He prefers to read the line "almost damn'd in a fair life," since he says, the gospel so judges men of whom all others speak well (3). In the middle to late eighteenth century the ground has shifted enough so that the connection between female fairness and male hell has loosened, but it has not shifted sufficiently to universally link male fairness with homophobic damnation.

At least in *Othello* texts during the long eighteenth century, the shift to automatically suspecting male–male physical contact that accompanied the suspicion of the discourse of male beauty happened quite late in the century. Throughout eighteenth-century *Othello* texts, editors, and critics do not worry about Iago's story about what happened while he and Cassio were sharing a bed:

> And then (Sir) would he gripe, and wring my hand:
> Cry, o sweet Creature: then kisse me hard,
> As if he pluckt vp kisses by the rootes
> That grew vpon my lippes, laid his Leg ore my Thigh,
> And sigh, and kisse. (TLN 2068–2072; 3.3.423–427)

Many editions retain the lines without a comment, and neither Griffith nor Lennox have anything to say about them.[38] But, toward the end of the century, the line that includes the word "thigh" was expendable. A 1764 acting edition cuts "then laid his Leg ore my Thigh." In the Bell edition (1777) with Gentleman's notes, "then laid his Leg ore my Thigh" is also missing. By the early nineteenth century, even more of this speech was cut on stage. In the Kemble revision, published in 1823, the lines "then Laid his Leg ore my Thigh, and sigh, and kisse" are missing from the play altogether. The heterosexual imaginary emerging in the eighteenth century resembled our own, but not completely. It tolerated a physical and emotional closeness between men that became anathema only in later in history.[39]

Othello's Defunct Appetite

The eighteenth-century reaction to another famous, stubborn crux in *Othello* indicates one aspect of the twentieth-century heterosexual imaginary that, as we have seen, entered dominant discourse much earlier in history: the link between masculinity and male (hetero)sexual potency. That stubborn crux appears near the beginning of a speech we looked at earlier in this chapter, the speech in which Othello denies that "light wing'd Toyes / Of feather'd *Cupid*" will ever blind his reason. In that speech, Othello asks the Duke to permit Desdemona to travel with him to Cyprus. He assures the Duke that he does not ask the favor for improper purposes:

> I therefore beg it not
> To please the pallate of my Appetite:
> Nor to comply with heat the yong affects
> In my defunct, and proper satisfaction,
> But to be free, and bounteous to her minde.
> (TLN 611–615; 1.3.162–166)

The syntax of this part of the speech is confusing and will remain so even with modern punctuation and Capell's substitution of "me defunct" for "my defunct," a substitution that is widely adopted to this day.[40] With or without the emendation, Othello seems to be claiming that he lacks sexual heat. In Shakespeare's world, this claim would impress the Duke, since it places Othello in the class of dominant men not controlled by their appetites. However, this claim rubbed up against the new eighteenth-century equation of masculinity with (hetero)sexual potency and appetite. A number of early-eighteenth-century editions, including Pope's, leave the passage as it stands in the folio and the quarto.[41] But, by the 1730s, the new equation seems to have put pressure on editors. Again, Theobald was the first to try to make (new common) sense of the passage. In order to do that, Theobald substituted "my distinct" for "my defunct." His note reads,

As this has been all along hitherto printed and stop'd [punctuated], it seems to me a Period of as stubborn Nonsense, as the Editors have obtruded upon poor *Shakespeare* throughout his whole Works. What a preposterous Creature is this *Othello* made, to fall in Love with, and marry, a fine young Lady, when *Appetite* and *Heat*, and *proper Satisfaction* are *dead* and *defunct* in him! (For, *defunct* signifies nothing else, that I know of, either primitively or metaphorically:) But if we may take

Othello's own Word in the Affair, when he speaks for himself, he was
not reduc'd to this fatal unperforming State. (396–397)

Theobald's outrage delineates his beliefs about marriage and male
sexual desire. In his mind, and in the minds of the critics who followed
him, the institution of marriage and the emotional/physiological
state of male sexual excitement for females are inextricably linked.
What, after all, would a man marry a "fine young Lady" for if he could
not become excited by her and perform sexually? Although not all
eighteenth-century critics would adopt Theobald's emendation,
none after Theobald could accept that Othello's appetite might be
"defunct"; Othello's "defunct" affects stuck in the craw of the emerging heterosexual imaginary. It could not countenance a claim by
Othello, an avatar of its new masculinity, that would sabotage
Othello's male identity.

Theobald's substitution of "distinct" for "defunct" proved popular
in the second half of the century. Hanmer accepts "distinct" and renders the lines in question as, "Nor to comply with heat [affects the
young,]/In my [distinct] and proper satisfaction" (457); (Hanmer's
"brackets" indicating his changes).[42] Although Hanmer's preferred
syntax seems at least as confusing as Shakespeare's, he considered it
superior to the folio's and quarto's. Alone among the editors in the
middle of the eighteenth century, Johnson read the passage to denote
"the passions of youth which I have now outlived," but his collabora-
tor, Steevens, could not let "defunct" stand.[43] Steevens comments,
"Theobald has observed the impropriety of making Othello confess,
that all youthful passions were *defunct* in him, and Hanmer's reading
may, I think, be received with only a slight alteration. I would read
'I beg it not,/To please the palate of my appetite,/Nor to comply with
heat, *and* young affects,/In my *distinct* and proper satisfaction;/But to
be,' &c" (389). Although they disputed the details, Steevens, Theobald,
and Hanmer agreed that "defunct" was impossible.

Critical solutions to Othello's "defunct" "affects" became ever
more creative as the century went on, extending to new definitions of
the adjective "defunct" and even to shuffling of the speech's lines.
Warburton agreed with Steevens's sentiment but managed to retain
"defunct" by redefining it. Warburton's note to "defunct and proper
Satisfaction" reads, "i. e. With that heat and new affections which the
indulgence of my appetite has raised and created. This is the meaning
of *defunct*, which has made all the difficulty of the passage" (298).
Somehow Warburton interpreted "defunct" to mean the opposite of

dead. In keeping with Theobald's common sense, if not with his emendation, Warburton makes Othello refer to an increase in sexual desire after his encounter with Desdemona, rather than to a lack of desire. Such a lack seemed unconscionable to these editors. Hugh Blair agreed completely, repeating Warburton's interpretation in his own edition (*Works of Shakespear* 208). Tyrwhitt showed even more creativity than Warburton, using two methods to get rid of the problem with "defunct." He switches line 265 and 266, so that the lines read: "Nor to comply with heat, the young affects;/But to be free and bounteous to her mind,/In my defunct and proper satisfaction." At this point, he offers another interpretation for "defunct": "And [I] would recommend it to consideration, whether the word *defunct* (which would be the only remaining difficulty) is not capable of a signification, drawn from the primitive sense of its Latin original, which could very well agree with the context" (5). If by "its Latin original," Tyrwhitt is referring to the past participle of *defungi*, he is using "defunct" here to mean something like "performed." Even after removing "defunct" from its indecent referent "affects," Tyrwhitt wanted Othello to boast of his sexual performance, instead of denying his sexual desire. The eighteenth-century Othello was a man with strong sexual desires, and, rather than debasing him and draining his potency, those desires made him masculine and potent. The editors disagree on the particulars of his speech, but they were virtually united in linking Othello's masculinity to his sexual heat.

Conclusion: *Othello*'s Decline and the Future of the Heterosexual Imaginary

By the middle of the twentieth century, *Othello*'s reputation had declined precipitously from Shakespeare's greatest tragedy to the poor cousin of the monumental plays, *Hamlet*, *Macbeth*, and *Lear*; but by the end of the eighteenth century much of *Othello*'s essential cultural work in relation to the emergence of heterosexuality had been done. The reasons for *Othello*'s decline are certainly overdetermined. Perhaps the Victorian revulsion at the play's open sexual language played a part (Rosenberg). More than possibly, with the hardening of racial categories and the dominance of racism, critics had difficulty countenancing a black hero of Shakespeare's greatest tragedy, however cleansed of his "Negro" identity. We can measure *Othello*'s decline in A.C. Bradley's turn-of-the-century lectures on Shakespeare.

Though admitting that *Othello* is the "most painfully exciting and the most terrible" of Shakespeare's tragedies, Bradley suggests that the play evokes feelings "of confinement to a comparatively narrow world" (176, 181). Bradley feels compelled to ask if there is

> a justification for the fact—a fact it certainly is—that some readers, while acknowledging, of course, the immense power of *Othello*, and even admitting that it is dramatically perhaps Shakespeare's greatest triumph, still regard it with a certain distaste, or, at any rate, hardly allow it a place in their minds beside *Hamlet*, *King Lear* and *Macbeth*? (183)

Bradley concludes that *Othello* "has not equally with the other three the power of dilating the imagination by vague suggestion of huge universal powers working in the world of individual fate and passion. It is, in a sense, less 'symbolic' " (185). After Bradley, one can document a twentieth-century trivialization of the play as "domestic."[44] Subsequently, in the late twentieth century, the feminist reaction against this trivialization produced essential criticism of gender relations in the play. If race played as well into *Othello*'s decline, race has also recently been a fabulously productive critical angle on the play. However, it is startling that the aspect of the play that made it less interesting for a critic such as A.C. Bradley was its major public selling point in the eighteenth century. *Othello*, unlike any other Shakespeare play, focused on a married man's love and desire for his wife. Seen through eighteenth-century eyes, Othello and Desdemona's relationship was exactly what the emerging heterosexual imaginary required; and, for that reason, it captured that century's imagination.

This history of *Othello* criticism provides yet another view of the contributions Shakespeare reception has made to the heterosexual imaginary. As this history shows, heterosexuality's assumptions easily became so naturalized as to dictate the truth of texts from the past, even when those texts directly contradict those assumptions. But nothing is forcing us to read the past or the future through heterosexuality's lens. Žižek says that an "ideology really succeeds when even the facts which at first sight contradict it start to function as arguments in its favour" (*Sublime* 49). For the most part, this is how nineteenth- and twentieth-century Shakespeare reception worked in relation to the ideology of heterosexuality. Restoration authors saw that Shakespeare contradicted what Restoration audiences believed about sex and men and women, so they emended his works to make them accord with those beliefs. As heterosexuality became really successful, in Žižek's terms, Shakespeare did not need to be fixed any more; and the Restoration's efforts to fix his works became twentieth-century trash. That trash, as we have seen, however, is abundant evidence that Shakespeare texts and Renaissance litera-ture are indeed "the facts which at first sight contradict" heterosexuality. I hope in this book to have contributed to the ongo-ing project of making that ideology and its complex and uneven development a bit more visible.

NOTES

Introduction

1. The heterosexuality of the "it" in Porter's song is indicated by lines such as, "folks in Siam do it; think of Siamese twins" and "why ask if shad do it; waiter bring me shad roe." Of course, the song leaves other options open: "some say in Boston even beans do it." Noel Coward's new lyrics for "Let's Do It" pursue homosexual implications (see Hoare 288, 417). See also Clum.

2. For a crucial expansion on Foucault's formulation, see Arnold Davidson.

3. See, among others, Bly, Bredbeck, DiGangi, Dollimore, Goldberg, Guy-Bray, Haggerty, Lanser, Masten, Orgel, Rambuss, Sinfield, Bruce Smith, Stallybrass, Traub, and James Grantham Turner; also see the collections edited by Goldberg, and Fradenburg and Freccero.

4. For historical work, see Abelove, Bray, Chauncy, Duberman et al., Halperin, Jonathan Ned Katz, and Trumbach; theoretical work includes Berlant, Bersani, Butler, Arnold Davidson, Rubin, Eve Kosofsky Sedgwick, and Michael Warner.

5. Trumbach argues forcefully for the appearance of modern heterosexuality in the late seventeenth century. He is not concerned with representation or with cause.

6. See Traub, *Renaissance*, especially 265–270, and Rackin "Foreign Country." In relation to the Middle Ages, see especially Schultz and Lochrie.

7. See Lochrie's important discussion on the natural and the normal (*Heterosyncracies*, especially xxii–xxiii).

8. I am using "dominant" and "emergent" as Raymond Williams defines these terms. See *Marxism* 121–127.

9. This, of course, is not the only function that these rewritings served. See Dobson, Marsden (*Re-Imagined*), Strier (*Resistant*), Taylor.

10. The discounting of rank as ultimately significant has also been true in relation to texts from the Middle Ages — see Schultz's work particularly.

11. See de Grazia ("Ideology") and Jones's and Stallybrass's work for the significance of possessions (property and objects) in relation to identity in the Renaissance.

12. The most powerful attempt to link the sexual license that appears in representations of the "lower stratum" to a general cultural celebration of sex appears in James Grantham Turner's work. Turner suggests that "The flourishing of libertine verse in the Restoration, brought to a gamy height by Rochester and his peers, had thus been prepared in the 'festive-violent' lower stratum, where obscene text and riotous gesture became equivalent, and transgressive verbal expression was 'licenced' by a ritual-performative context" (*Libertines* 55). I am suggesting quite a different relationship between early performance that lampoons and lambastes men for sexual misconduct and Restoration celebratory performance of sexual misconduct. The skimmington rites that Turner discusses (following the work of critics such as David Underdown) exist in an essentially sex-negative atmosphere. Their "celebrations" may exaggerate the penis and the vagina, but they do this in the service of punishment and humiliation. Rochester and his peers, in contrast, exaggerate for the purpose of celebration.

13. See, for an example of homogenization, Reay, who opens his textbook, *Popular Cultures in England 1550–1750*, with a chapter on "Sexualities."

14. On Donne's place within the homosocial imaginary, see Bach "(Re)placing John Donne."

15. On the controversy, see Henderson and McManus.

16. See Laqueur, and see Paster for crucial qualifications of Laqueur's thesis. See also Breitenberg and Schoenfeldt.

17. See Orgel and Fisher.

18. The first quotation comes from the Thomas Middleton play *The Phoenix* (C3v), the second from Middleton's *Blurt, Master-Constable* (C4v).

19. The knight calls the jeweler's wife "Revenue" and she calls him "Pleasure."

20. The evidence Traub cites from women's letters indicates that the English Renaissance allowed also for a very developed, unabashed love language between women (*Renaissance* 184–185).

21. See Orgel's chapter 2 in *Impersonations*. See also Belsey's *Shakespeare*.

22. See Hammond's discussion of the overlap between the words "friend" and "lover" in English Renaissance texts.

23. On the category of service, see Burnett.

24. See Burnett and Dolan (*Dangerous*).

25. See "Axiomatic" in *Epistemology* (246–250). In the same piece, Sedgwick warns about assumptions that there is one thing called homosexuality: "an unfortunate side effect of this move [historicizing sexuality] has been to implicitly underwrite the notion that 'homosexuality as we conceive of it today' itself comprises a coherent definitional field rather than a space of overlapping, contradictory, and conflictual definitional forces" (261). I take her point even though I would seem to be violating it when I keep writing about heterosexuality as if it is one

thing that can be known. But I think that, unlike homosexuality—that thing or things that has been around for about a hundred years—which has never been hegemonic, the heterosexual imaginary is one knowable thing, because of its hegemonic force. This is certainly not to say that it isn't contradictory—all hegemonies and ideologies are (think of American capitalism). It also is not to say that sex between a woman and a man is one knowable thing at all. See also Lochrie's introduction to *Heterosyncracies*.

26. I am using "hegemony" in Gramsci's sense. See his discussion of Croce (195). See also Raymond Williams's elaboration (*Marxism* 108–114). Žižek uses, and I will be using, the term "apparatuses" following Althusser's seminal formulation in his essay, "Ideology and Ideological State Apparatuses."

27. See Lochrie's similar list, *Heterosyncrasies* xiii.

28. Each of the items in this list should have the implicit qualification "mainstream."

29. Audre Lorde writes, "Traditionally, in american society, it is the members of oppressed, objectified groups who are expected to stretch out and bridge the gap between the actualities of our lives and the consciousness of our oppressor. For in order to survive, those of us for whom oppression is as American as apple pie have always had to be watchers, to become familiar with the language and manners of the oppressor, even sometimes adopting them for some illusion of protection" (114).

30. See Berlant's point, "how many times have I asked my own students to explain why, when there are so many people, only one plot counts as 'life' (first comes love, then . . .)?" (286).

31. On whiteness, see Dyer; on dominion, see Bach "Bearbaiting."

32. That battle is taking place on all fronts today: welfare legislation, the child care issue, and more prosaically but perhaps as importantly in the representational realm of children's magazines, television, and movies.

33. See Richlin's work and Halperin's response to that work ("Forgetting") for the debate about the sexual picture in the classical world.

34. For the differences between marriage and heterosexuality in the Middle Ages, see Schultz's work as well as Lochrie. This understanding of the historicity of marriage is filtering into general consciousness. See Shumway's review in the *Chronicle of Higher Education*: "Frye's argument about Greek comedy is that it's a celebration of community, and that marriage is a rite of renewal. By the time you get to the 19th century, we no longer think of marriage and weddings especially as having that function. They have become deeply personal. There is some evidence from historical studies that, whereas in earlier periods, weddings were almost always a celebration open to the community, they became increasingly private in the 19th century."

35. On *Othello*, see chapter 5. See Bergeron.
36. See Masten 71.
37. For one example, see Burton's dependence throughout *The Anatomy of Melancholy* on Augustine.
38. Burton, a devout Protestant vicar and rector as well as author, in his long address to the reader that prefaces *The Anatomy of Melancholy*, describes a perfect Protestant state in which "Murder, adultery, shall be punished by death" (105). (He is following Alfred's laws.) When Parliament took power in the Interregnum and instituted a Protestant government, it passed the Adultery Act of May 1650. This act, instituting the death penalty for adultery, may have been an attack on the Ranters.
39. See also Rubin, "Traffic," and Goldberg, *Sodometries* 69–70 on the issue of cultural differences.
40. See *Marxism and Literature*, when he used the terms "dominant," "residual," and "emergent."
41. McKeon does a nice job discussing the conflicts between historians on the presence or absence of the nuclear family in the English Renaissance (*Origins*). See also my "Homosocial Imaginary." What is most significant for the arguments I am advancing in this book is that no literature in the period shows us anything like a modern nuclear family.
42. Left out of this list are all the possibilities with all the animals, all the possibilities with objects, and whatever else people might think of. See Sedgwick, "Axiomatic."
43. Again, see McKeon on nobility and *virtu* (*Origins*). Of course, Christianity also challenged this belief. This idea was continually under assault in the Middle Ages.
44. See McKeon for an analysis of the historical process by which "regard for status . . . is subsumed under and accommodated to the more dominant and insistent regard for financial income and occupational identity" (McKeon, *Origins* 163). Bray describes the material contributions to this shift: changes in the architecture of great houses and shifts in where men slept (*Friend* 210).
45. See Sommerville for the collective effect of these on English religious culture.
46. See Bray's comment on the abandonment of traditional friendship: "The Enlightenment put aside this traditional ethic with contempt and put in its place a Fraternity that it claimed would be 'universal,' 'rational,' even 'scientific'" (*Friend* 304).
47. When later English Renaissance people looked to their monarchs for examples, they saw a chaste queen (Elizabeth) and a king with little interest in women (James I). Charles I and II, in contrast, showed their people kings devoted in their different ways to women. See Dolan, *Whores*, especially chapter 2 on Charles I.
48. See MacPherson.

49. See Pateman.
50. See Laqueur.
51. See Howard and Rackin on the rise of rape.
52. On the former, see Burnett; on the latter see Schiebinger. On the demographic crisis in the late seventeenth century, see also McKeon, *Origins* 153. Maximillian E. Novak says that "during the 1660's economists had disputed the utility of monogamy for the mercantilist state if it might be demonstrated that polygamy could produce more people and hence more wealth" ("Margery" 5).
53. See Abelove and Trumbach for theories about shifts in sexual practices.
54. Among the interesting rewritten plays for a history of heterosexuality that I have not had room in this book to pursue are the many rewrites of Shakespeare's history plays. See Crowne, Philips, Theophilous Cibber, Hill, Kenrick.
55. Again, see "Axiomatic" in *Epistemology*.
56. See Bly, *Queer*, for a foray into one subculture in London in the early seventeenth century.
57. On that analogy, see Kennedy's introduction.
58. The real difference here is in the way drinking was often linked in Shakespeare's time with effeminacy. For a history of ideas related to drinking, excess, and moderation, see Scodel.
59. Pollak's histories of the words "prude" and "coquette" are also pertinent (66).
60. See de Grazia and Stallybrass for the problems with the word "original" when talking about Shakespeare's texts. Their essay "Materiality" is essential reading.
61. See Williams, *Keywords* ("sex"), for a relevant history.
62. The wonderful essay on *King Lear* by de Grazia outlines the costs of using the term "early modern." She also gives a history of periodization that makes the term "Renaissance" a problem as well.

Chapter 1

The Homosocial *King Lear*: Sex, Men, and Women before the Valorization of Lust and Greed

1. Unlike chastity, service is a much more conditional ideal in the play. The play certainly adores Kent's service, but it frequently questions where service should begin and end. In contrast, *King Lear* never questions where chastity should begin and end. On service in the period see Burnett and Neill, *Putting*; also see the discussion of "domestic" tragedies in chapter 4.

2. "Renaissance Christian" is only a shorthand term for the many varieties of and quarrels over Christianity that animated Shakespeare's England. However, I will be arguing throughout that despite those quarrels and varieties, Christians in the Renaissance understood sex in similar ways to one another—that is, they saw sex as an issue of the soul. On the complexity of religion in Shakespeare's England see McEachern and Shuger 5–6.

3. See Thompson on this dynamic. McLuskie's reading of the play is an early and very important feminist critique. Garner and Sprengnether's collection *Shakespearean Tragedy and Gender* opens with a discussion of Jane Smiley's rewrite of *Lear*, *A Thousand Acres*. However, none of the essays in the volume treats *Lear* exclusively, and Neely's fine essay, which deals with *Lear*, *Hamlet*, and *Macbeth*, critiques *Lear*'s misogyny. *Lear* does not find a place in Comensoli and Russell's collection, *Enacting Gender on the English Renaissance Stage*.

4. See Neill, *Putting* 25–26, on Kent as the perfect servant and therefore the perfect man.

5. See de Grazia, "Ideology" 29–33, on lust and luxury.

6. Of course in later Freudian and psychoanalytic accounts, this love is always accompanied by unbridled aggression. Only the more intuitive (to the culture's beliefs) children's books, however, capture the essential ambivalence that these accounts say characterizes primal love bonds.

7. The quarto reads "womans wit" (Kv).

8. On the link between women's open mouths and their sexual looseness see Stallybrass, "Patriarchal." For the limits and dangers of this type of analysis, see Rackin, "Misogyny."

9. See *Our Bodies Ourselves* and then all of the appropriation of this originally revolutionary tenet. Now it is unusual to find a woman's magazine directed at "hip" younger women that does not talk about how to satisfy sexual desire.

10. The quarto reads "lets hit together" (C).

11. On the use of sexual desire to sell products, see any issue of *Cosmopolitan* magazine, as well as contemporary television. For a brief history of sex in American advertising, see Sivulka 372–377.

12. See Rackin, "Misogyny," for a timely reconsideration of the shape of misogyny in Shakespeare's world.

13. The other crucial division for the modern world is along racial lines. See chapter 5. For the change in women's positions with regard to work see Clark. Clark's work remains significant despite many later historians' questions and revisions. See Shoemaker for a summary.

14. For an introduction to this huge subject, see McKendrick, Brewer, and Plumb. Brewer offers a brief look at how women were implicated in the eighteenth-century consumer revolution.

15. In addition to the texts cited in the introduction see Lanser's work on Sapphism in the eighteenth century and Haggerty's work on male–male love in the eighteenth century.
16. See my discussion of *Richard III* in "Manliness."
17. The quarto reads here "change armes at home" (H3v).
18. The dictionary finds usages of "intrinsic" meaning "inherent, essential" as early as 1642.
19. For a simultaneously masculine and feminine use of nursing that connects it to God's grace, see Donne's image in a letter to Henry Goodyear about different forms of Christianity. Discussing Puritanism and Catholicism, Donne says, "The channels of God's mercies run through both fields; and they are sister teats of His graces" (*John Donne* 197).
20. One active strain of Renaissance misogyny accuses women of false-ness, counterfeiting, wearing makeup. The conjunction here of effeminate crying and truth is anti-misogynistic in the period.
21. Editors usually choose the quarto's "*histerica passio*." See Halpern for a fascinating reading of this crux.
22. See Neill, *Putting* 13–48.
23. By the Romantic period, passion has been fully approved—see chapter 6 for how this approval of passion for men has played out in *Othello* criticism. Brewer's work indicates the social battle over passion conducted during the eighteenth century.
24. According to the *Norton Shakespeare*, the quarto says "Bastard" throughout, and the folio says "Bastard" and "Edmond."
25. See Gordon Williams "thing."
26. The unevenness of ideological shifts is evident in these realms. Certain forms of Christian discourse have fought losing battles over drinking, for example. The history of American Prohibition is relevant here.
27. American beer commercials frequently play on male sexual desire for women. These commercials can also in misogynist fashion reject women in favor of male drinking buddies, but the rejection of women is never a rejection of sex—it is a rejection of the nagging wife, who represents men's responsibilities in relation to women and home.
28. See Scodel 199–224. See also Amussen, " 'The part of a Christian man' " 225.
29. The Renaissance codpiece functioned to display powerful men's ability to make male heirs. The prominent, decorated codpieces in portraits of Henry VIII are particularly suggestive in this regard.
30. See Bach, "Tennis Balls."
31. On "normal" sexuality, see Sedgwick and Michael Warner.
32. See Neely 90 and 92. The madmen in *The Duchess of Malfi* obsess about sex with women.
33. TLN 1865–1868, 1869–1872; 3.4.80–82, 84–86.

34. See Halpern, Danby, Delany, and John Turner in Holderness, Potter, and Turner. Halpern points out that Danby would not have identified himself as a Marxist critic, although his reading of the play anticipates Marxist accounts of proleptic class-struggle (Halpern 216).
35. See de Grazia, "Ideology" 33.
36. The quarto reads "small." The folio reads "great." A case can be made for "great"; perhaps all people have "great" vices, but they only show up in poor people. The rhetorical contrast in the passage seems to call for "small."
37. See Marcus 155 and Hotine. Remarkably, Shaheen ignores this liturgy when collecting the play's biblical references. Hassel makes a distinction between "genetic" works, written for a festival, and "affective" works, performed on holy days (18–19). He classifies *King Lear* as having an affective relationship to St. Stephen's Day. His view of *Lear*'s meaning, however, is wholly conditioned by a reading of the play as secular. See Elton 3–8 for a review of older critical readings that focus on the play's Christianity. This argument is still in progress, despite Kronenfeld's definitive work. For intelligent readings on both sides see Edwards (for Christianity in the play) and Strier "Shakespeare" (against Christianity in the play).
38. Donaldson translates these lines as "Thus you give your gold for glutton's well-being, / And squander it on scoundrels schooled in lechery" (Langland 425–426).
39. Danby is an exception here. See especially pages 186–189. Holbrook also is willing to speculate on the connections between Christianity and what he sees as the play's leftist criticism of society.
40. The modern American formulation of this problem leads to critiques of welfare mothers, where the premodern critique is concerned with fathers.
41. It is perhaps not surprising that this comment, which is so alien to modern sexual ideology, has provoked annoyance in the twentieth century. Bradley suggests that "one wishes [Edgar] had not said to his dying brother those words about their dead father" (305). Edwards, ninety-some years later, also finds these words distasteful.
42. See McKeon, *Origins*, for an account of the "rehabilitation" of greed (203).

Chapter 2

Restoration Shakespeare 1: Adultery and the Birth of Heterosexuality

1. On the connections between courtly love and adultery see Lewis's important study, *The Allegory of Love*. Lewis acutely understands how

Medieval and classical poetry does not depict heterosexuality as we know it (although he does not use the term heterosexuality). He is, however, as this book as a whole argues, mistaken in his attribution of what he calls "romantic love" to the Renaissance. See also Schultz's important new book on courtly love and sexuality.

2. See also Donne's sermon LXIV on David's adultery (*LXXX* 639–649). Donne refers to Augustine on this incident.

3. See Rackin, "Foreign" note 3, for commentary on this story. In many ways this chapter and the book as a whole follow Rackin's suggestion that a history of sexual desire might begin with this story and its implications. See Bersani for a late-twentieth-century reinterpretation of this story and its relation to desire.

4. See Halperin's comment on this translation (*How to* 68–71). He argues that the word " 'seducer' better captures some of the other dimensions of the word's meaning" (70). His invaluable discussion of the myth does not, I think, challenge the point that I am making, since the word indicated illicit sexual desire.

5. Tanner offers a similar survey, but for structuralist analysis, at the beginning of his book on adultery in the novel.

6. See Schwartz's analysis of David as violating his duty to fight with his men and also violating male property rights (141–142, 145–146). Schwartz comments that "David's adultery is set in stark relief . . . to Uriah's faithfulness to *God*. Under the injunctions of holy war, to sleep with his own wife would be faithless to God; it is that fidelity that Uriah maintains despite being plied with wine by the King, despite the apparent attractiveness of his wife, and it is that fidelity—to God—that he finally dies for" (148).

7. See Kipnis for an analysis of adultery in postmodern America. She suggests that adultery could be reimagined as "a counterlogic to the prevailing system" (298). Wheatley suggests that Restoration drama engaged in that project—what he calls "the celebration of adultery as a sublime rejection of the social order"—for a short time ("Thomas" 389). For a historical survey of materials related to adultery in the Restoration and early eighteenth century, see David M. Turner.

8. See James Grantham Turner, *Libertines*, who comments, "the category of Royal Mistress obstructed the attempt to corrall illicit sexuality into a nether zone" (152). Turner discusses as well how Charles's womanizing undermined his monarchy, enabling sometimes crippling critique—we can see in that criticism the not-yet-residual effects of the tradition that saw men as mastered by their desires and by the women they desired.

9. In the Fredson Bowers edition of Beaumont and Fletcher's works, Robert Kean Turner argues that *The False One* was written by Massinger and Fletcher. When I am writing about these texts as a group, I use the term "Cleopatra stories."

10. This anatomization is only one of the concerns of Shakespeare's *Antony and Cleopatra*. Strikingly, read in the context of all of the Cleopatra stories, Shakespeare's play is least concerned with the relationship that gives it its title. None of the other representations spends as much time on Caesar and his political maneuvers or on the political dealings among Romans that have little or nothing to do with Cleopatra.

11. Sedley's Caesar reveals his motivation in an aside.

12. See Klima and Starnes on Dryden's Shakespearean borrowings.

13. See Stallybrass, "Patriarchal," and Orgel.

14. See Evans, Gagen, and Kloesel for examples.

15. Shakespeare's play challenges the reality of Roman honor in myriad ways: in the conversation between Roman soldiers that reveals that Roman generals' military honor is really the production of his men; in Pompey's servant's offer to cut Pompey's partners' throats; and in its angle on Caesar's merciless machinations.

16. Also fascinating in this speech is this Restoration construction of Cleopatra as "white." Shakespeare's play depicts a tawny, black Cleopatra. See McDonald and Royster.

17. See the use of the vocabulary of melting in *Romeo and Juliet*.

18. See Schiebinger, *Nature's Body* 75. Schiebinger describes the argument about the status of apes. She implies a trajectory from Augustine's interpretation of apes as degenerate, outcast from human society during Genesis, to Rousseau and Monboddo's late-eighteenth-century conclusions that apes were "natural man." Sedley's construction of love is moving toward Rousseau's.

19. See David M. Turner 34.

20. The gradual loss of power for women in English history is a subject of historical debate. For a good summary of the historiography on the question, see Shoemaker. See also Rackin, *Shakespeare and Women*.

21. The dictionary finds its last usage of 4 in 1807, its last usage of 5 in 1785, 6 in 1677, 7 in 1708, and 8 in 1811.

22. The evidence from the other Renaissance Cleopatra texts has similar implications: Sidney uses the word "mistresse" once to describe the woman who mastered Hercules. The word does not appear in Daniel's *Letter*. It is used twice in Daniel's *Cleopatra*, both times to designate Cleopatra's position as mistress of her Egyptian servants. The word does not appear in Brandon's text. May's Titius disdains to fight to make Cleopatra "Mistris of the world and" Antony (B10; 2.2.107). May uses the word to denote Cleopatra's mastery over Antony. May's Cleopatra manipulates Antony by claiming that she hopes he sees her as more than the "mistris only of some looser houres" (B12; 2.3.71). Later in the play, Gallus, discussing Antony's disgraceful behavior at Actium, calls her "his Mistris *Cleopatra*" (C4v; 3.1.63). May also uses the word for Cleopatra's relationship with her servants. *The False One*, the latest of the seventeenth-century, pre-Restoration texts, has two

interesting more modern usages, both in the scene after Julius Caesar has chosen to attend to a display of Egypt's fortune instead of to Cleopatra. *The False One* is the first Cleopatra text that uses "mistress" in a way that would fit under the *OED*'s definition 11; however their Cleopatra is also recognizably a woman who sells her virginity, a whore in Renaissance terms. Fletcher and Massinger's Cleopatra is also a woman who dominates Caesar temporarily, to his grave disadvantage.

23. See Charnes's reading of the play as depicting the construction by Caesar of Antony and Cleopatra's story as a love story in order to ward off a political challenge (135–147).

24. See, for example, *Cymbeline*'s "tomboy" and "jay"; other words include "pinnace," "pung," "punk," "medlar," "aunt" (*Troilus and Cressida* 2.2.76), "daughter of the game," "drab," "fitchew," "guinea hen," "hobby-horse," "ramp," "puzzel," "callet," "trull," "kite," and "squall."

25. See Ann Rosalind Jones, *Currency*, on the Italian courtesan tradition. For crucial archival work on prostitution in Shakespeare's England and the representation of prostitution on stage, see Cristine Varholy's unpublished work.

26. It is hard to see how the *OED* categorized its first citation from John Lydgate's *Fall of Princes* under definition 11. The usage occurs in Scilla's presentation of her father's head to her beloved Minos. She says that she has disinherited herself for love of Minos:

> My selfe disinherited / for love of your persone
> Called in my countrey a false traytouresse
> Disconsolate stale away alone
> Of newe disfamed / and named a maistresse
> Of false murdre (fol. xiii)

27. The *OED* is very much a product of Victorian culture. See Willinsky; see also the recent biographies related to the dictionary. This shift also means that Shakespeare editors feel compelled to define the word in modern editions. Thus, in *The Norton Shakespeare*, a Frenchman in *Cymbeline* speaks of his "country mistresses." The note reads "The women of our country" (2973). The note seems accurate, but it is necessary because a reader today might automatically assume that the man was talking about established sexual partners.

28. See Todd for crucial work on women writers that documents this shift.

29. Shakespeare wrote a number of plays about women being slandered that can be read as helping to put pressure on this convention of female character, including *The Winter's Tale*, *Cymbeline*, *Othello*, and *Much Ado about Nothing*.

30. Cleopatra uses the word "whore" in one of Shakespeare's fabulous metadramatic references. She resolves to die before the Romans can represent her in the theater "I'th'posture of a Whore" (TLN 3464; 5.2.217). In that reference, Cleopatra denies that the word captures her

reality, as indeed it does not. Shakespeare's Cleopatra is, by definition, undefinable. Rackin's "Shakespeare's Boy" is still the best account of how Shakespeare achieves this effect. However that word circles her, and Antony even uses it to describe her. Fitz, in her survey of sexist *Antony and Cleopatra* criticism before 1977, shows the pitfalls and motivations of criticism that settles on defining Cleopatra as a whore.

31. Montaigne warns that men who think they can get away with chastely sleeping next to their wives are mistaken: "on the contrary, [women's] neede or longing is thereby encreased; for but the touch or company of any man whatsoeuer stirreth vp their heate, which in their solitude was husht and quiet, and laye as cinders raked vp in the ashes" (513). Wives are sexual fires waiting to start at the "touch or company of any man whatsoeuer."

32. See Candace Brook Katz for an analysis of a late-Restoration woman playwright's response to this dynamic.

33. See Canfield, "Jewel" 50. See also Yots's analysis of Elizabeth Boutell as Cleopatra.

34. Obviously Dennis's objections (see below) show that in Dryden's world this love could still be defined as sin. I am not arguing that the earlier frame disappears, just that it is losing the dominance it still maintained sixty years earlier.

35. On Cleopatra's rhetorical charms see Brandon's Octavia's claim: "No, tis hir wit hath thee bewitcht,/Hir sweet delighting tongue:/Which doth enchant thy wondring mind,/And makes thee stay this long" (*Octauia to Antonius* G7).

36. On the rivalry between Dryden and Shadwell, see Combe.

37. Hume argues that "the idea that even 1670's comedy is hostile to marriage as an institution is patently absurd." In this play, however, Evandra attacks not just "marriage of economic convenience" and "'forced' marriage" but also marriage in itself, which she defines as always economic in nature ("Myth" 28).

38. There are many examples of female characters in early-seventeenth-century plays driven to "immoral" behavior by fathers, brothers, or husbands bent on their own gain. Approved characters in these plays, however, are usually driven to marry, not to have sexual relationships outside of marriage. Frequently, also, those marriages are the marriages that would have been approved had the offending patriarch been properly cognizant of his own place and the marital exchanges proper to that place.

39. The natural coupling of "mistress" and "slave" is exploited to great effect in a text by De Scudery, translated into English in 1656. De Scudery writes a series of "harangues" by classical female characters. Briseis, the slave, taken as a "mistress" by Achilles provides an opportunity for De Scudery to exploit the literary potential of an

actual slave (who was the daughter of a king) in a love relationship with her captor. Briseis complains that she has lost Achilles to Polixena, his Trojan love. De Scudery treats the mistress/slave couple from the perspective of the homosocial imaginary. Briseis begs Achilles to love her: "I intreat you with humility; if I be yet your slave onely, and if I am yet both your Slave and Mistris, I command you" (222). I thank April Alliston for pointing me to this fascinating text.

40. See the *OED* 1c. Shakespeare often uses "slave" as a generalized insult.

41. "Slave" of course does not disappear from usage this way. For one among many examples, see Duke Moreno's embrace of Viola in William Burnaby's rewritten *Twelfth Night, Love Betray'd* (1703): "You make me more your Slave, than you was mine" (60).

42. See Neill's introduction to the Oxford edition for the use in Shakespeare editions of illustrations that drew from Dryden's play (26). In Shakespeare's *Cymbeline*, Iachimo tells Posthumus he saw in Imogen's bedroom a "tapestry of silk and silver; the story/Proud Cleopatra when she met her Roman" (2.4.69–70). In D'Urfey's Restoration rewriting of *Cymbeline*, Shattilion tells Ursaces he saw the same tapestry: "the Story / Was the Meeting of th'*Egyptian* Queen and *Anthony*, when *Cidnus* swell'd above the Banks / For pride, to bear that glorious Heroe / And his Mistress, that gave the World / For Love" (24).

43. See Ann Rosalind Jones, "Counterattacks," on the pamphlet war on women's character. For the general shape of Renaissance feminism, see Constance Jordan. See also Capp, *When Gossips* 15–25.

44. Brandon's text leads us to speculate about the character of "strange pleasures." Perhaps the pleasures of the Egyptian court are "strange" because they are pleasures that are supplied by strangers.

45. See Shakespeare's use of "leuities" in *Timon of Athens* (TLN 166; 1.1.138).

46. See also Sylvia's argument in Brandon's play (C2). Shakespeare gives versions of these arguments to Emilia in *Othello* and Iachimo in *Cymbeline*. See Parten 14.

47. This is essentially the same logic that animates the *Haec Vir* pamphlet.

48. Amussen, *Ordered*, concurs with Gowing (102). However, for some examples of this ubiquitous usage, see Burton 109, 115, 291, Shakespeare *1 Henry IV* 2.4.516, *King Lear* 1.2.116.

49. Quotations from *A Woman Killed* will be by signature from the 1607 publication and by scene and line number from Van Fossen's edition.

50. See also Capp, "*When Gossips*" 253. Shakespeare uses this same pairing in *All's Well that Ends Well*: "as a scolding queane to a wrangling knaue" (TLN 848–849; 2.2.22). Another Shakespearean use of "knave" to mean sexual criminal appears in *The Merry Wives of Windsor*: "*Falstaffes* a Knaue, a Cuckoldy knaue" (TLN 2593; 5.5.107). The pair, quean and knave, appears also in Middleton's *A Trick to Catch the Old One* (5.2.105–111). Capp asserts that " 'whore' was a far more damaging

insult than 'rogue' or 'knave' " (*When Gossips* 229). The literary evidence might make one question this assertion.

51. For further evidence of the influence of Thomas's work, see Ingram, "Family" 104; Ingram, *Church* (302–303 especially); David M. Turner 13; and Shoemaker 86. Although Turner is writing about the later historical period, the evidence that he cites in relation to Thomas's thesis is questionable. Again, read without that framework, Turner's evidence puts the transhistorical existence of the "double standard" in its modern form in question. Sharpe's early work is suggestive on this point. See especially 27–28.

52. See Edmunds.

53. Necessary, that is, to the emerging heterosexual imaginary. By this formulation I do not mean to suggest that this emergence was a historical necessity, just that for it to have succeeded as it did, the refiguration of adultery in these plays and Restoration culture was a necessary condition.

54. For traditional accounts see Edgar, Krutch, and Anthony. Marsden, "Female," offers a history of earlier and associated attacks on theatrical sexual display with particular attention to the effects on women viewers.

55. Dryden from the epilogue to Fletcher's *Pilgrim*.

56. See Augustine's disquisition on the David and Bathsheba story: "There is sin in thee, when thou takest pleasure; there reigneth, if thou shalt have consented. Carnal pleasure, *especially* if proceeding unto unlawful and strange objects, is to be bridled, not let loose: by government is to be tamed, not to be set up for government" (*Expositions on the Book* 190; my emphasis). Donne turns to this passage in his discussion of David and Bathsheba. See also Augustine's meditation in the *Confessions* on the pull of worldly pleasure: "Thus also, when above eternity delights us, and the pleasure of temporal good holds us down below, it is the same soul which willeth not that or this with an entire will, and is therefore torn asunder with grievous perplexities, while out of truth it prefers that, but out of custom forbears not this" (126).

57. See Hinnant on Collier's place in "the Patriarchalist Debate." Also see Hopes on Collier's "continued oppostition to the revolution" (161).

58. This reading of Dennis reading Collier on Ovid assumes that Dennis did not translate Collier's "wench" as "mistress" on purpose. Even if he did, however, Dennis knows that his readers know what a "mistress" is, which, by the end of the Restoration, any reader or theater patron would.

59. In his insistence on women's natural modesty, however, Collier is contributing to the gender shift that classified women as pure.

60. See Pateman. I am not suggesting that Collier belonged to an earlier world, only that he spoke for what he believed to be its principles. Neither am I suggesting that Collier's "moral" criticism was right in

the sense that the Victorian *Dictionary of National Biography* believes it to be right. However, Collier's affinity with the homosocial imaginary made him a more astute critic of Ben Jonson's *Epicoene* than Dryden when it comes to *Epicoene*'s sexual values. Dryden reads Dauphin as a lover who ends the play "with the hopes of enjoying all of his mistresses" (Preface to *An Evening's Love; or the Mock-Astrologer* quoted in *Of Dramatic Poesy and Other Critical Essays* I 151). Collier, more astutely, comments, "I grant *Dauphine* Professes himself in Love with the Collegiate Ladies at first. But when they invited him to a private Visit, he makes them no Promise; but rather appears tired, and willing to disengage" (153).

61. See Barnouw on Dennis's reversal of classical and Petrarchan notions of passion. See Heffernan on links between Dennis and Wordsworth. See also Albrecht.
62. See Hinnant. On the place of the Enlightenment generally in approving of sexual pleasure, see Roy Porter.

Chapter 3
Restoration Shakespeare 2: Friends and Libertines

1. See James Grantham Turner's "Pope's Libertine Self-Fashioning."
2. Compare, for example, these lines from a 1730 letter by John, Lord Hervey, to his friend Stephen Fox "I have often thought, if any very idle Body had Curiosity enough to intercept & examine my Letters, they would certainly conclude they came from a Mistress than a Friend" (quoted in Haggerty 71) to Pope's letter to Caryll in which Pope modestly disclaims Caryll's praise: "but one or two things you have said of me that I'm ashamed to thank you for, they are so extravagantly above my merit; and they prove it true, that a friend is as blind as a lover" (*Correspondence* 120). According to Pope, Caryll writes about him as a lover would. According to Hervey, he writes to Fox as a mistress would. Both Hervey and Pope are living in a world in which mistress and lover have been thoroughly redefined as sexual and essential positions for men and women. Both of these men in the early eighteenth century are willing to identify themselves within that system but in terms of their relationships with other men. Pope may well, as Haggerty suggests, have been eager to define Hervey as an illegitimate man, or a half-man half-woman, but Pope was not worried that his own insertion of male–male friendship into the mistress-lover relationship would compromise his own masculinity.
3. Flavius is not a friend, although "steward" is an ambiguous position. He is a servant, but a higher-level servant. See Burnett on degrees of service. Flavius is more like Adam in *As You Like It*, or Kent in

King Lear, other men who stay loyal to their masters. Enobarbus is also positioned between friend and mastered man. In Shadwell's *Timon*, Timon's steward Demetrius abandons him, wishing that he would be "gently turn'd/Out of [his] Office; lest [Timon] shou'd borrow all/I have gotten in his service" (35). Of course, this is Adam's dream in *As You Like It*; he wants only to give Orlando all that he has earned while in Orlando's father's service. It is also the offer that Evandra makes to Timon. The perfect mistress in this text is like the perfect friend/servant in earlier texts.

4. On the homoeroticism in this relationship see Goldberg, "Anus."

5. See Rackin, "Foreign" 70.

6. See also Masten's brilliant reading of these plays in relationship to one another in his chapter on male friendship, homoeroticism, and collaboration (28–62).

7. On the story of Damon and Pithias in the Renaissance, see Mills.

8. For a critique of that homophobia, see Haggerty 29.

9. James Grantham Turner's work is definitive on the question of libertinism and the libertine during the long eighteenth century. See also Chernaik. See Hume, "Myth," for the argument that rakes are not libertines and that Restoration drama does not promote libertine behavior. Canfield, "Religious," also argues that Restoration drama explicitly rejects "the affected, transient life of the libertine" (387).

10. On the relationship between these male identities, see Staves, "A Few Kind Words." Shakespeare never uses the word "rake" to denote a male identity. Shakespeare's use of "fop" is more complicated but also very infrequent.

11. The first quotation is from Spencer 100, the second from Kilbourne 129.

12. See also Goldberg's brilliant queer reading of Rosaline's place in the play ("*Romeo*").

13. See Amussen, " 'The Part of a Christian man,' " especially pages 217–220 on rape in the Renaissance.

14. See Staves, "A Few Kind," and Heilman on fop identities in Restoration.

15. That Shattilion is French rather than Italian may speak to D'Urfey's Hugenot sympathies.

16. James Grantham Turner, *Libertines and Radicals*, wants to argue for influence from the Continent on English sexual ideology. In the Renaissance, however, what we generally see is the Continent being stereotyped as sexually permissive and sinful. Before the Restoration, English sexual identity and practice were being defined in contrast to that stereotyping of the Continent.

17. Obviously "nation" is a difficult word to use in this period, but distinctions between place of origin are very clear on stage. On the construction of the English nation, see Baker, Helgerson, Mikalachki.

On race in the Renaissance see, among others, Bach, *Colonial*; Kim Hall; Loomba; McDonald; Hendricks and Parker.

18. See Lanser, "Befriending."

19. See Dolan, *Dangerous Familiars*, on the Renaissance reactions to "treasonous" servants.

20. See Neill, *Putting*; Jardine, *Still*; Burnett.

21. The folio dramatis personae defines him as a "fantastique." Thomas Overbury's compilation of characters has a relevant portrait of "A Phantastique," which includes the comment, "If all men were of his minde, all honesty would be out of fashion" (M4).

22. Lucio (of course) drinks excessively (and therefore accuses the Duke of being a drunk) and cannot control his mouth even when his social superiors require him to.

23. Being a Shakespearean play of the homosocial imaginary, *Much Ado* does not present that fear as wholly unreasonable. Beatrice herself makes cuckold jokes.

24. For a late-sixteenth-century treatment of this claim, see the story in Holinshed of John Ball's preaching to rebels. Holinshed calls the claim that "all men by nature were created alike" one of Ball's "fond and foolish toies" (437).

Chapter 4

"Domestic Tragedy" and Emerging Heterosexuality

1. Apparently John Payne Collier first coined the term "domestic tragedy" (437). See Orlin for a discussion of the constitution of the genre (*Private* 9–10).

2. See Orlin's 1995 catalogue for the Folger Exhibition, *Elizabethan Households*. That exhibition catalogue is a wonderful introduction to the differences between Renaissance households and modern households.

3. See Dolan, *Whores*, on the limitations of the term "companionate marriage," especially 71.

4. *The Fatal Error* was not performed. Victor published it in 1776, but his advertisement alludes to his having composed the play soon after reading *A Woman Killed with Kindness* in the Dodsley collection of 1743. I will be calling *The Fatal Error* a mid-eighteenth-century play.

5. This is the sense of character we see defensively invoked in such late-twentieth-century criticism as Harold Bloom's *Shakespeare and the Invention of the Human*. See Desmet and Sawyer's collection for cogent critical responses to this popular book. Pope's assessment of Shakespeare's dramatic characters is characteristic of

eighteenth-century responses. He calls Shakespeare's characters "so much of Nature her self," and he claims that "every single character in *Shakespear* is as much an Individual, as those in Life itself" (Introduction to *Works of Shakespeare* 1723 ii, iii). Yet Pope is happy to banish to the bottom of the page those speeches and words that he finds indecorous and, therefore, out of character.

6. As Diana Henderson suggests, "bourgeois sentimental drama . . . did not emerge until more than a century later [than *A Woman Killed with Kindness*] and reflected a very different 'reality' " ("Many" 291).

7. See Pollak's analysis of women's place in the early eighteenth century. Pollak suggests that "[a]dultery committed by a woman—no matter what the circumstance—was an unforgivable violation of every prevailing notion of honor and virtue and carried serious social consequences" (69).

8. Panek calls *A Woman Killed* "a domestic tragedy centering on a man's discovery and punishment of his wife's unfaithfulness" (357). Wentworth argues that the play brings the Medieval morality play into the domestic sphere where, rather than being judged by God, "Anne is to be judged by her husband" (156). Cook focuses on Anne and Frankford, suggesting that "between husband and wife there exists a steady but altogether subdued affection" (355). Although Kiefer acknowledges that "the playwright emphasizes the network of ties binding people together," he says that Heywood focuses on the "triangular relationship of Anne, John and Wendoll" and "the seemingly idyllic Frankford household "into which Wendoll intrudes" (83–84).

9. For an analysis that further decenters our notion of children as denoting and constituting the domestic family see Fumerton's chapter "Exchanging Gifts: The Elizabethan Currency of Children and Romance." See Newman, "Sundry," for an analysis of sixteenth-century letters that challenges Fumerton's conclusions.

10. Quotations from *A Woman Killed* will be by signature from the 1607 publication and by scene and line number from Van Fossen's edition.

11. In response particularly to those who see the subplot, as Adams did, as filler that "continually interferes with and interrupts the important main action" (156), critics have developed thematic parallels between the two plots. See Baines 81, Bromley, Canuteson, Cook, Ribner 53, Townsend.

12. See Felperin 153, Coursen 184n., and Levin 93.

13. Gutierrez notes "the play upon the concepts of 'kind' (kindness) and 'kin' (kinship) especially link [*sic*] the treatment of women in the two plots" (280). Her new historicist treatment of the play shares some of the premises of this argument, most importantly that "Heywood . . . represents the problematic position of women in the family, especially in relation to male bonding outside the family unit" (282). But Gutierrez focuses on Anne and Frankford as a couple and on the adultery that destroys that couple.

14. For a good discussion of the problems with the terminology of class in discussions of Renaissance England, see Laslett 23. See also Cressy, "Describing," and O'Dair.
15. See Ezell.
16. Thus like Orlin, in her brilliant reading of the play in terms of Renaissance ideals of friendship and companionate marriage, I too see "a conceptual pattern that contrasts the two women only superficially (characterologically) and that conflates them functionally (ethically) by submerging any prospect of their agency" (*Private* 175).
17. See Orlin, *Private* 159–160.
18. This is where I differ from Orlin's analysis of the play. Heywood is not valuing companionate marriage over companionate friendship. When, in the eighteenth century, companionate marriage became valued more than companionate friendship, *A Woman Killed* looked ridiculous.
19. Renaissance drama does criticize aristocratic excess, but it also is invested in preserving the identity of a true, purified aristocracy, both chaste and honorable. Some of that drama's criticism of aristocratic excess may be related to humanist scholars' efforts to construct a social space for themselves. See Stewart xxxiv–xliv.
20. For cogent analyses of the social efficacy of Petrarchan love language, especially for courtiers, see Marotti and Montrose.
21. By the Restoration, poets and dramatists felt the need to differentiate English and foreign literary form. See, for example, the beginning of Dryden's preface to *The Tempest or The Enchanted Island*:

    The writing of Prefaces to Plays, was probably invented by some very ambitious Poet, who never thought he had done enough: Perhaps by some Ape of the French Eloquence, which uses to make a business of a Letter of Gallantry an examen of a Farce; and, in short, a great pomp and ostentation of words on every trifle. This is certainly the Talent of that Nation, and ought not to be invaded by any other. They do that out of gaiety, which would be an imposition upon us. (Davenant and Dryden A2).

22. See David M. Turner's discussion of the periodical press' advice about revealing affairs (77); see also his discussion of the evolving demarcations of public and private space (158–160).
23. Within the servant world, Humphry acts as a knowlegable conscience, as his dialogue with Richard, the servant who has returned from London with Sir Charles, shows. The naive Richard is a foil for both Humphry's upright character and for the play's general critique of aristocratic behavior.
24. *Arden of Faversham* has a less developed critical tradition than *A Woman Killed with Kindness*, although it has attracted a lot of attention as an apocryphal Shakespeare play. See Youngblood's defense of the play in 1963. Dolan notes that the play "has been considered

undistinguished and homely" (*Dangerous* 71). Attwell in 1991 feels compelled to claim that there is "sufficient reason for us to look closely at the play today" (329). For a detailed bibliography of the criticism of the play prior to the early 1970s, see Levenson's contribution to Logan and Smith 240–252.

25. See, for example, Lieblein, who suggests that "the counterpart to Alice's adultery is Arden's ruthless upward social mobility" (186).

26. See Schutzman's fine article for another reading of the play that breaks down this modern binary. Schutzman brilliantly details Alice's intricate maneuvers to create her own space. My only difficulty with this reading is the positive valence Schutzman attaches to Alice's maneuvers. I would argue that this positive valence comes from our late modern feminist desire to see women's power in positive terms.

27. See Raymond Chapman 15; Wine's 1973 introduction to the play, especially lxxiii; and White's introduction to the Revels edition, especially xxv.

28. In fact some of Alice's language sounds remarkably similar to that paradigm of sexual excess, Chaucer's Wife of Bath. In order to distract Arden from his suspicions, Alice declares:

> ah me accurst,
> To lincke in lyking with a frantick man,
> Hence foorth Ile be thy slaue, no more thy wife:
> For with that name I neuer shall content thee.
> If I be merry thou straight waies thinks me light.
> If sad thou saiest the sullens trouble me.
> If well attyred thou thinks I will be gadding,
> If homely, I seeme sluttish in thine eye.
> Thus am I still, and shall be whill I die,
> Poore wench abused by thy misgouernment.
> (TLN 1944–1953, 13.104–112)

Alice sounds as if she had taken a leaf from the Wife's book of ways to disarm old, suspicious husbands. See Lochrie's brilliant analysis of the Wife's unnatural excess (*Covert* 202–203).

29. As Orlin notes, "in the sources there is little distinction made between Arden the man of business and Arden the husband, for it is his greed that makes him a willing cuckold" ("Man's" 72).

30. Dolan argues that for a wife to desire another man and for a servant to desire his master's place "is to challenge the whole social order that regulates sexuality and reproduction, the distribution of property, and the hierarchies of authority and submission" (*Dangerous* 57).

31. See, however, Whigham's attempt to hear Will as the voice of the disempowered (95–107).

32. All quotations from *Arden of Faversham* are given both from the Malone Society reprint of the 1592 quarto by through line number(s)

and from the New Mermaids edition edited by White by scene and line number(s).

33. See Bray on the significance of oaths in the homosocial imaginary (*Friend* 135–136). See also Sommerville 140–143.

34. See the marginal gloss at the point in which Black Will enters Holinshed's chronicle account of the murder: "Marke how the deuill will not let his organs or instruments let slip either occasio[n] or opportunitie to commit most heinous wickednesse" (Holinshed 1063). Although the playwright alters the chronicle account to suit his or her dramatic purposes, Black Will is a constant between the source and the play. Lake also makes this point about Alice and Black Will (69). See also Lake's lovely discussion of Black Will (116–118).

35. See Enobarbus's comment in *Antony and Cleopatra*: "*Anthony* onely, that would make his will/Lord of his Reason" (TLN 2156–2157; 3.13.3–4). See also Masten's discussion of the word "will" (35).

36. When Nick first encounters Wendoll in *A Woman Killed with Kindness* he distrusts him immediately, proposing to himself (and the audience) that "The Deuill and he are all one in mine eye" (C, 4.88). Wendoll, like Black Will, is the most willful man in his play. In theological terms, both of their wills ally them to the devil.

37. See also Whigham, who posits Mosby and Alice's search for "a 'truer' marriage" (85), and Comensoli, who argues that Alice "gives voice to a radical discourse of desire" (88).

38. I am not suggesting that audience members would not enjoy watching Alice's fantastic flaunting of her transgression of moral codes. I am suggesting that there is a significant difference between enjoyment and identification. Although neither precludes the other, they are also not necessarily connected. We can witness this dynamic in the interest of so much of the contemporary public in viewing extreme violence. The vast majority of people who watch extremely violent films do not themselves intend to commit violence, nor do they necessarily condone it. Many viewers condemn violence and yet enjoy viewing it. This is a simple point, but I think it is often forgotten. *Arden of Faversham* presents Alice in such a demonized light that it comes close to precluding identification with her even though that same demonized light might have made her extremely enjoyable to watch. Obviously, as with all representation, it is always possible that someone would identify with her. Our critical tendency to see her side when she professes atheistic desire, however, has more to do with the generally secular character of the modern academy than it does with her character in the Renaissance play. See Knapp. See also Sommerville's pertinent comment on the misunderstanding "that the demonic or the sacrilegious belong in the category of the secular" (10).

39. See also Perkins: "For the husband that is a Christian is married two waies: First with Christ, and secondly with his wife. The former

mariage is made in Baptisme, and is a more holy coniunction, then is the latter" (107).

40. This quotation is from Rose's edition of the Wakefield Mystery Plays. The fall of man piece of the first play in the cycle, *The Creation*, is missing from the manuscript of the Wakefield Plays. Rose replaced it with a section of the York Cooper's play, *The Fall of Man*, which dates from earlier than 1376.

41. Because representation is always wonderfully open to reading against the grain, the language of love in musicals, especially, has been taken up by gay culture and been simultaneously constitutive of gay culture. However, such appropriations do not necessarily change the power of dominant representation to reinforce dominant culture. As Clum observes, "[t]hroughout its history, the musical accommodated itself to this mainstream prejudice, while managing at the same time to" support gay men (2). See also Miller.

42. See Marotti.

43. When Lord Cheiny meets Franklin on the road, he says, "My Lord protectors man I take you to bee" (TLN 1546; 9.32–33). The playwright seems to be playing with the metaphorical power of Somerset's title, "Protector."

44. See Sharpe's example from York in 1592, 16.

45. On the revised *Arden*'s stage history and popularity see Wine's introduction, especially xlviii–xlix.

46. See my discussion of the coupled histories of the words "mistress" and "slave" in chapter 2.

47. See the Shakespearean usages the *OED* cites: Don Pedro, in *Much Ado about Nothing*, calling Borachio (whom he thinks has committed a sexual crime with Hero) "most like a liberall villaine" (TLN 1752; 4.1.91); and Desdemona, in *Othello*, asking Cassio whether the loose-tongued Iago, who has just engaged her in sexualized banter, is a "most prophane, and liberall Counsailor" (TLN 938–939; 2.1.165). M.R. Ridley in the *Arden Othello* also points to Gertrude in *Hamlet* commenting on the garlands Ophelia, before her death, made from "long Purples, That liberall Shepheards giue a grosser name" (TLN 3161–3162; 4.7.140–141; Ridley 58, note to line 163). *The Norton Shakespeare* notes, "Among the recorded names for the purple orchis are 'priest's pintle' (penis), 'dog's cullions' (testicles), 'goat's cullions,' and 'fool's ballochs' " (1740n.1).

48. This representational change is not a response to a shifting economic system in which women were purchased in the earlier world and are not purchased in the later world. Pollak argues that as the middle class gains dominance, marriage becomes more, not less, of an economic bargain. Instead what we see is a shift in the way the purchase of women is related to male identity.

49. Arden is using "groom" here as meaning a "serving-man." See *OED* "groom" 3. The *OED* also finds "groom" meaning "man-child" or "boy"

in earlier centuries (*OED* 1.). Given the "contemptuous" usage here and in the *OED* usages collected under definitions 2 and 3, we might speculate that "groom" may have retained that age-related derogatory meaning through the Renaissance.

50. The context of this phrase indicates that Mosby is talking about Arden's economic seat. However, it very likely also signifies sexually, just as "seat" does in Iago's speech in *Othello*: "I do suspect the lustie Moore/Hath leap'd into my Seate" (TLN 1078–1079; 2.1.282–283). The double resonance of "seat" is just one more indication of the inseparability of lust and greed in the homosocial imaginary.

51. For some examples, see Bach, "Manliness."

52. See also Franklin's comment, "No nobleman will count'nance such a peasant" (TLN; 1.31).

53. The original *Arden* evokes the night and the day to glorify Mosby's previous life as a contented worker: "My daily toil begat me night's repose, / My night's repose made daylight fresh to me" (8.13–14). It is possible that the eighteenth-century speech was sparked by this speech of Mosby's although the imagery of night and day is too conventional to enable me to make this claim with any certainty. If he was thinking of this speech of Mosby's, which has no place in his reconceived *Arden*, the movement of this imagery from a speech that lauds the honest work of a manual workman to a speech that lauds Cupid is provocative.

54. See, however, Klein's attempt to complicate these categories as they are used to analyze eighteenth-century culture.

55. The dialogue concerning the bed runs as follows:

> *Michael* My M. would desire you come to bed.
> *Franklin* Is he himselfe already in his bed:
> *Michael* He is and faine would haue the light away. (4.55–57)

56. See Sedgwick's discussion of "homosexual panic" (*Between Men* 83–90). In *Epistemology*, Sedgwick usefully elaborates this concept. See particularly 19–21 and chapter four.

57. See Orlin's discussion of Renaissance texts that explore these dangers (*Private*). See also Bray (*The Friend*).

58. See also Jardine 248.

Chapter 5

Othello in the Seventeenth and Eighteenth Centuries and the Colonial Origins of Heterosexuality

1. See Floyd-Wilson on Ophelia's character. Like the staged and cut *Othello* explored in this chapter, the *Hamlet* that eighteenth-century

audiences saw was fodder for the emerging heterosexual imaginary. Wilson notes that "the emendations to the script of the revived *Hamlet* stress the romance between Ophelia and Prince Hamlet" (399).

2. See Stallybrass, "Patriarchal." See also Orlin, "Desdemona's" 180–181. See Garner for a discussion of Desdemona as a complex character, both sensual and innocent. Magnusson's discussion of character as a result of social interaction with its codes of politeness is a very persuasive model for understanding Desdemona's inconsistency. See her analysis of Katherine in *Henry VIII* (29).

3. For heterosexuality as the story of life see Berlant 286. Pearson speculates that Othello was popular in the Restoration because, "Alone among Shakespeare's mature tragedies, *Othello* is a domestic play in which heterosexual love is shown in contention with, and is ultimately given priority over, a public world of war and politics" (13). Although I would quarrel with her terms, Pearson's essay on women dramatists' rewritings of ethnic stereotypes is fascinating. See Pearson also for the connections between sexuality and blackness.

4. Othello is just one Shakespearean example. For another, think of Armado in *Love's Labour's Lost* whose Spanish ethnicity translates into his passionate and debasing love of Jacquenetta. Since in Shakespeare, Italian identities are so often screens for English identity, those ethnic identities are less stereotyped in some cases, although not in all.

5. See Fisher's work on beards.

6. Smith's description of the Crym-Tartars is compiled from two texts collected by Samuel Purchas, but the "taffity" seems to be Smith's addition.

7. See Vaughan, *Othello* 50–56, for additional references. See also Winthrop Jordan 32–40, Barthelemy 5–6, and Tokson 82–105.

8. Like Smith's description of the Crym-Tartars, Loke's story about the Garamantes derives from a thirteenth-century text. See Eldred Jones 3. Also see Jones for more evidence of "the association of dark peoples with lust" (8).

9. See Newman, " 'And Wash' " 147.

10. Within the history of *Othello* criticism in the eighteenth century, we can also find documentation of English antisemitism. The eighteenth-century editors often chose the folio reading "base Judean" in Othello's last speech. Their comments sometimes reveal virulent prejudice. See especially Steevens's notes quoted in Johnson's and Steevens's edition 518–519.

11. These are modern categories, of course. Most editors, as we have seen, use the editorial apparatus to voice critical opinions. There were, however, critics who did not function as editors, notably most of the women who published on Shakespeare in the eighteenth century.

12. This history has been largely forgotten in the late twentieth century. See the latest Arden editor, Honigmann's, discussion of why the play

has not been considered Shakespeare's greatest in his introduction to the play. On *Othello*'s popularity in the Restoration and early eighteenth century see Taylor 28, 32, 58.

13. See, for example, Theobald's long diatribe against Rymer, which ends with the dismissive comment "but such Reflexions require no serious Answer" (*Works* 372).

14. Here we see evidence of Shakespeare's sonnet 116 functioning within emerging heterosexuality as it will continue to function in English history, despite its significance, in its original context, as a love poem from one man to another. In the early twentieth century, Knight says of Othello and Desdemona, "This is the harmonious marriage of true and noble minds" (122). The sonnet is also used for heterosexual-true-love effect in the film *Shakespeare in Love*. On the history of sexuality in relation to Shakespeare's sonnets, see Stallybrass, "Editing," and De Grazia, "The Scandal."

15. Coleridge's diction indicates the fear of racial mixture that lies behind his criticism. He reacts in horror to the idea that Desdemona would "conceive" with a Negro.

16. See Neill, "Unproper," on nineteenth-century racist reactions to *Othello*.

17. The quotation is from Rosenberg 21. See Rosenberg's section on the cuts in the Smock Alley quarto (20–25). See also Vaughan, *Othello* 97–98.

18. The redefinition of masculinity away from violence occupied several centuries and is still being negotiated in modern culture, as it probably will be as long as people fight wars to settle disputes. It is however a process. See Staves, "Money for Honor" 293, for more on this process in the eighteenth century. On the question of male violence in the English Renaissance, see Appelbaum and Cahill.

19. See also Lennox's comment that "The Virtues of *Shakespear*'s *Moor* are no less characteristic than the Vices of *Cinthio*'s; they are the wild Growth of an uncultivated Mind, barbarous and rude as the Clime he is born in; thus, his Love is almost Phrensy; his Friendship Simplicity; his Justice cruel; and his Remorse Self-Murder" (134). Again, this comment shows how racism can interact with emerging heterosexuality. Lennox can approve of the love match and even find Desdemona virtuous because of it, but Lennox finds in Othello's "rude" "Clime" the origins of his too violent love.

20. This attitude has never completely disappeared. Whereas love for a woman and especially sexual desire for women has become a marker of masculinity, modern English and American cultures have retained many forms of misogyny from the past. In fact, this form of misogyny may be becoming more prevalent.

21. The *OED*'s citations for "blandishment" are as informative as those for "nice." The dictionary cites very negative examples from the sixteenth century, such as Spenser's "he gan enquire . . . of the Foxe,

and his false blandishment" (*Mother Hubbard*) and (figuratively) Robert Greene's "bear hence these wretched blandishments of sin" from *A Looking Glasse for London and England*. From the eighteenth century, however, the dictionary records Addison's "Nature has given all the Arts of Soothing and Blandishment to the Female" from *Spectator* (*OED* "blandishment").

22. On the multiple texts of *Othello*, see Berger. I use "quarto" in this chapter to signify Q1. Berger argues that the second quarto of *Othello* is already a conflated and an authoritative text.

23. See the textual note in the *Norton Shakespeare* 2098–2099.

24. On Rowe's edition, see Taylor 74–83. Taylor says that Rowe did consult *Othello*'s quarto for his edition (83).

25. The seventeenth-century quartos are all printed from the first quarto and read "sighs." The only exception to this trend in the eighteenth century that I have found is a 1710 *Othello* that the Folger catalogue says is a reprint by Thomas Johnson of the folio text.

26. See, for example, Markley on the emergence of a "sexual ideology that insists on the indivisibility of feminine chastity and [dominant] feminine identity" (116).

27. Even an editor who retained the word "wretch" retained it because he saw it as derogatory. Heath's 1765 *A Revisal of Shakespear's Text, wherein the Alterations introduced into it by the more modern Editors and Critics are particularly considered* includes a long note on "Excellent wretch," which reads, "His assurance in her faith and virtue is already somewhat staggered; and he begins to consider it as a thing possible, that she may be unworthy of his love. To this state of mind this exclamation is admirably well adapted, expressing the utmost fondness, and at the same time a distrust growing upon him" (561). In this edition' eyes, "wretch" is appropriate because it is slightly condemnatory, although it still expresses Othello's "utmost fondness" for Desdemona.

28. One of the signs of modernity in gender and sexual terms is the diminution of sexual terms for women in the eighteenth century. As we have seen, early-seventeenth-century texts abound with sexualized terms for women (chapter 2). Many of these terms either drop out of discourse or are reinterpreted as not sexual. Some examples are the words "trull," "callet," and "guinea hen." Gentleman glosses the word "callet" in Æmilia's complaint about Othello's language, "could not have laid such terms upon his callet": "*Callet* here, means trull, or scold: to *callet*, is used at present, for to scold" (67). The easy slippage between scold and whore is less possible in Gentleman's time. In 1765, Johnson glosses Iago's term "guinea-hen" as "A showy bird with fine feathers" (351). In the 1773 Johnson and Steevens edition, Steevens notes, "A *Guinea-hen* was anciently the cant term for a prostitute" (392). As woman was redefined away from automatic association with whore, the myriad terms for whore become part of an "ancient" vocabulary.

29. This dance of purification between *Othello* and *Antony and Cleopatra* can and did work both ways. In the 1907 New Variorum edition of *Antony and Cleopatra*, Horace Howard Furness comments on "wench" in Agrippa's speech: "This is by no means always a derogatory term. In the most tragic moment of his life Othello calls his dead Desdemona 'O ill-starr'd wench!'" (119n.)

30. See also Claudio's comment to Hero in *Much Ado about Nothing*: "But you are more intemperate in your blood,/Than *Venus*" (TLN 1716–1717; 4.1.57–58); and Prince Harry's comment on Falstaff's kissing the whore Doll Tearsheet, "*Saturne* and *Venus* this yeere in Coniunction? (2 *Henry IV* TLN 1288; 2.4.237–238). The Dauphin in *1 Henry VI* calls Joan (whom Shakespeare depicts as a whore) "Bright Starre of *Venus*" (TLN 351; 1.3.123). A servant in *Troilus and Cressida* calls the adultress Helen "the mortall *Venus*" (TLN 1508–1509; 3.1.30–31). "*Venus*," according to the evil Aaron, "gouerne[s]" the "desires" of the sexually voracious adultress Tamora in *Titus Andronicus* (TLN 766; 2.3.30).

31. James Grantham Turner discusses images of Venus placed in eighteenth-century gardens to construct a space of coy mystery, what he calls the "proper concealment" of the "perfect mistress." Although he does not discuss this transition from lascivious Venus to proper Venus, his one Renaissance example indicates the trajectory I am suggesting ("Sexual Politics" 360).

32. See Honigmann's comment: "unexplained. Perhaps a line deleted by Shakespeare" (116n.).

33. See *Othello* 1710, 1724, 1734, 1734b.

34. In contrast, under the fully developed heterosexual imaginary, a man's leadership ability is suspect if he is not married. The significant flaunting of wives in American presidential campaigns is one example of this phenomenon.

35. I am not accusing either Cressida or Cleopatra of actual infidelity, just asserting that the texts make them flirt with infidelity enough to lead their lovers to believe in it.

36. See the 1747 *Othello*, which leaves a big space after Cassio's name: "*Michael Cassio*; the *Florentine*'s 'A fellow almost damn'd in a fair wife.'" Also see the 1749 *Othello*, printed in Dublin, which puts the phrase in parentheses: "—(The Florentine's/A fellow almost damn'd in a fair wife—)." In the folio, the parentheses start before the "A".

37. As in the case of racism, within *Othello* criticism we can see features of this homophobia. For one example, see Honigmann's discussion of Iago's potential "homosexuality" (50–52); Honigmann appears to dismiss the possibility but then, almost unbelievably, finishes the discussion with the observation, "That said, it remains true that Iago's perverted nature sets him apart from the more 'normal' men and women of the tragedy" (52).

38. See Rowe (1709), Pope (1723), Theobald (1733), Hanmer (1744), Warburton (1747), Johnson (1765), the 1765 *Revisal* (Heath), Capell (1767), Jennens (1770–1774), Blair (1773), Johnson and Steevens (1773), and numerous individual *Othellos* (1724, 1734a and b, 1747, 1749, 1753, 1755, 1761).

39. We can also see the late-eighteenth- and nineteenth-century removal of Æmilia from the death tableaux at the end of the play as a denial of or an erasure of the intimate bonds between women that character-ized the homosocial imaginary. The late eighteenth century and nine-teenth century were uncomfortable with a tableaux on the bed that included more than what was seen as the essential isolated heterosex-ual couple. For the removal of Æmilia from the bed, see Neill, "Unproper" 204.

40. See the extended note in the Ridley *Arden*. See also the Honigmann *Arden* that adopts "me." The 1997 *Norton Shakespeare* adopts "me" as well.

41. The folio omits the comma after "heat." Pope follows the folio.

42. My brackets here stand for Hanmer's marks that denote his changes. They look like forward and backward half slashes.

43. Johnson reproduces all the earlier editors on the "young affects in my defunct." He comments, "I do not think that Mr. *Theobald*'s emenda-tion clears the text from embarrassment . . . Dr. *Warburton*'s explana-tion is not more satisfactory: what made the difficulty, will continue to make it . . . *Affects* stands here, not for *love*, but for *quality*, for that by which anything is affected. *I ask it not*, says he, *to please appetite, or satisfy loose desires*, the passions of youth which I have now outlived, or *for any particular gratification of myself, but merely that I may indulge the wishes of my wife* (348–349).

44. See Knight: "*Othello* is eminently a domestic tragedy" (120).

BIBLIOGRAPHY

Editions of Shakespeare, Works

Shakespeare, William. *The First Folio of Shakespeare. The Norton Facsimilie*. Ed. Charlton Hinman. New York: W. W. Norton, 1968.

———. *The Works of Mr. William Shakespeare*. Ed. Nicholas Rowe. London, 1709.

———. *The Works of Mr William Shakespear*. Ed. Alexander Pope. London, 1723.

———. *The Works of Shakespeare*. Ed. Lewis Theobald. London: Printed for A. Bettesworth and C. Hitch, J. Tonson, F. Clay, W. Feales, and R. Wellington, 1733. Vol. 7 (7 vols.).

———. *The Works of Mr William Shakespear*. Ed. Thomas Hanmer. Oxford: Printed at the Theatre, 1744. Vol. 6 (6 vols.).

———. *The Works of Shakespear* in 8 vols. Ed. Mr. Pope and Mr. Warburton London, 1747. Vol. 8.

———. *The Plays of William Shakespeare* in 8 vols. Ed. Samuel Johnson. London, 1765. Vol. 8.

———. *William Shakespeare His Comedies, Histories, and Tragedies* in 10 vols. Octavo. Ed. Edward Capell. London, 1767. Vol. 10.

———. *The Works of Shakespear*. Ed. Hugh Blair. Edinburgh, 1773. Vol. 8.

———. *The Plays of William Shakespeare*. Ed. Samuel Johnson and George Steevens. London, 1773. Vol. 10.

———. *Five Plays of Shakespeare*. Ed. Charles Jennens. London, 1770–1774. Vol. 2 (2 vols.).

———. *The Norton Shakespeare*. Ed. Stephen Greenblatt, Walter Cohen, Jean E. Howard, and Katherine Eisaman Maus. New York: W. W. Norton, 1997.

Editions of *Othello* Cited

Shakespeare, William. *Othello. The Arden Shakespeare*. Ed. Mr. R. Ridley. London: Methuen and Co. Ltd, 1958.

———. *Othello, The Moor of Venice. A Tragedy*. London, 1681.

———. *Othello, The Moor of Venice. A Tragedy*. London, 1710. [Reprint by Thomas Johnson printed in the Hague–Folger card catalogue.]

Shakespeare, William. *Othello, The Moor of Venice; A Tragedy, As it hath been divers times Acted at the* Globe, *and at the* Black-Friers: *And now at the* Theater-Royal, *by His Majesty's Servants.* London: 1724.

———. *Othello, The Moor of Venice. A Tragedy. As it is Acted at the Theatres.* London, 1734.

———. *Othello, The Moor of Venice. A Tragedy.* London: 1734b.

———. *Othello, The Moor of Venice. A Tragedy. As it is now Acted By His Majesty's Servants.* London, 1747.

———. *Othello, The Moor of Venice. A Tragedy.* Dublin, 1748.

———. *Othello The Moor of Venice A Tragedy.* Dublin, 1749.

———. *Othello, the Moor of Venice A Tragedy As it is now Acted by His Majesty's Servants.* London, 1753.

———. *Othello, the Moor of Venice. A Tragedy. As it is now acted At the Theatre Royal in Covent Garden.* London: 1755 [a modern note says that the date is wrong; apparently the cast first played in 1760].

———. *Othello, The Moor of Venice. A Tragedy. As it is now acted at the Theatre Royal in Covent-Garden.* London, 1761.

———. *Othello, The Moor of Venice. A Tragedy.* London: Printed exactly to the Representation by Halhed Garland, 1764.

———. *Othello, The Moor of Venice. A Tragedy. As it is now acted at the Theatres Royal in Drury-Lane and Covent-Garden.* London, 1771.

———. *Othello. A Tragedy, by Shakespeare, As performed at the Theatre-Royal, Drury-Lane. Regulated from the Prompt-Book, with Permission of the Managers, By Mr. Hopkins, Prompter. An Introduction, and Notes Critical and Illustrative, are added by the Authors of the Dramatic Censor.* Notes by Francis Gentleman. London: Printed for John Bell 1777.

———. *Othello, The Moor of Venice, A Tragedy* Revised by J.P. Kemble. As performed at the Covent Garden, New York and Boston Theatres Boston; Published by Richardson and Lord, J.H.A. Frost, Printer, 1823.

———. *Othello. A New Variorum Edition of Shakespeare.* Vol. 6. Ed. Horace Howard Furness. Philadelphia: J.B. Lippincott Company, 1886. 2nd edition.

———. *Othello. The Arden Shakespeare.* Ed. M.R. Ridley. London: Methuen and Co. Ltd, 1958.

———. *Othello. The Arden Shakespeare.* Ed. E.A.J. Honigmann. Surrey: Thomas Nelson and Sons Ltd., 1997.

Other Shakespeare Works Cited

Shakespeare, William. *Venvs and Adonis.* London, 1593.

———. *His True Chronicle Historie of the Life and Death of King Lear* . . . London, 1608.

———. *The Tragedie of Anthonie and Cleopatra. A New Variorum Edition of Shakespeare.* Ed. Horace Howard Furness. Philadelphia: Lippincott, 1907.

Shakespeare, William. *Shakespeare Quarto Facsimilies*. London: The Shakespeare Association, 1939.

———. *The Tragedy of Anthony and Cleopatra*. Ed. Michael Neill. Oxford: Oxford University Press, 1994.

Non-Shakespearean Works Cited

Abelove, Henry. "Some Speculations on the History of Sexual Intercourse during the Long Eighteenth Century in England." *Genders* 6 (Fall 1989): 125–130.

Adams, Henry Hitch. *English Domestic Or, Homiletic Tragedy 1575 to 1642*. New York: Columbia University Press, 1943.

Albrecht, W.P. "John Dennis and the Sublime Pleasure of Tragedy." *Studies on Voltaire and the Eighteenth Century* 87 (1972): 65–86.

Althusser, Louis. "Ideology and Ideological State Apparatuses (Notes toward an Investigation)." *Mapping Ideology*. Ed. Slavoj Žižek. London: Verso, 1994. 100–140.

Amussen, Susan Dwyer. *An Ordered Society: Gender and Class in Early Modern England*. Oxford: Basil Blackwell Ltd., 1988.

———. " 'The Part of a Christian Man': The Cultural Politics of Manhood in Early Modern England." *Political Culture and Cultural Politics in Early Modern England*. Ed. Susan D. Amussen and Mark A. Kishlansky. New York: Manchester University Press, 1995. 213–233.

Anderson, Michael. *Approaches to the History of the Western Family*. London: The Macmillan Press Ltd., 1980.

Andreadis, Harriette. *Sappho in Early Modern England*. Chicago: University of Chicago Press, 2001.

Anthony, Sister Rose. *The Jeremy Collier Stage Controversy*. Milwaukee: Marquette University Press, 1937.

Appelbaum, Robert. " 'Standing to the Wall': The Pressures of Masculinity in *Romeo and Juliet*." *Shakespeare Quarterly* 48.3 (1997): 251–272.

Aquinas, St. Thomas. *Summa Theologica*. in 5 vols. Trans. Fathers of the English Dominican Province. Benziger Brothers, Inc., 1948. Vol. 4.

Arden of Feversham (The Lamentable and Trve Tragedie of M.). London, 1592. The Malone Society Reprints. Oxford: Oxford University Press, 1940 (1947).

Arden of Faversham (The Tragedy of). Ed. M.L. Wine. London: Methuen & Co., Ltd., 1973.

Arden of Faversham. Ed. Martin White. London: A & C Black, 1982.

Armistead, Jack M. "Dryden's Prospero and His Predecessors." *South Atlantic Review* 50.1 (1985): 23–33.

Armstrong, Nancy and Leonard Tennenhouse. *The Ideology of Conduct: Essays in Literature and the History of Sexuality*. New York: Methuen, 1987.

Attwell, David. "Property, Status, and the Subject in a Middle-Class Tragedy: *Arden of Faversham*." *ELR* 21.3 (1991): 328–338.

Auberlen, Eckhard. "*The Tempest* and the Concerns of the Restoration Court: A Study of *The Enchanted Island* and the Operatic *Tempest*." *Restoration* 15.2 (1991): 71–88.

Augustin. *The Confessions and Letters of St. Augustin. A Select Library of the Nicene and Post-Nicene Fathers of the Christian Church*. Ed. Philip Schaff. New York: Charles Scribner's Sons, 1907. Vol. 1.

Augustin. *Expositions on the Book of the Psalms. A Select Library of the Nicene and Post-Nicene Fathers of the Christian Church*. Ed. Philip Schaff. New York: Charles Scribner's Sons, 1907. Vol. 8.

Bach, Rebecca Ann. "Bearbaiting, Dominion, and Colonialism." *Race, Ethnicity, and Power in the Renaissance*. Ed. Joyce Green McDonald. Madison: Fairleigh Dickinson Press, 1997.

———. "The Homosocial Imaginary of *A Woman Killed with Kindness*." *Textual Practice* 12.3 (1998): 503–524.

———. *Colonial Transformations: The Cultural Production of the New Atlantic World 1580–1640*. New York: Palgrave, 2000.

———. "Tennis Balls: *Henry V* and Testicular Masculinity, or, According to the *OED*, Shakespeare Doesn't Have Any Balls." *Renaissance Drama* 30 (2001): 3–23.

———. "Manliness before Individualism: Masculinity, Effeminacy, and Homoeroticism in Shakespeare's History Plays." *The Blackwell Companion to Shakespeare's History Plays*. Ed. Richard Dutton and Jean Howard. Oxford: Blackwell, 2003. 220–245.

———. "(Re)placing John Donne in the History of Sexuality." *ELH* 72 (2005): 259–289.

Bacon, Francis. *Francis Bacon: A Critical Edition of the Major Works*. Oxford: Oxford University Press, 1996.

Baker, David J. *Between Nations: Shakespeare, Spenser, Marvell, and the Question of Britain*. Stanford: Stanford University Press, 1997.

Baines, Barbara J. *Thomas Heywood*. Boston: G.K. Hall & Co., 1984.

Barnouw, Jeffrey. "The Morality of the Sublime: To John Dennis." *Comparative Literature* 35.1 (1983): 21–42.

Barthelemy, Anthony Gerard. *Black Face, Maligned Race: The Representation of Blacks in English Drama from Shakespeare to Southerne*. Baton Rogue: Louisiana State University Press, 1987.

Belsey, Catherine. "Alice Arden's Crime." *Renaissance Drama* n. s. 13 (1982): 83–102.

———. *The Subject of Tragedy: Identity and Difference in Renaissance Drama*. London: Routledge, 1985.

———. *Shakespeare and the Loss of Eden: The Construction of Family Values in Early Modern Culture*. New Brunswick, N.J.: Rutgers University Press, 1999.

Berger, Thomas L. "The Second Quarto of *Othello* and the Question of 'Textual Authority.' " *Critical Essays on Shakespeare's* Othello. Ed. Anthony Gerard Barthelemy. New York: G.K. Hall & Co., 1994. 144–161.

Bergeron, David M. *King James and Letters of Homoerotic Desire.* Iowa City: University of Iowa Press, 1999.

Berkeley, David S. "A Vulgarization of Desdemona." *SEL* 3.2 (1963): 233–239.

Berlant, Lauren. Introduction to *Intimacy: A Special Issue. Critical Inquiry* 24.2 (1998).

Bernbaum, Ernest. *The Drama of Sensibility.* Gloucester, Mass.: Peter Smith, 1958.

Bersani, Leo. *Homos.* Cambridge: Harvard University Press, 1995.

Bevington, David. Introduction. *Romeo and Juliet. The Complete Works of Shakespeare.* Ed. David Bevington. New York: Harper Collins, 1992. 4th ed. 977–979.

Bly, Mary. "Bawdy Puns and Lustful Virgins: The Legacy of Juliet's Desire in the Comedies of the Early 1600s." *Shakespeare Survey* 49 (1996): 97–109.

———. *Queer Virgins and Virign Queans on the Early Modern Stage.* Oxford: Oxford University Press, 2000.

Boswell, James. *Boswell's Life of Johnson.* Ed. George Birkbeck Hill. Rev. L.F. Powell. Oxford: Clarendon Press, 1934. 6 vols.

Bowers, Fredson. *The Dramatic Works in the Beaumont and Fletcher Canon.* Cambridge: Cambridge University Press, 1992. Vol. 8.

Bowers, Rick. "*A Woman Killed with Kindness*: Plausibility on a Smaller Scale." *Studies in English Literature 1500–1900* 24 (1984): 293–306.

Bradley, A.C. *Shakespearean Tragedy: Lectures on* Hamlet, Othello, King Lear, Macbeth. London: Macmillan, 1960.

Branam, George C. *Eighteenth-Century Adaptations of Shakespearean Tragedy.* Berkeley: University of California Press, 1956.

Brandon, Samuel. *The Tragicomoedi of the Vertuous Octavia.* London, 1598.

Braude, Benjamin. "The Sons of Noah and the Construction of Ethnic and Geographical Identities in the Medieval and Early Modern Periods." *William and Mary Quarterly* 3rd ser., 54.1 (1997): 103–142.

Bray, Alan. *Homosexuality in Renaissance England.* London: Gay Men's Press, 1982.

———. "Homosexuality and the Signs of Male Friendship in Elizabethan England." *Queering the Renaissance.* Ed. Jonathan Goldberg. Durham: Duke University Press, 1994. 40–61.

———. *The Friend.* Chicago: The University of Chicago Press, 2003.

Bredbeck, Gregory. *Sodomy and Interpretation: Marlowe to Milton.* Cornell: Cornell University Press, 1991.

Breitenberg, Mark. *Anxious Masculinity in Early Modern England.* Cambridge: Cambridge University Press, 1996.

Brewer, John. " 'The Most Polite Age and the most vicious.' Attitudes towards Culture as a Commodity, 1660–1800." *The Consumption of Culture: 1600–1800.* Ed. Ann Bermingham and John Brewer. London: Routledge, 1995. 341–361.

Brodwin, Leonora Leet. *Elizabethan Love Tragedy.* New York: New York University Press, 1971.

Bromley, Laura G. "Domestic Conduct in *A Woman Killed with Kindness*." *Studies in English Literature 1500–1900* 26 (1986): 259–276.

Brown, Laura. *English Dramatic Form, 1660–1760: An Essay in Generic History*. New Haven: Yale University Press, 1981.

Burnaby, William. *Love Betray'd*. London, 1703.

Burnett, Mark Thornton. *Masters and Servants in English Drama and Culture: Authority and Obedience*. New York: St. Martins, 1997.

Burton, Robert. *The Anatomy of Melancholy*. Ed. Thomas C. Faulkner, Nicolas K. Kiessling, and Rhonda L. Blair. Oxford: The Clarendon Press, 1989. Vol. 1.

Butler, Judith. *Gender Trouble: Feminism and the Subversion of Identity*. New York: Routledge, 1990.

———. *Bodies that Matter: On the Discursive Limits of "Sex."* New York: Routledge, 1993.

Cahill, Patricia Ann. " 'Tales of Iron Wars': Martial Bodies and Manly Economies in Elizabethan Culture." Dissertation, Columbia University, 2000.

Callaghan, Dympna, ed. *A Feminist Companion to Shakespeare*. Malden, Mass.: Blackwell, 2000.

———. "Shakespeare and Religion." *Textual Practice* 15.1 (2001): 1–4.

Campbell, Oscar James. "The Salvation of Lear." *ELH* 15.2 (1948): 93–109.

Canfield, J. Douglas. "The Jewel of Great Price:" Mutability and Constancy in Dryden's *All for Love*." *ELH* 42.1 (1975): 38–61.

———. "Religious Language and Religious Meaning in Restoration Comedy." *SEL* 20 (1980): 385–406.

Canny, Nicholas. *The Upstart Earl: A Study of the Social and Mental World of Richard Boyle, First Earl of Cork 1566–1643*. Cambridge: Cambridge University Press, 1982.

Cantor, Muriel G. "Prime-Time Fathers: A Study in Continuity and Change." *Critical Studies in Mass Communications* 7 (1990): 275–285.

Canuteson, John. "The Theme of Forgiveness in the Plot and Subplot of *A Woman Killed with Kindness*." *Renaissance Drama* n.s. 2 (1969): 123–141.

Capp, Bernard. "The Double Standard Revisited: Plebian Women and Male Sexual Reputation in Early Modern England." *Past and Present* 162 (1999): 70–100.

———. *When Gossips Meet: Women, Family, and Neighborhood in Early Modern England*. Oxford: Oxford University Press, 2003.

Cary, Elizabeth. *The Tragedy of Mariam: The Fair Queen of Jewry*. Ed. Barry Weller and Margaret W. Ferguson. Berkeley: The University of California Press, 1994.

The Cassell Dictionary of Slang. Ed. Jonathan Green. London: Cassell, 1998.

Chapman, George, Ben Jonson, and John Marston. *Eastward Hoe. Ben Jonson*. Ed. C.H. Herford and Percy Simpson. Oxford: Clarendon Press, 1932.

Chapman, Raymond. "*Arden of Faversham*: Its Interest Today." *English* XI (1956): 15–17.

Chappell, William. *Old English Popular Music*. Revised by H. Ellis Wooldridge. New York: Jack Brussel, 1961.

Charnes, Linda. *Notorious Identity: Materializing the Subject in Shakespeare*. Cambridge: Harvard University Press, 1993.

Chaucer, Geoffrey. "The Pardoner's Tale." *The Riverside Chaucer*. Ed. Larry D. Benson. Boston: Houghton Mifflin, 1987. 3rd ed. 196–202.

Chauncy, George Jr. *Gay New York: Gender, Urban Culture, and the Making of the Gay Male World, 1890–1940*. New York: Basic Books, 1994.

Chernaik, Warren. *Sexual Freedom in Restoration Literature*. Cambridge: Cambridge University Press, 1995.

Cibber, Colley. *An Apology for the Life of Mr. Colly Cibber, Comedian*. London, 1740. 2nd ed.

Cibber, Theophilous. *An Historical Tragedy of the Civil Wars in the Reign of King Henry VI (Being a Sequel to the Tragedy of Humfrey Duke of Gloucester: And an Introduction to the Tragical History of King Richard III)*. Alter'd from Shakespear, in the year 1720. London, 1720.

Clark, Alice. *Working Life of Women in the Seventeenth Century*. London: Frank Cass and Company Limited, 1968.

Cleaver, Robert and John Dod. *A Godly Forme of Household Gouernment, For the ordering of priuate Families, according to the direction of Gods Word*. London, 1630.

Cloud, Random. " 'The Very Names of the Persons': Editing and the Invention of Dramatick Character." *Staging the Renaissance: Reinterpretations of Elizabethan and Jacobean Drama*. New York: Routledge, 1991. 88–96.

Clum, John M. *Something for the Boys: Musical Theater and Gay Culture*. New York: St. Martin's Press, 1999.

Cohen, Walter. Introduction. *The Two Noble Kinsmen*. By William Shakespeare. *The Norton Shakespeare*. Gen. ed. Stephen Greenblatt. New York: W.W. Norton & Co., 1997. 3195–3203.

Coleridge, Samuel Taylor. *The Complete Works of Samuel Taylor Coleridge*. Ed. Professor Shedd. New York: Harper and Brothers, 1854. Vol. 4 (7 vols.).

Collier, Jeremy. *A Short View of the Immorality, and Profaneness of the English Stage, Together with the Sense of Antiquity upon this Argument*. London, 1698.

Collier, John Payne. *The History of English Dramatic Poetry*. London: G. Bell & Sons, 1879.

Combe, Kirk. " 'But Loads of Sh- Almost Choked the Way': Shadwell, Dryden, Rochester, and the Summer of 1676." *Texas Studies in Literature and Language* 37.2 (1995): 127–164.

Comensoli, Viviana. *'Household Business': Domestic Plays of Early Modern England*. Toronto: University of Toronto Press, 1996.

Comensoli, Viviana and Anne Russell, eds. *Enacting Gender on the English Renaissance Stage*. Urbana and Chicago: University of Illinois Press, 1999.

Cook, David. "*A Woman Killed with Kindness*: An Unshakespearean Tragedy." *English Studies* 45 (1964): 353–372.

Coursen, Herbert R. Jr. "The Subplot of *A Woman Killed with Kindness*." *English Language Notes* 2.3 (1965): 180–185.

Cressy, David. "Describing the Social Order of Elizabethan and Stuart England." *Literature and History* 3 (1976): 29–44.

———. "Kinship and Kin Interaction in Early Modern England." *Past and Present* 113 (1986): 38–69.

———. "Foucault, Stone, Shakespeare and Social History." *English Literary Renaissance* 21.2 (1991): 121–133.

Crowne, John. *Henry the Sixth, The First Part with the Murder of Humphrey Duke of Glocester*. London, 1681.

———. *Henry the Sixth, The Second Part of the Misery of Civil War*. London, 1681.

Danby, John F. *Shakespeare's Doctrine of Nature: A Study of* King Lear. London: Faber and Faber, 1949.

Daniel, Samuel. *The Tragedie of Cleopatra. The Works of Samuel Daniel*. Newly augmented. London, 1602.

———. *A Letter from Octauia to Marcus Antonius* (1599). *The Complete Works in Verse and Prose of Samuel Daniel*. Ed. Alexander B Grosart. London, 1885. Vol. 1 (4 vols.).

D'Avenant, William. *The Law against Lovers. The Works of Sir William Davenant*. London, 1673. First performed 1662.

D'Avenant, William and John Dryden. *The Tempest, or the Enchanted Island*. London, 1676.

Davidson, Arnold I. "Sex and the Emergence of Sexuality." *Critical Inquiry* 14 (1987): 16–48.

Davidson, Clifford. "*Timon of Athens*: The Iconography of False Friendship." *The Huntington Library Quarterly* 43.3 (1980): 181–200.

De Grazia, Margreta. "The Scandal of Shakespeare's Sonnets." *Shakespeare Survey* 46 (1994): 35–49.

———. "The Ideology of Superfluous Things: *King Lear* as Period Piece." *Subject and Object in Renaissance Culture*. Ed. Margreta De Grazia, Maureen Quilligan, and Peter Stallybrass. Cambridge: Cambridge University Press, 1996. 17–42.

———. "*Hamlet* before Its Time." *Modern Language Quarterly* 62.4 (2001): 355–372.

De Grazia, Margreta and Peter Stallybrass. "The Materiality of the Shakespearean Text." *Shakespeare Quarterly* 44.3 (1993): 255–283.

Dekker, Thomas. *The Honest Whore*. London, 1604.

———. *The Honest Whore, Part I. The Dramatic Works of Thomas Dekker*. Ed. Fredson Bowers. Vol. 2. Cambridge: Cambridge University Press, 1955.

Dekker, Thomas and Thomas Middleton. *The Roaring Girle or Moll Cut-Purse*. London, 1611.

The Roaring Girl. The Dramatic Works of Thomas Dekker. Ed. Fredson Bowers. Cambridge: Cambridge University Press, 1966. Vol. 3 (4 vols.).

Delany, Paul. "*King Lear* and the Decline of Feudalism." *PMLA* 92 (1977): 429–440.

Dennis, John. *The Usefulness of the Stage, To the Happiness of Mankind. To Government, and To Religion.* London, 1698.

———. *The Critical Works of John Dennis.* Ed. Edward Niles Hooker. Baltimore: The Johns Hopkins Press, 1943. 2 vols.

De Scudery, Monsieur. *A Triumphant Arch Earected and Consecrated to the Glory of the Feminine Sexe.* Englished by I.B. London, 1656.

Desmet, Christy and Robert Sawyer, eds. *Harold Bloom's Shakespeare.* New York: Palgrave, 2002.

Dictionary of American Slang. Ed. Harold Wentworth and Stuart Berg Flexner. New York: Thomas Y. Crowell Co., 1975. Second supplemented edition.

Dictionary of National Biography. Ed. E.T. Williams and C.S. Nicholls. Oxford: Oxford University Press, 1981.

DiGangi, Mario. "Queering the Shakespearean Family." *Shakespeare Quarterly* 47.3 (1996): 269–290.

———. *The Homoerotics of Early Modern Drama.* Cambridge: Cambridge University Press, 1997.

Dobson, Michael. " 'Remember / First Possess his Books': The Appropriation of *The Tempest* 1700–1800." *Shakespeare Survey* 43 (1990): 99–108.

———. *The Making of the National Poet: Shakespeare, Adaptation, and Authorship 1660–1769.* New York: Oxford University Press, 1994.

Dodsley, R., ed. *A Select Collection of Old Plays.* London, 1744. Vol. 1 (12 vols.).

Dolan, Frances E. *Dangerous Familiars: Representations of Domestic Crime in England, 1550–1700.* Ithaca: Cornell University Press, 1994.

———. *Whores of Babylon: Catholicism, Gender and Seventeenth-Century Print Culture.* Ithaca: Cornell University Press, 1999.

Dollimore, Jonathan. *Sexual Dissidence: Augustine to Wilde, Freud to Foucault.* Oxford: Clarendon Press, 1991.

Donne, John. *LXXX Sermons Preached by that Learned and Reverend Divine, John Donne, Dr In Divinitie.* London, 1640.

———. *ΒΙΑΘΑΝΑΤΟΣ.* London, 1648.

———. *The Elegies and the Songs and Sonnets.* Ed. Helen Gardner. Oxford: Clarendon Press, 1965.

———. *The Divine Poems.* Ed. Helen Gardner. Oxford: Oxford University Press, 1978.

———. *John Donne: A Critical Edition of the Major Works.* Ed. John Carey. Oxford: Oxford University Press, 1990.

Doran, Madeleine. *Endeavors of Art.* Madison: University of Wisconsin Press, 1954.

Dryden, John. *Troilus and Cressida, or Truth Found too Late.* London, 1679.

———. *Of Dramatic Poesy and Other Critical Essays.* Ed. George Watson. London: J.M. Dent & Sons, 1962. 2 vols.

———. *All for Love, or The World Well Lost.* Ed. David M. Vieth. Lincoln: University of Nebraska Press, 1972.

Duberman, Martin, Martha Vicinus, and George Chauncy, Jr. *Hidden from History: Reclaiming the Gay and Lesbian Past.* New York: Penguin Books, 1989.

Duffy, Eamon. *The Stripping of the Altars: Traditional Religion in England 1400–1580*. New Haven: Yale University Press, 1992.

D'Urfey, Thomas. *The Injured Princess, or the Fatal Wager*. London, 1682.

Dyer, Richard. *White*. London: Routledge, 1997.

Edgar, Irving I. *Essays in English Literature and History*. New York: Philosophical Library, 1972.

Edmunds, John. " 'Timon of Athens' Blended with 'Le Misanthrope': Shadwell's Recipe for Satrirical Tragedy." *Modern Language Review* 64.3 (1969): 500–507.

Edwards, Michael. "*King Lear* and Christendom." *Christianity and Literature* 50:1 (2000): 15–29.

Elton, William R. King Lear *and the Gods*. San Marino: The Huntington Library, 1966.

Evans, David R. " 'Private Greatness': The Feminine Ideal in Dryden's Early Heroic Drama." *Restoration* 16.1 (1992): 12–19.

Everett, Barbara. "The New King Lear." *Critical Quarterly* 2 (1960): 325–339.

Ezell, Margaret J.M. *The Patriarch's Wife: Literary Evidence and the History of the Family*. Chapel Hill: The University of North Carolina Press, 1987.

Felperin, Howard. *Shakespearean Representation*. Princeton: Princeton University Press, 1977.

Fisher, Will. "The Renaissance Beard: Masculinity in Early Modern England." *Renaissance Quarterly* 54 (2001): 155–187.

Fitz, L.T. "Egyptian Queens and Male Reviewers: Sexist Attitudes in *Antony and Cleopatra* Criticism." *Shakespeare Quarterly* 28.3 (1977): 297–316.

Fletcher, Anthony. *Gender, Sex, and Subordination in England, 1500–1800*. New Haven: Yale University Press, 1995.

Fletcher, John. *The False One. The Dramatick Works of Beaumont and Fletcher*. Ed. George Colman, the Elder. London, 1778 [1619–1623?; orig. pub. 1647]. Vol. 4 (10 vols.).

———. *The Pilgrim, A Comedy*. Written Originally by Mr. Fletcher, and now very much Alter'd with several Additions. Likewise A Prologue, Epilogue, Dialogue and Masque, Written by the late Great Poet Mr. Dryden . . . London, 1700.

Fletcher, John [and Nathan Field and Philip Massinger]. *The Bloody Brother*. London, 1639.

Floyd-Wilson, Mary. "Ophelia and Femininity in the Eighteenth Century: 'Dangerous Conjectures in Ill-Breeding Minds.' " *Women's Studies* 21 (1992): 397–409.

Foakes, R.A. Hamlet *versus* Lear: *Cultural Politics and Shakespeare's Art*. Cambridge: Cambridge University Press, 1993.

Foucault, Michel. *The History of Sexuality: Volume 1*. Trans. Robert Hurley. New York: Random House, 1978.

Fradenburg, Louise and Carla Freccero. *Premodern Sexualities*. New York: Routledge, 1996.

Fumerton, Patricia. *Cultural Aesthetics*. Chicago: University of Chicago Press, 1991.

Gagan, Jean. "Love and Honor in Dryden's Heroic Plays." *PMLA* 77.3 (1962): 208–220.

Gainsford, Thomas. *The Rich Cabinet Furnished with Varietie of Excellent Discriptions, Exquisite Characters, Witty Discourses, and Delightfull Histories, Deuine and Morrall*. London, 1616.

Garner, S.N. "Shakespeare's Desdemona." *Shakespeare Studies* 9 (1976): 233–252.

Garner, Shirley Nelson and Madelon Sprengnether, eds. *Shakespearean Tragedy and Gender*. Bloomington: Indiana University Press, 1996.

Garrick, David. *The Letters of David Garrick*. Ed. David M. Little and George M. Kahrl. Cambridge: Harvard University Press, 1963. Vol. 3.

Geneva Bible. Facs. of 1560 ed. Madison: University of Wisconsin Press, 1969.

Gervinus, Georg Gottfried. *Shakespeare Commentaries*. Trans. under the author's superintendence by F. E. Burnett. New ed. rev. by the translator. London: Smith, Elder, 1875.

Gildon, Charles. *The Works of Mr William Shakespear*. Ed. Nicholas Rowe. Printed for E. Curll and E. Sanger, London, 1710. Vol. 7.

Goldberg, Jonathan. *Sodometries*. Stanford: Stanford University Press, 1992.

———. "*Romeo and Juliet*'s Open Rs." *Queering the Renaissance*. Durham: Duke University Press, 1994. 218–235.

———, ed. *Queering the Renaissance*. Durham: Duke University Press, 1994.

———. "The Anus in *Coriolanus*." *Historicism, Psychoanalysis, and Early Modern Culture*. Ed. Carla Mazzio and Douglas Trevor. New York: Routledge, 2000. 260–271.

Gouge, William. *Of Domesticall Dvties*. London, 1622.

Gowing, Laura. *Domestic Dangers: Women, Words, and Sex in Early Modern London*. Oxford: Clarendon Press, 1996.

Gramsci, Antonio. *An Antonio Gramsci Reader*. Ed. David Forgacs. New York: Schoken Books, 1988.

Griffith, Mrs Elizabeth. *The Morality of Shakespeare's Drama Illustrated*. London, 1775.

Guffey, George R. "Politics, Weather, and the Contemporary Reception of the Dryden-Davenent *Tempest*." *Restoration* 8.1 (1984): 1–9.

Gutierrez, Nancy A. "The Irresolution of Melodrama: The Meaning of Adultery in *A Woman Killed with Kindness*." *Exemplaria* 1.2 (1989): 265–291.

Guy-Bray, Stephen. *Homoerotic Space: The Poetics of Loss in Renaissance Literature*. Toronto: University of Toronto Press, 2002.

Haggerty, George E. *Men in Love: Masculinity and Sexuality in the Eighteenth Century*. New York: Columbia University Press, 1999.

Hakluyt, Richard. *The Principal Navigations, Voiages, Traffiques and Discoueries of the English Nation*. London, 1599. Vol. 2.

Hall, Kim F. *Things of Darkness: Economies of Race and Gender in Early Modern England*. Ithaca: Cornell University Press, 1995.

Hall, Stuart. "Notes on Deconstructing the 'Popular.'" *People's History and Socialist Theory*. Ed. Raphael Samuel. London: Routledge & Kegan Paul Ltd., 1981. 227–240.

———. "The Rediscovery of 'Ideology': Return of the Repressed in Media Studies." *Culture, Society and the Media*. Ed. Michael Gurevitch, Tony Bennett, James Curran, and Janet Woolacott. London: Methuen. 1982. 56–90.

Hall, Stuart. "The Problem of Ideology: Marxism without Guarantees." *Stuart Hall: Critical Dialogues in Cultural Studies*. Ed. David Morley and Kuan-Hsing Chen. London: Routledge, 1996. 25–46.

Halperin, David M. "Forgetting Foucault: Acts, Identities, and the History of Sexuality." *Representations* 63 (1998): 93–120.

———. *One Hundred Years of Homosexuality*. New York: Routledge, 1990.

———. *How to Do the History of Homosexuality*. Chicago: The University of Chicago Press, 2002.

Halpern, Richard. *The Poetics of Primitive Accumulation: English Renaissance Culture and the Genealogy of Capital*. Ithaca: Cornell University Press, 1991.

Hammond, Paul. *Figuring Sex between Men from Shakespeare to Rochester*. Oxford: The Clarendon Press, 2002.

Haralovich, Mary Beth. "Sitcoms and Suburbs: Positioning the 1950s Homemaker." *Quarterly Review of Film and Video* 11.1 (1989): 61–83.

Hareven, Tamara K. "Modernization and Family History: Perspectives on Social Change." *Signs* 2.1 (1976): 190–206.

Hassel, R. Chris Jr. *Renaissance Drama and the English Church Year*. Lincoln: University of Nebraska Press, 1979.

Heath, Benjamin. *A Revisal of Shakespear's Text, wherein the Alterations introduced into it by the more modern Editors and Critics are particularly considered*. London, 1765.

Heffernan, James A.W. "Wordsworth and Dennis: The Discrimination of Feelings." *PMLA* 82.5 (1967): 430–436.

Heilman, Robert B. "Some Fops and Some Versions of Foppery." *ELH* 49.2 (1982): 363–395.

Heinemann, Margot. "'Demustifying the Mystery of State': *King Lear* and the World Upside Down." *Shakespeare Survey* 44 (1991): 75–83.

Helgerson, Richard. *Forms of Nationhood: The Elizabethan Writing of England*. Chicago: University of Chicago Press, 1992.

Heller, Dana. *Family Plots: The De-Oedipalization of Popular Culture*. Philadelphia: University of Pennsylvania Press, 1995.

Henderson, Diana E. "Many Mansions: Reconstructing *A Woman Killed with Kindness*." *SEL* 26 (1986): 277–294.

———. "*A Woman Killed with Kindness* and Domesticity, False or True." *Connotations* 5.1 (1995/1996): 49–54.

Henderson, Katherine Usher and Barbara F. McManus. *Half Humankind: Contexts and Texts of the Controversy about Women in England, 1540–1640*. Urbana: University of Illinois Press, 1985.

Hendricks, Margo, and Patricia Parker, eds. *Women, "Race," and Writing in the Early Modern Period*. London: Routledge, 1994.

Heywood, Thomas. *A Woman Kilde with Kindnesse*. London, 1617.

———. *A Woman Killed with Kindness*. Ed. R.W. Van Fossen. Cambridge: Harvard University Press, 1961.

———. *A Woman Killed with Kindness*. Ed. Brian Scobie. New York: W.W. Norton and Company, Inc., 1985.

Hill, Aaron. *King Henry the Fifth Or, The Conquest of France, by the English*. London, 1723.

Hinnant, Charles H. "Colier, Congreve and the Patriarchalist Debate." *Eighteenth-Century Life* 4.4 (1978): 83–85.

Hoadly, John and George Lillo. *Arden of Feversham*. London, 1759.

Hoare, Philip. *Noël Coward: A Biography*. New York: Simon and Schuster, 1995.

Hogan, Charles Beecher. *Shakespeare in the Theatre 1701–1800*. Oxford: Clarendon Press, 1952–1957. 2 vols.

Holbrook, Peter. "The Left and *King Lear*." *Textual Practice* 14.2 (2000): 343–362.

Holderness, Graham, Nick Potter, and John Turner. *Shakespeare and the Play of History*. Iowa City: University of Iowa Press, 1987.

Holinshed, Raphael. *The Chronicles of England, From William the Conquerour . . . untill this present yeare of Grace 1585*. London, 1587. Vol. 3 [STC 13569 U. Penn.].

Hopes, J. "Politica and Morality in the Writings of Jeremy Collier." *Literature and History* 8 (1978): 159–174.

Hotine, Margaret. "Two Plays for St. Stephen's Day." *Notes and Queries* 227.29 (April 1982): 119–121.

Howard, Jean E. and Phyllis Rackin. *Engendering a Nation: A Feminist Account of Shakespeare's English Histories*. New York: Routledge, 1997.

Howard, Jean E. and Scott Shershow, eds. *Marxist Shakespeares*. London: Routledge, 2001.

Howe, Elizabeth. *The First English Actress: Women and Drama, 1660–1700*. Cambridge: Cambridge University Press, 1992.

Hume, Robert D. *The Development of English Drama in the Late Seventeenth Century*. Oxford: Clarendon Press, 1976.

———. "The Myth of the Rake in 'Restoration' Comedy." *Studies in the Literary Imagination* 10.1 (1977): 25–55.

Hutson, Lorna. *The Usurer's Daughter: Male Friendship and Fictions of Women in Sixteenth-Century England*. London: Routledge, 1994.

Ingram, Martin. *Church Courts, Sex and Marriage in England, 1570–1640*. Cambridge: Cambridge University Press, 1987.

———. "Family and Household." *A Companion to Renaissance Drama*. Ed. Arthur F. Kinney. Oxford: Blackwell, 2002.

Jameson, Anna Brownwell. *Shakspeare's Heroines*. London: George Bell & Sons, 1897.

Jameson, Fredric. *The Political Unconscious: Narrative as a Socially Symbolic Act*. Ithaca: Cornell University Press, 1981.

Jankowski, Theodora A. *Pure Resistance: Queer Virginity in Early Modern English Drama*. Philadelphia: University of Pennsylvania Press, 2000.

Jardine, Lisa. *Still Harping on Daughters: Women and Drama in the Age of Shakespeare*. New York: Columbia University Press, 1989.

Jardine, Lisa. "Companionate Marriage versus Male Friendship: Anxiety for the Lineal Family in Jacobean Drama." *Political Culture and Cultural Politics in Early Modern England*. Ed. Susan D. Amussen and Mark A. Kishlansky. New York: Manchester University Press, 1995. 234–254.

Jones, Ann Rosalind. "Counteratttacks on 'the Bayter of Women': Three Pamphleteers of the Early Seventeenth Century." *The Renaissance Englishwoman in Print: Counterbalancing the Canon*. Ed. Anne M. Haselkorn and Betty S. Travitsky. Amherst: The University of Massachusetts Press, 1990.

———. *The Currency of Eros: Women's Love Lyric in Europe, 1540–1620*. Bloomington: University of Indiana Press, 1990.

Jones, Ann Rosalind and Peter Stallybrass. *Renaissance Clothing and the Materials of Memory*. Cambridge: Cambridge University Press, 2000.

———. "Fetishizing the Glove in Renaissance Europe." *Critical Inquiry* 28 (2001): 114–132.

Jones, Eldred. *Othello's Countrymen: The African in English Renaissance Drama*. London: Oxford University Press, 1965.

Jordan, Constance. *Renaissance Feminism: Literary Texts and Political Models*. Ithaca: Cornell University Press, 1990.

Jordan, Winthrop D. *White Over Black: American Attitudes toward the Negro, 1550–1812*. Chapel Hill: The University of North Carolina Press, 1968.

Katz, Candace Brook. "The Deserted Mistress Motif in Mrs. Manley's *Lost Lover, 1696*." *Restoration and Eighteenth Century Theatre Research* 16.1 (1977): 27–39.

Katz, Jonathan Ned. *The Invention of Heterosexuality*. New York: Dutton, 1995.

Kavanagh, James H. "Shakespeare in Ideology." *Alternative Shakespeares*. Ed. John Drakakis. London: Methuen, 1985. 144–165.

Kelly, Joan. "Did Women Have a Renaissance." *Women, History, and Theory*. Chicago: The University Of Chicago Press, 1984. 19–50.

Kennedy, Gwynne. *Just Anger: Representing Women's Anger in Early Modern England*. Carbondale: Southern Illinois University Press, 2000.

Kenrick, William. *Falstaff's Wedding*. London, 1760.

Kiefer, Frederick. "Heywood as Moralist in *A Woman Killed with Kindness*." *Medieval and Renaissance Drama in England* 3 (1986): 83–98.

Kilbourne, Frederick. *Alterations and Adaptations of Shakespeare*. Boston: Gotham Press, 1906.

Kipnis, Laura. "Adultery." *Critical Inquiry* 24.2 (1998): 289–327.

Kirkman, James Thomas. *Memoirs of the Life of Charles Macklin, Esq*. London, 1799. 2 vols.

Klein, Lawrence E. "Gender and the Public/Private Distinction in the Eighteenth Century: Some Questions about Evidence and Analytic Procedure." *Eighteenth-Century Studies* 29.1 (1996): 97–109.

Klima, S. "Some Unrecorded Borrowings from Shakespeare in Dryden's *All for Love*." *Notes and Queries* 208.10 (1963): 415–418.

Kloesel, Lynn F. "The Play of Desire: Vulcan's Net and Other Stories of Passion in *All for Love*." *The Eighteenth Century: Theory and Interpretation* 31.3 (1990): 227–244.

Knapp, Jeffrey. *Shakespeare's Tribe: Church, Nation, and Theater in Renaissance England*. Chicago: The University of Chicago Press, 2002.

Knight, G. Wilson. *The Wheel of Fire: Essays in Interpretation of Shakespeare's Sombre Tragedies*. London: Oxford University Press, 1930.

Korda, Natasha. *Shakespeare's Domestic Economies: Gender and Property in Early Modern England*. Philadelphia: University of Pennsylvania Press, 2002.

Kronenfeld, Judy. King Lear *and the Naked Truth: Rethinking the Language of Religion and Resistance*. Durham: Duke University Press, 1998.

Krutch, Joseph Wood. *Comedy and Conscience after the Restoration*. New York: Columbia University Press, 1949.

Lacey, John. *Sauny the Scott: or, the Taming of the Shrew*. London, 1698.

Lake, Peter with Michael Questier. *The Antichrist's Lewd Hat: Protestants, Papists and Players in Post-Reformation England*. New Haven: Yale University Press, 2002.

Langland, William. *Piers Plowman: The C Version*. Ed. George Russell and George Kane. London: The Athlone Press, 1997.

———. *Piers Plowman*. Trans. E. Talbot Donaldson. *The Longman Anthology of British Literature*. Ed. David Damrosch. New York: Longman, 2003. Vol. 1A. 2nd. ed. 424–454.

Lanser, Susan S. "Befriending the Body: Female Intimacies as Class Acts." *Eighteenth-Century Studies* 32.2 (1998–1999): 179–198.

———. "Sapphic Picaresque, Sexual Difference and Challenges of Homo-Adventuring." *Textual Practice* 15.2 (2001): 251–268.

———. "Bluestocking Sapphism and the Economies of Desire." *Huntington Library Quarterly* 65 (2002): 257–276.

Laqueur, Thomas. *Making Sex: Body and Gender from the Greeks to Freud*. Cambridge: Harvard University Press, 1990.

Laslett, Peter. *The World We Have Lost Further Explored*. New York: Charles Scribner's Sons, 1984.

Lennox, Charlotte. *Shakespear Illustrated: or the Novels and Histories, on which the Plays of Shakespear are Founded, Collected and Translated from the Original*

Authors. with Critical Remarks in Two Volumes. by the Author of the FEMALE QUIXOTE. London: 1753.

The Letters of David Garrick. Ed. David M. Little and George M. Kahrl. Cambridge: Belknap Press, 1963.

Levin, Richard. *The Multiple Plot in English Renaissance Drama*. Chicago: University of Chicago Press, 1971.

Levine, Laura. *Men in Women's Clothing: Antitheatricality and Effeminization, 1579–1642*. Cambridge: Cambridge University Press, 1994.

Lewis, C.S. *The Allegory of Love*. New York: Oxford University Press, 1936.

Lieblein, Leanore. "The Context of Murder in English Domestic Plays, 1590–1610." *Studies in English Literature 1500–1900* 23 (1983):181–196.

Lithgow, William. *The Totall Discourse, of the Rare Aduentures, and the painefull Peregrinations of long nineteene Yeares Trauayles, from SCOTLAND, to the most Famous Kingdomes in Europe, Asia and Africa*. London, 1632.

Little, Arthur L. Jr. "'An Essence that's Not Seen': The Primal Scene of Racism in *Othello*." *Shakespeare Quarterly* 44 (1993): 304–324.

Lochrie, Karma. *Covert Operations: The Medieval Uses of Secrecy*. Philadelphia: University of Pennsylvania Press, 1999.

———. *Heterosyncrasies: Female Sexuality When Normal Wasn't*. Minneapolis: University of Minnesota Press, 2005.

Logan, Terence P. and Denzell S. Smith, eds. *The Predecessors of Shakespeare: A Survey and Bibliography of Recent Studies in Renaissance Drama*. Lincoln: University of Nebraska Press, 1973.

Loomba, Ania. *Gender, Race, Renaissance Drama*. Delhi: Oxford University Press, 1992.

———. *Shakespeare, Race, and Colonialism*. Oxford: Oxford University Press, 2002.

Lorde, Audre. *Sister Outsider*. Trumansburg, N.Y.: The Crossing Press, 1984.

Luhmann, Niklas. *Love as Passion: The Codification of Intimacy*. Trans. Jeremy Gaines and Doris L. Jones. Cambridge: Harvard University Press, 1986.

Lydgate, John. *Here begynneth the boke of Johan Bochas discrying the fall of pri[nces]/princessses/and other nobles*. London, 1527.

MacFarlane, Alan. *The Origins of English Individualism*. New York: Cambridge University Press, 1978.

Mack, Maynard. *King Lear in Our Time*. Berkeley: University of California Press, 1972.

MacPherson, C.B. *The Political Theory of Possessive Individualism*. London: Oxford University Press, 1962.

Magnusson, Lynne. *Shakespeare and Social Dialogue: Dramatic Language and Elizabethan Letters*. Cambridge: Cambridge University Press, 1999.

Marcus, Leah S. *Puzzling Shakespeare: Local Reading and Its Discontents*. Berkeley: University of California Press, 1988.

Markley, Robert. "'Be Impudent, Be Saucy, Forward, Bold, Tonzing and Leud': The Politics of Masculine Sexuality and Feminine Desire in Behn's

Tory Comedies." *Cultural Readings of Restoration and Eighteenth-Century English Theater*. Ed. J. Douglas Canfield and Deborah C. Payne. Athens: University of Georgia Press, 1995. 114–140.

Marmion, Shakerly. *The Antiquary*. London, 1641.

Marotti, Arthur. " 'Love Is Not Love.': Elizabethan Sonnet Sequences and the Social Order." *ELH* 49.2 (1982): 396–428.

Marsden, Jean I. *The Re-Imagined Text: Shakespeare, Adaptation, and Eighteenth-Century Literary Theory*. Lexington: University of Kentucky Press, 1995.

———. "Female Spectatorship, Jeremy Collier, and the Anti-Theatrical Debate." *ELH* 65 (1998): 877–898.

Marx, Karl. *Capital: A Critique of Political Economy*. Trans. Samuel Moore and Edward Aveling. New York: The Modern Library, 1906.

Masten, Jeffrey. *Textual Intercourse: Collaboration, Authorship, and Sexualities in Renaissance Drama*. Cambridge: Cambridge University Press, 1997.

Matteo, Gino J. *Shakespeare's Othello: The Study to the Stage 1604–1904*. Salzburg: Universität Salzburg, 1974.

Maurer, Shawn Lisa. "Reforming Men: Chaste Heterosexuality in the Early English Periodical." *Restoration* 16:1 (1992): 38–55.

Maus, Katherine Eisaman. " 'Playhouse Flesh and Blood': Sexual Ideology and the Restoration Actress." *ELH* 46 (1979): 595–617.

May, Thomas. *The Tragedie of Cleopatra Queen of Ægypt*. London (acted 1626), 1639.

———. *The Trageody of Cleopatra Queene of Ægypt*. Ed. Denzell S. Smith. New York: Garland, 1979.

McDonald, Joyce Green. *Women and Race in Early Modern Texts*. Cambridge: Cambridge University Press, 2002.

McEachern, Claire and Debora Shuger. *Religion and Culture in Renaissance England*. Cambridge: Cambridge University Press, 1997.

McHenry, Robert W. Jr. "Betrayal and Love in *All for Love* and *Bérénice*." *SEL* 31 (1991): 445–459.

McKendrick, Neil, John Brewer, and J.H. Plumb. *The Birth of a Consumer Society: The Commercialization of Eighteenth-Century England*. Bloomington: Indiana University Press, 1982.

McKeon, Michael. *The Origins of the English Novel 1600–1740*. Baltimore: The Johns Hopkins University Press, 1987.

———. "Historicizing Patriarchy: The Emergence of Gender Difference in England, 1660–1760." *Eighteenth-Century Studies* 28.3 (1995): 295–322.

McLuskie, Kathleen. " 'Tis But a Woman's Jar': Family and Kinship in Elizabethan Domestic Drama." *Literature and History* 9.2 (1983): 228–239.

———. "The Patriarchal Bard: Feminisit Criticism and Shakespeare: *King Lear* and *Measure for Measure*." *Political Shakespeare: New Essays in Cultural Materialism*. Ithaca: Cornell University Press, 1985. 88–108.

Middleton, Thomas. *Blvrt Master-Constable*. London, 1602.

Middleton, Thomas. *The Phoenix*. London, 1607.

———. *A Trick to Catch the Old One*. London, 1608.

Mikalachki, Jodi. *The Legacy of Boadicea: Gender and Nation in Early Modern England*. London: Routledge, 1998.

Miller, D.A. *Place for Us: Essay on the Broadway Musical*. Cambridge: Harvard University Press, 1998.

Mills, Lauren J. *One Soule in Bodies Twain: Friendship in Tudor Literature and Stuart Drama*. Bloomington: Principia, 1937.

Montaigne, Michaell de. *The Essayes or Morall, Politike and Millitarie Discourses of Lord Michaell de Montaigne*. Trans. John Florio. London, 1603.

Montrose, Louis Adrian. *The Purpose of Playing: Shakespeare and the Cultural Politics of the Elizabethan Theatre*. Chicago: The University of Chicago Press, 1996.

Murfin, Ross and Supryia M. Ray. *The Bedford Glossary of Critical and Literary Terms*. New York: Bedford/St. Martin's, 2003. 2nd ed.

Neely, Carol Thomas. " 'Documents in Madness': Reading Madness and Gender in Shakespeare's Tragedies and Early Modern Culture." *Shakespearean Tragedy and Gender*. Ed. Shirley Nelson Garner and Madelon Sprengnether. Bloomington: Indiana University Press, 1996. 75–104.

Neill, Michael. "Unproper Beds: Race, Adultery, and the Hideous in *Othello*." *Critical Essays on Shakespeare's* Othello. Ed. Anthony Gerard Barthelemy. New York: G.K. Hall & Co., 1994: 187–215.

———. *Putting History to the Question: Power, Politics, and Society in English Renaissance Drama*. New York: Columbia University Press, 2000.

Newman, Karen. " 'And Wash the Ethiop White': Femininity and the Monstrous in *Othello*." *Shakespeare Reproduced: The Text in History and Ideology*. Ed. Jean E. Howard and Marion F. O'Connor. New York: Methuen, 1987. 143–162.

———. "Sundry Letters, Worldly Goods: The Lisle Letters and Renaissance Studies." *Journal of Medieval and Early Modern Studies* 26.1 (1996): 139–152.

Novak, Maximillian E. "Margery Pinchwife's 'London Desease': Restoration Comedy and the Libertine Offensive of the 1670's." *Studies in the Literary Imagination* 10.1 (1977): 1–23.

———. "Criticism, Adaptation, Politics, and the Shakespearean Model of Dryden's *All for Love*." *Studies in Eighteenth Century Culture* 7 (1978): 375–387.

O'Dair, Sharon. *Class, Critics, and Shakespeare: Bottom Lines on the Culture Wars*. Ann Arbor: University of Michigan Press, 2000.

Orgel, Stephen. *Impersonations: The Performance of Gender in Shakespeare's England*. Cambridge: Cambridge University Press, 1996.

Orlin, Lena Cowen. " 'Man's House as His Castle in *Arden of Feversham*." *Medieval and Renaissance Drama in England* 2 (1985): 57–89.

———. *Private Matters and Public Culture in Post-Reformation England*. Ithaca: Cornell University Press, 1994.

———. *Elizabethan Households: An Anthology*. Washington, D.C.: The Folger Shakespeare Library, 1995.

Orlin, Lena Cowen. "Desdemona's Disposition." *Shakespearean Tragedy and Gender*. Ed. Shirley Nelson Garner and Madelon Sprengnether. Bloomington: Indiana University Press, 1996.

———. "Chronicles of Private Life." *The Cambridge Companion to English Literature 1500–1600*. Ed. Arthur F. Kinney. Cambridge: Cambridge University Press, 2000. 241–264.

Ornstein, Robert. *The Moral Vision of Jacobean Tragedy*. Madison: The University of Wisconsin Press, 1965.

Otway, Thomas. *The History and Fall of Caius Marius. A Tragedy*. As it is Acted at the Duke's Theatre. London, 1680.

Overbury, Sir Thomas. *His Wife. With Additions of New Characters*. London, 1627.

Oxford English Dictionary. Oxford: Oxford University Press, 1971.

Panek, Jennifer. "Punishing Adultery in *A Woman Killed with Kindness*." *Studies in English Literature 1500–1900* 34.2 (1994): 357–378.

Parker, Patricia. *Shakespeare from the Margins: History, Language, Context*. Chicago: Chicago University Press, 1996.

Parten, Anne. "Masculine Adultery and Feminine Rejoinders in Shakespeare, Dekker and Sharpham." *Mosaic* 17.1 (1984): 9–18.

Partridge, Eric. *A Dictionary of Slang and Unconventional English*. Ed. Paul Beale. London: Routledge and Kegan Paul, 1984.

Paster, Gail Kern. *The Body Embarrassed: Drama and the Disciplines of Shame in Early Modern England*. Ithaca: Cornell University Press, 1993.

———. *Humoring the Body: Emotions and the Shakespearean Stage*. Chicago: The University of Chicago Press, 2004.

Pateman, Carole. *The Sexual Contract*. Stanford: Stanford University Press, 1988.

Patterson, Lee. "On the Margin: Postmodernism, Ironic History, and Medieval Studies." *Speculum* 65.1 (1990): 87–108.

Pearson, Jacqueline. "Blacker than Hell Creates: Pix Rewrites *Othello*." *Broken Boundaries: Women and Feminism in Restoration Drama*. Ed. Katherine Quinsey. Lexington: The University Press of Kentucky, 1996. 13–30.

Perkins, M.W. *Christian Oeconomie: Or A Short Survey of the Right Manner of erecting and ordering a Familie, according to the Scriptures*. Translated from the Latin by Thomas Pickering London, 1609.

Philips, Ambrose. *Humfrey, Duke of Gloucester. A Tragedy*. London, 1723.

Plato. *Symposium*. Trans. Michael Joyce. *The Collected Dialogues of Plato*. Ed. Edith Hamilton and Huntington Cairns. New York: Bollingen Foundation, 1961.

Pollak, Ellen. *The Poetics of Sexual Myth: Gender and Ideology in the Verse of Swift and Pope*. Chicago: The University of Chicago Press, 1985.

Pope, Alexander. *The Correspondence of Alexander Pope*. Ed. George Sherburn. Oxford: Clarendon Press, 1956. Vol. 1 (2 vols.).

Poovey, Mary. *Uneven Developments: The Ideological Work of Gender in Mid-Victorian England*. Chicago: University of Chicago Press, 1988.

Porter, Joseph A. "Marlowe, Shakespeare, and the Canonization of Heterosexuality." *The South Atlantic Quarterly* 88.1 (1989): 127–147.

Porter, Roy. "Mixed Feelings: The Enlightenment and Sexuality in Eighteenth-Century Britain." *Sexuality in Eighteenth-Century Britain.* Ed. Paul-Gabriel Boucé. Totowa: Manchester University Press, 1982.

Rackin, Phyllis. "Shakespeare's Boy Cleopatra, the Decorum of Nature, and the Golden World of Poetry." *PMLA* 87.1 (1972): 201–212.

———. "Foreign Country: The Place of Women and Sexuality in Shakespeare's Historical World." *Enclosure Acts.* Ed. Richard Burt and John Michael Archer. Ithaca: Cornell University Press, 1994. 68–95.

———. "Misogyny Is Everywhere." *A Feminist Companion to Shakespeare.* Ed. Dympna Callaghan. Oxford: Blackwell, 2000. 42–56.

———. "Shakespeare's Crossdressing Comedies." *A Companion to Shakespeare's Works: Volume III The Comedies.* Ed. Richard Dutton and Jean E. Howard. Oxford: Blackwell, 2003.

———. *Shakespeare and Women.* New York: Oxford University Press, 2005.

Rambuss, Richard. *Closet Devotions.* Durham: Duke University Press, 1998.

Random House Historical Dictionary of American Slang. Ed. J.E. Lighter. New York: Random House, 1994.

Ravenscroft, Edward. *Titus Andronicus, or the Rape of Lavinia* A Tragedy alter'd from Mr Shakespears works. London, 1687.

Reay, Barry. *Popular Cultures in England, 1550–1750.* London: Longman, 1998.

Ribner, Irving. *Jacobean Tragedy.* New York: Barnes & Noble Inc., 1962.

Rich, Adrienne. "Compulsory Heterosexuality and Lesbian Existence." *Blood, Bread, and Poetry: Selected Prose 1979–1985.* New York: Norton, 1986.

Richlin, Amy. "Not before Homosexuality: The Materiality of the *Cinaedus* and the Roman Law against Love between Men." *Journal of the History of Sexuality* 3.4 (1992/1993): 523–573.

Rogers, Pat. "The Breeches Part." *Sexuality in Eighteenth-Century Britain.* Ed. Paul-Gabriel Boucé. Manchester: Manchester University Press, 1982. 244–258.

Rose, Mary Beth. *The Expense of Spirit: Love and Sexuality in English Renaissance Drama.* Ithaca: Cornell University Press, 1988.

Rosenberg, Marvin. *The Masks of Othello.* Berkeley: University of California Press, 1961.

Royster, Francesca T. *Becoming Cleopatra: The Shifting Image of an Icon.* New York: Palgrave, 2003.

Rubin, Gayle. "The Traffic in Women: Notes on the 'Political Economy' of Sex." *Toward an Anthropology of Women.* Ed. Rayna R. Reiter. New York: Monthly Review Press, 1975. 157–210.

———. "Thinking Sex: Notes for a Radical Theory of the Politics of Sexuality." *Pleasure and Danger: Exploring Female Sexuality.* Ed. Carole S. Vance. Boston: Routledge, 1984. 267–319.

———. "Sexual Traffic." With Judith Butler. *differences* 6 (1994): 62–99.

Runge, Laura L. "Beauty and Gallantry: A Model of Polite Conversation Revisited." *Eighteenth-Century Life* 25.1 (2001): 43–63.

Rymer, Thomas. *The Critical Works of Thomas Rymer*. Ed. Curt A. Zimansky. New Haven: Yale University Press, 1956.

Saunders, Benjamin. "Circumcising Donne: The 1633 *Poems* and Readerly Desire." *Journal of Medieval and Early Modern Studies* 30.2 (2000): 375–399.

Scarry, Elaine. "Donne: 'But yet the body is his booke.'" *Literature and the Body: Essays on Populations and Persons*. Baltimore: Johns Hopkins University Press, 1989.

Schiebinger, Londa. *Nature's Body: Gender in the Making of Modern Science*. Boston: Beacon Press, 1993.

Schoenfeldt, Michael C. *Bodies and Selves in Early Modern England: Physiology and Inwardness in Spenser, Shakespeare, Herbert, and Milton*. Cambridge: Cambridge University Press, 1999.

Schultz, James A. *Courtly Love, the Love of Courtliness, and the History of Sexuality*. Chicago: University of Chicago Press, 2006.

Schutzman, Julie R. "Alice Arden's Freedom and the Suspended Moment of *Arden of Faversham*." *Studies in English Literature* 36 (1996): 289–314.

Schwartz, Regina M. "Nations and Nationalism: Adultery in the House of David." *Critical Inquiry* 19 (1992): 131–150.

Scodel, Joshua. *Excess and the Mean in Early Modern Literature*. Princeton: Princeton University Press, 2002.

Sedgwick, Eve Kosofsky. *Between Men: English Literature and Male Homosocial Desire*. New York: Columbia University Press, 1985.

———. *Epistemology of the Closet*. Berkeley: University of California Press, 1990.

Sedley, Sir Charles. *Antony and Cleopatra: A Tragedy*. London, 1677.

Shadwell, Thomas. *The History of Timon of Athens, the MAN-HATER*. London, 1678.

Shaheen, Naseeb. *Biblical References in Shakespeare's Tragedies*. Newark, Delaware: University of Delaware Press, 1987.

Shannon, Laurie. *Sovereign Amity: Figures of Friendship in Shakespearean Contexts*. Chicago: University of Chicago Press, 2002.

Shapiro, James. *Shakespeare and the Jews*. New York: Columbia University Press, 1996.

Sharpe, J.A. *Defamation and Sexual Slander in Early Modern England: The Church Courts at York*. York: Borthwick Institute of Historical Research, 1980.

Shoemaker, Robert B. *Gender in English Society, 1650–1850*. London: Longman, 1998.

Shumway. David R. *The Chronicle of Higher Education* August 9, 2002. B4.

Sidney, Mary. *The Countess of Pembroke's Antonie* (1592). Trans. of Robert Garnier, *M. Antonie* (1578). Ed. Alice Luce. Weimar: Verlag Von Emil Felber, 1897.

Sinfield, Alan. "How to Read *The Merchant of Venice* without Being Heterosexist." *Alternative Shakespeares II*. Ed. Terence Hawkes. London: Routledge, 1996.

Sivulka, Juliann. *Soap, Sex, and Cigarettes: A Cultural History of American Advertising*. Belmont, Calif.: Wadsworth Publishing Company, 1998.

Smith, Bruce R. *Homosexual Desire in Shakespeare's England: A Cultural Poetics*. Chicago: University of Chicago Press, 1994.

———. *Shakespeare and Masculinity*. Oxford: Oxford University Press, 2000.

Smith, Captain John. *The Complete Works of Captain John Smith (1580–1631)* in three volumes. Ed. Philip L. Barbour. Chapel Hill: The University of North Carolina Press, 1986.

Smith, Marion Bodwell. *Marlowe's Imagery and the Marlowe Canon*. Philadelphia, 1940.

Sommervile, C. John. *The Secularization of Early Modern England: From Religious Culture to Religious Faith*. Oxford: Oxford University Press, 1992.

Spencer, Hazelton. *Shakespeare Improved: The Restoration Versions in Quarto and On the Stage*. Cambridge: Harvard University Press, 1927.

Spencer, Theodore. *Shakespeare and the Nature of Man*. New York: Collier Books, 1942.

Spenser, Edmund. *The Faerie Queene*. Ed. Thomas P. Roche, Jr. New York: Penguin Books, 1978.

Stallybrass, Peter. "Patriarchal Territories: The Body Enclosed." *Rewriting the Renaissance*. Ed. Margaret W. Ferguson, Maureen Quilligan, and Nancy J. Vickers. Chicago: University of Chicago Press, 1986. 123–146.

———. "Transvestism and the 'Body Beneath': Speculating on the Boy Actor." *Erotic Politics: Desire on the Renaissance Stage*. New York: Routledge, 1992. 64–83.

———. "Editing as Cultural Formation: The Sexing of Shakespeare's Sonnets." *Modern Language Quarterly* 54.1 (1993): 91–103.

Starnes, D.T. "Imitation of Shakespeare in Dryden's *All for Love*." *Texas Studies in Literature and Language* 6 (1964): 39–46.

Staves, Susan. "A Few Kind Words for the Fop." *SEL* 22 (1982): 413–428.

———. "Money for Honor: Damages for Criminal Conversation." *Studies in Eighteenth- Century Culture* 2 (1982): 279–297.

———. "Where Is History But in Texts? Reading the History of Marriage." *The Golden & The Brazen World: Papers in Literature and History, 1650–1800*. Ed. John M. Wallace. Berkeley: the University of California Press, 1985. 125–145.

———. "The Secrets of Genteel Identity in *The Man of the Mode*: Comedy of Manners vs. the Courtesy Book." *Studies in Eighteenth Century Culture* 19 (1989): 117–128.

Stewart, Alan. *Close Readers: Humanism and Sodomy in Early Modern England*. Princeton: Princeton University Press, 1997.

Stone, Lawrence. *Family, Sex and Marriage in England 1500–1800*. New York: Harper & Row, 1977.

Strier, Richard. *Resistant Structures: Particularity, Radicalism, and Renaissance Texts*. Berkeley: University of California Press, 1995.

———. "Shakespeare and the Skeptics." *Religion and Literature* 32.2 (2000): 171–196.

Sullivan, Garrett A. Jr. " 'Arden Lay Murdered in That Plot of Ground': Surveying, Land, and *Arden of Faversham*." *ELH* 61 (1994): 231–252.

Swinburne, Algernoon Charles. *A Study of Shakespeare*. London: Chatto & Windus, 1895.

Tanner, Tony. *Adultery in the Novel: Contract and Transgression*. Baltimore: Johns Hopkins University Press, 1979.

Tate, Nahum. *The History of King Lear. Acted at the Duke's Theatre. Reviv'd with Alterations*. London, 1681.

———. *Ingratitude of a Common-Wealth: Or, the Fall of Caius Martius Coriolanus asit is acted at the Theatre-Royal*. London, 1682.

Taylor, Gary. *Reinventing Shakespeare: A Cultural History from the Restoration to the Present*. London: The Hogarth Press, 1989.

Thomas, Keith. "The Double Standard." *Journal of the History of Ideas* 20 (April 1959): 195–216.

Thompson, Ann. "Are there any Women in *King Lear*." *The Matter of Difference: Materialist Feminist Criticism of Shakespeare*. Ed. Valerie Wayne. Ithaca: Cornell University Press, 1991.

Todd, Janet. *The Sign of Angellica: Women, Writing and Fiction, 1660–1800*. New York: Columbia University Press, 1989.

Tokson, Elliot H. *The Popular Image of the Black Man in English Drama, 1550–1688*. Boston: G.K. Hall and Co., 1982.

Townsend, Freda. "The Artistry of Thomas Heywood's Double Plots." *Philological Quarterly* 25 (1946): 97–119.

Traub, Valerie. *Desire and Anxiety*. London: Routledge, 1992.

———. *The Renaissance of Lesbianism in Early Modern England*. Cambridge: Cambridge University Press, 2002.

Trull, Mary. "Public Privacies: Household Intimacy in Renaissance Genres." Dissertation, University of Chicago, 2002.

Trumbach, Randolph. "Kinship and Marriage in Early Modern England and France." *Annals of Scholarship* 2.4 (1981): 113–128.

———. *Sex and the Gender Revolution: Homosexuality and the Third Gender in Enlightenment London*. Chicago: The University of Chicago Press, 1998.

Turner, David M. *Fashioning Adultery: Gender, Sex and Civility in England, 1660–1740*. Cambridge: Cambridge University Press, 2002.

Turner, James Grantham. "The Sexual Politics of Landscape: Images of Venus in Eighteenth-Century Poetry and Landscape Gardening." *Studies in Eighteenth-Century Culture* 2 (1982): 343–366.

———. "Properties of Libertinism." *Eighteenth-Century Life* 9 n. s. 3 (1985): 75–87.

———. "The Culture of Priapism." *Review* 10 (1988): 1–34.

———. "Pope's Libertine Self-Fashioning." *The Eighteenth-Century: Theory and Interpretation* 29 (1988): 123–144.

———. "The Libertine Sublime: Love and Death in Restoration England." *Studies in Eighteenth-Century Culture* 19 (1989): 99–115.

———. "Sex and Consequence." *Review* 11 (1989): 133–177.

Turner, James Grantham. *Libertines and Radicals in Early Modern London: Sexuality, Politics, and Literary Culture 1630–1685*. Cambridge: Cambridge University Press, 2002.

———. *Schooling Sex: Libertine Literature and Erotic Education in Italy, France, and England, 1534–1685*. Oxford: Oxford University Press, 2003.

Tyrwhitt, Thomas. *Observations and Conjectures upon some Passages of Shakespeare*. Oxford: Clarendon Press, 1766.

Ure, Peter. "Marriage and the Domestic Drama in Heywood and Ford." *English Studies* 32 (1951): 200–216.

Vanita, Ruth. " 'Proper' Men and 'Fallen' Women: The Unprotectedness of Wives in *Othello*." *SEL* 34.2 (1994): 341–356.

Varholy, Cristine. "Representing Prostitution in Tudor and Stuart England." Dissertation, University of Wisconsin, Madison, 2000.

Vaughan, Virginia Mason. *Othello: A Contextual History*. Cambridge: Cambridge University Press, 1994.

———. "Race Mattered: *Othello* in Late Eighteenth-Century England." *Shakespeare Survey* 51 (1998): 57–66.

Vickers, Nancy. "Diana Described: Scattered Woman and Scattered Rhyme." *Critical Inquiry* 8.2 (1981): 265–279.

Victor, Benjamin. *The History of the Theatres of London and Dublin from the year 1730 to the present time*. London, 1761. 3 vols.

———. *The Fatal Error: a Tragedy. Original Letters, Dramatic Pieces and Poems* in 3 vols. London: Printed for T. Becket, 1776.

The Wakefield Mystery Plays. Ed. Martial Rose. New York: W.W. Norton & Company, 1961.

Wall, Wendy. "Forgetting and Keeping: Jane Shore and the English Domestication of History." *Renaissance Drama* 27 (1996): 123–156.

———. *Staging Domesticity: Household Work and English Identity in Early Modern Drama*. Cambridge: Cambridge University Press, 2002.

Warner, Michael. *The Trouble with Normal: Sex, Politics, and the Ethics of Queer Life*. New York: The Free Press, 1999.

Warner, William B. "Realist Literary History: McKeon's New Origins of the Novel." *Diacritics* 19.1 (1989): 62–81.

Weber, Harold. "Carolinean Sexuality and the Restoration Stage: Reconstructing the Royal Phallus in *Sodom*." *Cultural Readings of Restoration and Eighteenth-Century English Theater*. Ed. J. Douglas Canfield and Deborah C. Payne. Athens: University of Georgia Press, 1995. 67–88.

Wentworth, Michael. "Thomas Heywood's *A Woman Killed with Kindness* as Domestic Morality." *Traditions and Innovations*. Ed. David G. Allen and Robert A. White. Newark: University of Delaware Press, 1990.

Westhauser, Karl E. "Friendship and Family in Early Modern England: The Sociability of Adam Eyre and Samuel Pepys." *Journal of Social History* 27.3 (1994): 517–536.

Whately, William. *A Bride-Bush: Or a Direction for Married Persons Plainely Describing the Dvties Common to Both, and peculiar to each of them. By performing of which, marriage shall prooue a great helpe to such, as now for want of performing them, doe find it a little hell.* London, 1619.

Wheatley, Christopher J. "Thomas Durfey's *A Fond Husband*, Sex Comedies of the Late 1670s and Early 1680s, and the Comic Sublime." *Studies in Philology* 90.4 (1993): 371–390.

———. " 'But speak every thing in its Nature': Influence and Ethics in Durfey's Adaptations of Fletcher." *Journal of English and Germanic Philology* 95.4 (1996): 515–533.

Whigham, Frank. *Seizures of the Will in Early Modern English Drama.* Cambridge: Cambridge University Press, 1996.

Wikander, Matthew H. " 'The Duke My Father's Wrack': The Innocence of the Restoration *Tempest*." *Shakespeare Survey* 43 (1990): 91–98.

Wilkinson, Robert. *The Merchant-Royal: or Woman a Ship.* London, 1607. *Conjugal Duty: Set Forth in a Collection of Ingenious and Delightful Wedding-Sermons.* London: J. Watson, 1732.

Williams, Gordon. *A Dictionary of Sexual Imagery in Shakespearean and Stuart Literature.* London: The Athlone Press, 1994. 3 vols.

———. *Shakespeare, Sex and the Print Revolution.* London: Athlone, 1996.

Williams, Raymond. *Marxism and Literature.* Oxford: Oxford University Press, 1977.

———. *Keywords.* New York: Oxford University Press, 1985.

Willinsky, John. *Empire of Words: The Reign of the OED.* Princeton: Princeton University Press, 1994.

Wrightson, Keith. *English Society 1580–1680.* New Brunswick, N.J.: Rutgers University Press, 1982.

Wyatt, Sir Thomas. *Collected Poems of Sir Thomas Wyatt.* Ed. Kenneth Muir. Cambridge: Harvard University Press, 1950.

Wycherley, William. *The Country Wife.* Ed. Thomas H. Fujimura. Lincoln: University of Nebraska Press, 1965.

Yots, Michael. "Dryden's *All for Love* on the Restoration Stage." *Restoration and Eighteenth Century Theatre Research* 16.1 (1977): 1–10.

Youngblood, Sarah. "Theme and Imagery in *Arden of Feversham*." *SEL* 3.2 (1963): 207–218.

Youings, Joyce. *Sixteenth Century England.* London: Penguin Books Ltd., 1984.

Žižek, Slavoj. *The Sublime Object of Ideology.* London: Verso, 1989.

———. "The Spectre of Ideology." *Mapping Ideology.* Ed. Slavoj Žižek. London: Verso, 1994.

INDEX

REBECCA ANN BACH is Associate Professor of English
at the University of Alabama at Birmingham.
She is the author of
*Colonial Transformations: The Cultural Production of the
New Atlantic World, 1580-1640* (Palgrave, 2001).
She has published articles on Renaissance drama and culture
in many journals and collections, including *ELH,
Renaissance Drama, Textual Practice,* and *SEL.*

Printed in the United States
103560LV00003BA/10/P